South Sudan
Elites, Ethnicity, Endless Wars and the Stunted State

Peter Adwok Nyaba

PUBLISHED BY
Mkuki na Nyota Publishers Ltd
P. O. Box 4246
Dar es Salaam, Tanzania
www.mkukinanyota.com

© Peter Adwok Nyaba, 2019

ISBN 978-9987-083-66-4

All rights reserved. No part of this publication may be reproduced, stored in a retrieval system or transmitted in any form or by any means, electronic, mechanical, photocopying, recording, or otherwise, without the prior written permission of Mkuki na Nyota Publishers Ltd.

Visit www.mkukinanyota.com to read more about and to purchase any of Mkuki na Nyota books. You will also find featured authors interviews and news about other publisher/author events. Sign up for our e-newsletters for updates on new releases and other announcements.

Distributed worldwide outside Africa by African Books Collective.
www.africanbookscollective.com

Contents

Dedication v
Acronynms. vi
Acknowledgements. viii
Foreword. x
Preface. xiii
Introduction. 1

CHAPTER ONE
Elites, Ethnic Politics, and the Stunted State. 14
Evolution of Political Action in Southern Sudan 20
The Genesis of Sociopolitical Duplicity 23
The Elite's Sociopolitical Duplicity and Challenges of Transition 46

CHAPTER TWO
The Revolution that Wasn't. 60
Was the SPLM/A a Reincarnation of SANU 75
Promotion of Militarism: A culture of Fear and Self-Preservation . . . 83
Political and Ideological Subversion of the Revolution 86
Ethnicity and the Upsurge of Ethnic Nationalism in the SPLM/A. . . 106
The Ideological Shift to the Right and the Search for Peace 117
Corruption in the SPLM/A: The Evolution of the Parasitic
    Capitalist Class. 127
The SPLM/A: A Revolution that Wasn't. 140

CHAPTER THREE
The Civil War was Not Inevitable 150
Spinning Rumours into a Dangerous Narrative 153

Leaders' Incompatibility becomes South Sudan's Predicament 156
How and why Salva Kiir Did what He Did 170
Preparation for Military Action Against Riek Machar.............173
Fighting in the Presidential Guards and Massacre of Ethnic Nuer ..179
Riek Machar Declares a Rebellion 183
The Commoditization of Rebellion 188
The IGAD Peace Agreement and Its Collapse....................199
The IGAD High Level Revitalization Forum.....................203
President Kiir and Riek Could have Averted the Catastrophe 204

CHAPTER FOUR
**To Fix South Sudan we Must Complete the
National Democratic Revolution**..............................210
The stage of National Democratic Revolution...................220
National Democratic Revolution Versus the
    IGAD Peace Mediation......................................222
Common Ownership of Means of Production 236
IGAD, HLRF, and the National Democratic Revolution...........239
What Should We Do...241

EPILOGUE
My journey to and from the SPLM/A-IO: A Personal Account....245
The Decision to Join SPLM/A-IO 252
The SPLM/A-IO in a Deadly Dilemma 257
Managing Relations with other Opposition Groups 260
The Decision to Quit SPLM/A-IO 264
Here to Where — *Qua Vadis?* 266

References..268

Dedication

To my children and grandchildren and more specifically, my life partner, Hon. Abuk Payiti Ayik, for whom I quote these lines from a song by Don Williams:

> Some days I seem so far away from where I want to be,
> And the things that I've accomplished seem so small.
> When I'm weary of the struggle, and I feel I can't go on,
> You love me through it all.
>
> Your love gives me a balance when I'm standing on the edge.
> You keep me going when my dreams have stalled,
> And you're always building bridges when I'm building walls.
> You love me through it all.

Acronyms

ANF	African Nationalist Front
ARCISS	Agreement on the Resolution of the Conflict in South Sudan
CPA	Comprehensive Peace Agreement
CIDA	Canadian International Development Agency
CPS	Communist Party of the Sudan
CTSAMM	Ceasefire and Transitional Security Arrangements Monitoring Mechanism
CUSS	Council for Unity of Southern Sudan
EAC	East African Community
ECC	Equatoria Central Committee
EPLF	Eritrean People's Liberation Front
EPRDF	Ethiopian People's Revolutionary Democratic Front
GoSS	Government of South Sudan
HEC	High Executive Council
HLRF	High Level Revitalization Forum
ICGLR	International Conference on Great Lakes Region
IGAD	Inter-Governmental Authority on Development
IMF	International Monetary Fund
JCE	Jieng (Dinka) Council of Elders
JMEC	Joint Monitoring and Evaluation Commission
NCP	National Congress Party

NDA	National Democratic Alliance
NDR	National Democratic Revolution
NUP	National Unionist Party
PDP	People's Democratic Party
POCs	Protection of Civilians sites
PRA	People's Regional Assembly
SAC	Sudan African Congress
SAF	Sudan Armed Forces
SAP	Structural Adjustment Programme
SANU	Sudan African National Union
SDF	Sudan Defence Force
SPLM/A	Sudan People's Liberation Movement/Army
SPLM/A–IO	Sudan People's Liberation Movement/Army–In Opposition
SPLM-DC	Sudan People's Liberation Movement–Democratic Change
SSLA	South Sudan Legislative Assembly
SSLM	Southern Sudan Liberation Movement
SSPA	Southern Sudan Political Association
SRRA	Sudan Relief and Rehabilitation Association
SSU	Sudan Socialist Union
SWF	Student Welfare Front
TGoNU	Transitional Government of National Unity
WB	World Bank
WFP	World Food Programme
UNMISS	United Nations Mission in South Sudan
UN/OLS	United Nations/Operation Lifeline Sudan
UP	Umma Party
UPDF	Ugandan People's Defence Force

Acknowledgements

South Sudan: Elites, Ethnicity, Endless Wars and the Stunted State is a modest contribution to the growing knowledge, through books, research papers, and reports, on South Sudan and its people. This knowledge production is borne out of political activism rather than pure academic scholarship suggesting that eagle-eyed scholars will find it theoretically inadequate. This is deliberate given that the intention is to ignite or stimulate popular discourse among South Sudan's political elite on the questions of state formation and nation-building processes. The ethnic cum provincial power wrangles within the political elite have shattered any semblance of unity and thrown the country off the transition course.

The absence of challenging tasks in the SPLM/A-IO gave me enough time to write these pages. I shared the second draft of the manuscript with many friends and colleagues in the hope of soliciting critical comments and possible peer review.

I am thankful to Prof. Amir Idris, professor and chair of the Department of African and African-American Studies at Fordham University, New York, for taking time from his academic schedule. In his remarks, Amir wrote that the manuscript "provided a deep and nuanced understanding of how South Sudan's political elite has failed to identify the problem and to transform South Sudan's socio-economic formation, but the manuscript uses elitism narrowly." I deeply appreciate these remarks.

Dr. Peter Obadaya Tingwa read the manuscript and came up with meticulous and insightful details, which I incorporated into the text without veering away from the thrust of my analysis of those events. I sincerely would like to thank Peter Tingwa and also appreciate his rich experience with UN peacekeeping missions in Liberia and Somalia.

It is not lost on me that some of the friends were still reading the manuscript by the time I sent it to the publishers. They have forwarded me their comments, in time to make changes where necessary. I take this opportunity to thank Dr. David Bassouni, Dr. Halle Jørn Hanssen, and Prof. Eisei Kurimoto for their encouragement and kind words.

Dr. Carol Berger rendered the manuscript linguistically palatable with her editing. I am indebted to her and thank her for this priceless assistance, and also for gracing this book with a foreword.

Last but not least, my sincere thanks go to Walter Bgoya and his colleagues at Mkuki na Nyota Publishers for publishing my book.

Foreword

The author of this book, Peter Adwok Nyaba, is both a prolific writer and a man who has been at the centre of South Sudan's dramatic history for more than five decades. He was born during the colonial era, when Sudan was under British rule. In the 1960s, he was among the many South Sudanese students who joined the bush war to fight northern Sudanese rule, that conflict ending with the 1972 Addis Ababa Agreement. By the mid-1980s, he was once again in a training camp, this time inside Ethiopia territory, as a fighter with the Sudan People's Liberation Army (SPLA).

Nyaba survived the 21-year war, and was present in Juba on 9 July 2011 when the flag of the newly independent nation of South Sudan was raised for the first time. He was also there on 15 December 2013, cowering with his family inside their home in Hai Jebel, when Dinka-led troops of the SPLA went house to house massacring ethnic Nuer. In the days that followed, as Nyaba writes, President Salva Kiir Mayardit told his troops to spare Nyaba's life but to place him under house arrest. He managed to slip out of South Sudan, defying his house arrest and going into exile in Nairobi, Kenya. From there he joined Riek Machar's rebellion.

Nyaba is a Shilluk, or Chollo, from the region of Northern Upper Nile, bordering Sudan to the north and Ethiopia to the east. This area is on the frontline of the now five-year civil war, which has displaced millions and, according to a report by the London School of of Hygiene and Tropical Medicine, caused the deaths of almost 400,000 people.. Like many of South Sudan's senior figures, Nyaba has shifted his loyalties, several times, between political organisations and between the state and opposition. In his case, moving between the Southern Front, Sudanese Communist Party, SPLM/A, and Machar's SPLM/A-In Opposition, the latter of which he recently ended his association.

In this book, Nyaba's perhaps most important contribution to a better understanding of the current war is his account of the ways that the Dinka-led state has used ethnic nationalism to upend intercommunal relations throughout the country. He acknowledges that the leaders of other cultural groups have also used the power of ethnic identification to further their ambitions. As he writes in *South Sudan: Elites, Ethnicity, Endless Wars and the Stunted State*, "The collective weakness is our inability to liberate ourselves from the claws of negative ethnicity."

He continues, "We need to make our people understand that ethnicity and ethnic politics — as fronted for by the JCE [Jieng (Dinka) Council of Elders], the elders of Nuer, Chollo, Bari, and all kinds of elder formations and ethnic associations — are nothing but tools of subjugation and exploitation. These elders, like the political, military, and business elites, are bloodsuckers. We must combat them through education."

I have a long history in Sudan and South Sudan, first in the 1980s as a reporter for the BBC and, since 2005, as an anthropologist. I have lived for extended periods in the Dinka heartland of the former Lakes State and travelled widely in the country. I had known of Nyaba for some years before we finally met. He is a tall man, with a ready smile. He is generous with people who want to talk about his country's history. But at the end of a lengthy conversation, he may have difficulty standing and relies on a cane.

In May 1987, in what was known as the Battle of Jekau, Nyaba, then a guerrilla fighter, was seriously wounded. The SPLA were attacked inside Ethiopian territory by Khartoum-backed forces of the Anya-nya II. By chance, I happened to be in the then-Sudanese town of Malakal, across the border from Ethiopia, as the battle was being fought. It was from Malakal that an officer of the Sudan Armed Forces was commanding the Anya-nya II forces, ordering them to attack the South Sudanese rebels inside Ethiopia. Nyaba survived but lost his right leg. That he lived was due to the presence of a Cuban medical team in the nearby Ethiopian town of Gambela. If you meet a South Sudanese veteran who lost a limb during the North-South war (1983–2005), chances are that he was injured within the vicinity of Gambela, where medical support was available. Fighters with serious injuries rarely survived, such was the lack of even basic medical care. That same year, an SPLA fighter from the Bor Dinka also lost his leg when a shell exploded during training at a camp in Bilpam. Like Nyaba, his life was saved by the Cuban medics based in Gambela. He is today a member of the Jieng Council of Elders, blamed by many, including the author of this book, for the upsurge in Dinka ethnic nationalism.

I refer to this long ago battle to illustrate the intimate nature of the current civil war. The senior military and political figures who have turned community against community, unleashed soldiers to force villagers from their homes, to rape and kill civilians, the very men who, as of early September 2018, were preparing to initial yet another peace agreement in Addis Ababa, spent their youths together in training camps, in guerrilla battalions, and, later, became commanders within the national army, state governors, and members of parliament in the newly independent South Sudan. Their fates have been intertwined for almost 40 years. In recent years, however, as far back as independence in 2011, each has retreated to his home constituency, his ethnic origin, for legitimacy and power.

South Sudan: Elites, Ethnicity, Endless Wars and the Stunted State is an important book. Nyaba provides an insider's account of the country's unfolding events. As the author stresses, the country remains impoverished and literacy is a rare gift. Whether or not the reader agrees with his suggested solution to this state of affairs — "a national democratic revolution" — there is no disputing that few people in South Sudan have the means to write or even to read.

The international community is ever ready to finance a new project in support of "peace-building", most often little more than staged efforts led by those in power, and "stabilisation", a term that remains without a definition. Western and regional powers could do worse than provide support for a Marshall Plan of basic literacy, not only for the young but also for those who are compelled to fight, whose lives are spent in uniform within the country's police stations and army barracks. As Nyaba writes, education is the tool that could bring to a close the never-ending wars of South Sudan.

Carol Berger
18 September 2018
Cairo

Preface

As this book goes to press, it is worth noting that the IGAD-led peace talks in Khartoum, begun in June 2018, had come to a wobbly conclusion. The main opposition — the SPLM/A-IO, South Sudan Opposition Alliance, and National Salvation Front — which until 1 September was still opposed to the agreement, initialled the document on outstanding governance issues, pending the signing ceremony scheduled for 13 September in Addis Ababa.[1] This was after the desperate intervention of Sudan's President Omer al Bashir. This delay came as no surprise. From the word go the IGAD mediation mischaracterized the fundamental contradiction at the root of the conflict. It belaboured the issues of "power sharing" and "superficial reforms" rather than the need to transform the system. Attempting to resolve the two issues is unlikely to take South Sudan out of the current political impasse.

The sticking point is that President Salva Kiir Mayardit has vowed to never again work with Riek Machar Teny-Dhurgon. Their two face-to-face meetings, hosted by the IGAD Chair and Ethiopian Prime Minister Abiy Ahmed (Addis Ababa) and Sudanese President Omer al Bashir (Khartoum), were failures. Indeed, Kiir's longstanding refusal to engage with Machar was the trigger for the start of the conflict in 2013. For the sake of the people and the country, and since the whole struggle has boiled down to the issue of power sharing, Machar should have surrendered the leadership of the SPLM/A-IO to his chosen deputy, Henry Odwar. Machar, due to his own actions, and considering the

---

[1] Statement by the chairman of the National Salvation Front, Gen. Thomas Cirillo Swaka, entitled "Why the National Salvation Front has not initialled the Khartoum Peace Agreement," dated 1 September 2018.

regional and international climate, has left the SPLM/A-IO with only one option: "retreat" in order to "advance" at a later time.

The present social, economic, and political context of South Sudan does not allow its leaders to behave like the biblical woman who insisted on cutting the child into two. Both current and former members of the SPLM/|SPLA are responsible for the crisis. They built Salva Kiir into what he is — an imperial president. Now, at the height of his power, he will not surrender or share it with anybody. In 2013, he told Pagan Amum, "I will not to leave it to anybody [and] will make it difficult for anybody to benefit from it after me." It is very sad that many of us, particularly the Jieng intellectuals who continue to support Salva Kiir on account of ethnicity or provincialism, did not realize in 2013 that he would never relent on the question of power. It calls to mind Kiir's reaction in 2003 to the proposal that Machar be named as deputy to Dr. John Garang in the SPLM/SPLA hierarchy. Those present at the meeting recall that Salva Kiir held onto the chair he was sitting on, next to Garang, in such a manner as if to physically prevent Machar from taking it. Kiir's attitude to power comes from a place of raw ambition, an attitude held so strongly that it can only lead to self-destruction.

The objective reality is that the opposition has failed to dislodge Kiir from power. But while he may be the president of the republic, he is presiding over a dying state. This is a situation that must invoke patriotic sensibilities in each and every South Sudanese, as well as a clear understanding that all of us are mortal. A few more years of misrule by a despot can be tolerated if the people of South Sudan are spared further suffering and deprivation, as they have experienced for the past five years. In fact, in terms of state violence, the current situation is similar to the Turko-Egyptian (1824–1885) and Mahdiyya (1885–1898) eras in the Sudan, when communities if not whole ethnicities became extinct. This suggests that to survive, people have to accept the Revitalized Agreement on the Resolution of the Conflict in South Sudan, if only to prevent the country's total collapse. If this occurs, South Sudan will become a protectorate of Sudan (Bashir) and Uganda (Yoweri Museveni), the very men who midwifed the "Khartoum Declaration of Agreement", which Kiir and Machar signed on 26 June 2018.

People across the sociopolitical spectrum are full of bitterness and hatred as a result of their experience with Kiir's rule over the last 13 years. So much so that the government's division of the country into 32 (or more) states is gaining acceptance as a means of buying peace. But people do not realise the danger that the state creation carries. Many communities that have experienced marginalization and oppression at the hands of their neighbours no longer want a return to the ten-state or three-region configuration of South Sudan. This is rationalised by the call for federation as a solution to inter- and intra-ethnic tensions, although it is more likely that this supposed federalism will only compound these problems. The best option, of course, would be that in the best tradition of forgiveness and reconciliation, which our people have long practised, South Sudanese accept the situation, forgive each other and reconcile in order to stop the violence, particularly against innocent civilians. This would create the conditions necessary for the internally displaced and refugees to return to their homes and rebuild their lives.

It will be difficult, if not impossible, to avoid living together as long as we identify as South Sudanese. Many nations have been forged through hardship, toil, and blood. More importantly, there has been self-sacrifice. What happened in South Sudan over the last five years is not unique to us alone. I am convinced that once we stop this violence against ourselves we will never again confront such a combination of factors, the outcome of which has been the dehumanisation of our political elite. We have sacrificed a lot for this country. Let us now, working together without anger or division, build it.

Peter Adwok Nyaba
Nairobi, 9 September 2018

Introduction

> First, it is clear to me and I am sorry to say so, but I have never seen a political elite with so little interest in the well-being of its people.
> UN Secretary-General António Guterres[2]

As the year 2017 closed on South Sudan and its people, I wrote a short paper entitled "Make 2018 a Year of Decisive Action," which circulated on social and electronic media. South Sudan had just marked the fourth anniversary of the skirmishes in the Tiger Battalion, the Presidential Guards in Juba. The fighting that evening heralded the beginning of the civil war. The Agreement on the Resolution of the Conflict in South Sudan (ARCISS), brokered by the Intergovernmental Authority on Development (IGAD) and signed in Addis Ababa and Juba, respectively on 17 and 26 August 2016, did not completely end the war. The parties to the conflict formed the Transitional Government of National Unity (TGoNU) on 29 April 2016, but barely two months later the war rekindled. Both the TGoNU and ARCISS collapsed, the war escalated to engulf the whole country with the proliferation of armed and political opposition to the regime. South Sudan entered into another period of humanitarian crisis. By the end of 2017, more than five million South Sudanese were refugees in Uganda, DR Congo, Sudan, Ethiopia, and Kenya, or in United Nations Protection of Civilians (PoC) sites in Juba, Bor, Bentiu, Wau, and Malakal, or in the bushes and swamps of South Sudan.

---

[2] Remarks made at the UN/IGAD/AU Consultative Meeting on South Sudan in Addis Ababa, Ethiopia, on 30 March 2018.

There was a reason for writing that paper, which called for decisive action to change this horrible stalemate. There was a state of passivity and apathy in the opposition. The lack of unity, because of varied and contradictory objectives among the more than ten different groups, was a situation that could not inspire hope. The government launched military operations throughout the country, pursuing a scorched-earth policy against the civilian population, razing their villages and crops, and pushing them into neighbouring countries. The Obama administration had pressured the IGAD region to recognize the post-July 2016 government in Juba. The Joint Monitoring and Evaluation Commission (JMEC) spent two years pretending to monitor and evaluate ARCISS implementation, in full knowledge that the second largest of the parties to it was already back in the bush. It could not have been anything but malicious cynicism. I was then in the early stages of writing this book. I believe it is now more important than ever to publish a full account of what has occurred since the war broke out.

In February 2017, Amir Idris asked a number of South Sudanese scholars and political activists to contribute to a book on South Sudan, focusing on post-independence dilemmas. I chose to write on the curse of elitism (Idris, 2018: 19). The words of UN Secretary-General António Guterres, quoted above, could not have come at a more opportune time. I have used them to underscore the fact that it does not matter on which side of the political divide in South Sudan a person stands: he or she is nonetheless culpable in this senseless war. I have seen it all, from the first gunshot in Juba on 15 December 2013. The fighting that night within the Presidential Guards was so close and traumatizing.

I consider the writing of this book part of a personal struggle to generate knowledge about the pathetic situation in South Sudan, in order to help construct trajectories for transforming it. The South Sudan political elite has become a farcical replica of the dominant elite in the Sudan, which Mansour Khalid described in his book *The Government They Deserve*. South Sudan was bound to follow in Sudan's footsteps in its journey as an independent country. Only a change of attitudes and a correct perception of reality among the people of South Sudan, in their many different social formations, will prevent the escalation of this human tragedy. However, this change could come only from knowledge and scientific understanding of the social and political factors that have contributed to the situation at hand. This knowledge can come about only from individual participants who are sensitive, and also courageous enough to investigate, to diligently expose even their own part in the carnage. That was one reason for writing this book. Five years of civil war has so numbed and desensitized many of my compatriots that they do not recognise the immense dehumanization of the South Sudan person that the war has caused. This is particularly true of my compatriots in government whose motive is to turn the tragedy into a minting machine for themselves and their families. It is difficult to imagine how long it will take to re-moralize or re-humanize all of us — the victims of our own actions.

I intended this book to carry my feelings and thoughts about the anguish, bitterness, frustration, and suffering of the almost 200,000 South Sudanese who since December 2013 have been living in UN-protected camps. The situation of people in the swamps of Leer in Unity State, Aburoch, and Kal Agany in the Shilluk Kingdom in Upper Nile State, and other areas in Equatoria and Western Bahr el Ghazal, counted as "internally displaced", is of great concern. The government forces and tribal militias perpetually harass, brutalize, and rape them, further exacerbating their wretchedness. Every time the peace talks in Addis Ababa, Ethiopia, postpone or stall a few more people collapse and die of frustration and hopelessness. I am also concerned about the two million South Sudanese who elected with their feet to walk to the refugee camps, for a second or even third time, in Uganda, DR Congo, Sudan, Ethiopia, and Kenya. When will their suffering cease? I know the answer lies with the political elite in government and in the opposition.

Five years into the civil war and suffering and still no light seems to flicker at the end of the tunnel while the so-called stakeholders rummage in regional capitals for power or its sharing. This does not at all inspire hope. The writing of these pages is partly out of disillusionment with the opposition, which I elected to join in July 2014. It is also partly to pull myself apart in order to look at the situation objectively. It has given me a burst of mental activity in the midst of political stagnation and passivity. Like many others in the main opposition, I am able to explain the reasons for the stagnation. Unfortunately, it will not be easy to make the necessary changes to lift us out of our morass. This speaks loudly to the lack of ideological unity and wide difference in perceptions of the problem and the principal objectives of the war. The lack of clarity as to whether it is a liberation movement or a social revolution is a source of discomfort in the leadership, and has worsened the disunity. Despite the many difficulties, including military logistics and the lack of material support, the foot soldiers have put on brave faces and continue to struggle.

In some ways, writing critically is an attempt to think outside the political box we have placed ourselves. When the internal political environment is suffocating for lack of democratic exchanges, writing is the best way to ventilate, to create truths that speak to those in power, in the hope of bringing them more in touch with reality. It is also a way of speaking to those on the other side of the river, the ones who have been forced out by a president who is doing nothing other than appointing and disappointing even his own people. As in my previous writings I have tried to be objective in my description and analysis of the situation. I have always appreciated that my audience — the South Sudanese intelligentsia, in particular — reads me correctly because I speak directly to them.

I am more convinced than at any other time that the problem of South Sudan and its people is not British colonialism or the different Sudanese regimes that governed from Khartoum after 1956. Political oppression, exploitation, discrimination, and wars have been part of humanity since time immemorial. They are not peculiar to South Sudanese people; looking around us in sub-Saharan Africa and the Middle East these woes feature in the lives of all people. However, once people have extricated themselves from these negative sociopolitical realities, as at independence, they have always tried to not recreate the very conditions that led to their misery. This is where the difference now lies. In 2011, the world eagerly expected that the people of South Sudan would rebuild their lives and their young country in peace, harmony and security; that they would build a vibrant economy anchored on agriculture, with oil money lubricating the wheels of this economy. Success in building a state and society based on law and order, respect for human rights, fundamental freedoms, and a vibrant economy would justify the 21-year war the people of South Sudan fought.

Unfortunately, this strong international goodwill for South Sudan's success did not translate into a national readiness to succeed. Instead, the leaders turned against each other to gain what they had lost during the struggle for independence. They quarrelled and fought among themselves and turned the innocent masses against each other. Now the world hears nothing about South Sudan but news of war, death, displacement, and hunger. The problem of South Sudan is now identified as the work of its very sons and daughters — the South Sudanese political, military, and business elite. The political class that evolved in the context of the people's struggle for freedom, justice, fraternity, and prosperity transformed in a space of only ten years into a pack of hyenas devouring not only the people but also the country and its resources, replaying the very games that the different Khartoum regimes have played since 1956. And they are doing this with the help of their foreign friends. The reason is simple and links to the nature of the South Sudanese intellectuals themselves. Many suffer from collective amnesia and cerebral dystrophy. Like warthogs, many have short memories. Nor have they engaged in critical self-education, reading to learn or to unlearn the outmoded ideas and concepts. Because of this, they quickly recreated the very conditions they had struggled against just a short while ago.

This book is about South Sudan, a country that upon its birth enjoyed enormous goodwill from its people and the peoples of the world. That is why the United Nations Security Council recognized South Sudan on 8 July 2011, even before its flag was raised the following day to the thunderous applause of tens of thousands braving the blazing sun on the grounds of the Dr. John Garang Memorial. Since then there has been no positive news from South Sudan, except for the fortunes made by cowboy contractors and those who came to extract and loot. There are many places in South Sudan that have never experienced peace. Soon after signing the peace agreement in 2005, as if that was a signal for renewed conflict, they rekindled the old feuds long supressed by the war. The Luach and Paweny went against each other through the agency of their sons who were competing generals in the SPLA. The Aguok and Apuk in Gogrial, the Agar clans against themselves as well as against the Gok, their neighbours in Rumbek. The Ciec, Atuot, and Aliab in the swamps of Yirol also did not spare each other. In Jonglei, the Lou Nuer, Murle, and Dinka sections had sporadic skirmishes. Near the capital Juba, the Bari and Mundari were at each other throats over land.

In 2009, President Salva Kiir brought war to the Shilluk Kingdom and, two years later, in 2010, to northern Jonglei. In Western Equatoria, Yei District included, where the sedentary tribes have been living in harmony for many years, armed Dinka pastoralists, escaping the mutual cattle raids in their areas, encroached into these areas and sparked fights with the locals over destruction of crops in Mundri (2005); and over poor relations in Yambio (2005), Maridi (2015) and Yei (2016). Many of the herds belonged to senior SPLA Dinka officers. The same could be said about conflict in Western Bahr el Ghazal. Consequently, many parts of South Sudan have known nothing but perpetual strife, largely through the proliferation of firearms. Most of these arms came from the stores of the Sudan People's Liberation Army (SPLA), the national defence force.

This book speaks to the failure of South Sudan's political elite and tries to analyse and identify the problems that have brought us to where we are today. Given the failures, one is compelled to ask how this elite succeeded in convincing people to make enormous sacrifices during the first two civil wars. Unlike many others who have contributed to knowledge generation about South Sudan, I write from the standpoint of an active participant and contributor, in one way or the other, to the situation. My intention, therefore, is to help move the political discourse forward towards conflict resolution, and to chart a course for the socioeconomic and political development of South Sudan. I come from a political school of thought to which many intellectuals in South Sudan have become resistant.

I have come to conclude that perhaps the SPLM/A meant to achieve in the war of national liberation not only independence but also a mass of people desensitized to the destiny for which they have struggled, sacrificed lives, and missed socioeconomic development opportunities. The objective of teaching Marxism-Leninism and its ideals of freedom, justice, fraternity and prosperity while practicing the very opposite of these concepts was, in fact, to produce hatred and contempt for socialist ideology. This has rendered many intellectuals in South Sudan resistant to revolutionary ideas; resistant also to a correct and scientific knowledge of a social and economic transformation of backwardness in South Sudan. This is completely and specifically true of the current brand of leaders, former officers, and combatants who in the SPLM/A now lead the country, most of whom benefited from revolutionary courses in Ethiopia and Cuba. They are the targets of my criticism. In particular, I am completely disgusted with the compatriots who believe they are opposed to the ethnocentric kleptocratic totalitarianism and yet practice the same ideology in their political outfits. The weakness of the opposition forces has granted the regime a new lease on life to continue creating humanitarian disasters throughout the country.

This is not criticism just for the sake of it. The objective is to stimulate honest debate in order to generate a correct and scientific understanding of the socioeconomic and political crisis in the country, discern its negative impact on the lives of the people and to chart ways for its transformation. My reference to the SPLM/A is in relation to the evolution of the culture of self-preservation, indifference, intrigue, short-changing, and double-talk, which evolved over the course of 21 years of struggle. It is imperative that we combat this culture as a means of emancipating ourselves from the greed and selfishness that has rendered the intellectuals oblivious to their historical responsibility to uplift the masses. This culture, it would appear, evolved because those who joined the SPLM/A were not selfless volunteers but rent-seekers who were looking for opportunities that they could not realize in peacetime. It is no wonder that comrades in the SPLM/A have undermined each other in order to rise up within the hierarchy of power. Comrades were left to sink deeper into trouble, the cynical attitude typified by the common war-time remark, "Let him increase his charges." They allowed people to commit as many mistakes as possible before those in power eventually made an arrest and laid charges.

This attitude seems to originate from the Dinka-Nuer popular wisdom: "Do not advise somebody on his way going. Advise him when he returns." The logic being that one stands to benefit from the failure of the other. It is a backward-looking social psychology which could easily create a situation of mutual blocking — because I don't want you to benefit from what I am doing, then I will not do it — and prevent a society's progress. No wonder society has remained stagnant for the last 200 years. It is a culture of silent intrigue. Which may explain why no one among the close confidantes of President Salva Kiir, particularly the top intelligence and security officers and the members of Jieng Council of Elders (JCE), is able to tell him the truth about what is happening in the country. It may be that as a dictator Kiir might not want to hear anything negative and could easily harm those who tell him the truth.

The manner in which the IGAD region has dealt with the civil war in South Sudan and the humanitarian catastrophe it has caused brings to mind the anecdote of the hippos in Malakal. One day in 1976, two angry hippos took their fight out of the River Nile and onto the land. Oblivious of the danger awaiting both of them, they charged at each other again and again, until hunters shot and killed them for food. The flipside of the civil war is that it has benefited the economies of neighbouring countries, the very same countries that are now mediating the failed peace talks. The government of the Republic of South Sudan is a member of IGAD and attends the organisation's council of ministers, as well as its summit meetings on the conflict in South Sudan, which makes it possible for the state to influence and overturn any negative reporting. It raises genuine suspicions that some of these regional leaders, particularly those who openly support President Salva Kiir, might be fuelling the conflict for their own economic advantage.

I have talked before of Jieng (Dinka) think tanks — namely the Sudd Institute and the Ebony Centre — having joined the choir and produced policy papers that effectively accelerate the downward slide of the country. These think tanks produced three studies that President Salva Kiir later passed into law. The implementation of their recommendations exacerbated the national political situation. The first was Establishment Order 36/2015, which created 28 states. It fragmented and turned South Sudan into ethnic cantons with no economic basis for viability. This is tantamount to negation of the nation-building process. The other study was on "national dialogue." Put into practice, the National Dialogue is a case of the regime dialoguing with itself. It is not possible to engage in dialogue while the war rages. The third study was on the proposed "reunification" of the feuding SPLM factions categorised as SPLM in Government (Salva Kiir Mayardit), the SPLM/A in Opposition (Riek Machar Teny-Dhurgon) and the SPLM Former Detainees (Pagan Amum). Given the animosity between the factions, attempts to achieve "reunification" are nothing more than chasing a mirage.

The book consists of this introduction, four chapters, and an epilogue, the latter of which includes a personal reflection on my participation in the SPLM/A-IO political process. It is my sincere wish that South Sudan intellectuals and the political elite take the time to read and digest these lines.

The current social configuration of South Sudan and its people is a product of historical developments that have affected the Nile Valley and surrounding areas for the last one or even two millennia. The past 200 years have witnessed the dramatic consequences of European intrusion and colonial occupation and pacification. State formation in the Sudan was by no means easy and straightforward. South Sudan is a product of the socioeconomic and political engineering processes of the Sudanese state. The condition of extreme power asymmetry, in its political and economic dimensions, started during the colonial times and continued uninterrupted upon independence and throughout national sovereignty. In Chapter One I discuss the sociopolitical duplicity (defined as attitudes, behaviours, and negative psychosocial syndromes) that emerged from conditions of extreme asymmetry in political power, wealth, and knowledge. This plays out in political exclusion, economic neglect or marginalization, and social discrimination based on ethnicity, language, and culture.

Southern Sudan and its people have always featured as a particular subset, or secondary interest, of the Sudan. Territorially, it counted as a third of the country and its people were referred to as animist. When it came to dispensing state power and resources, Southern

Sudan started to experience political exclusion, social discrimination, and economic marginalization. The stigma of the Arabic word *abeed* (slave) and other discriminatory attitudes inherited from history have defined the relations of South Sudanese with their northern Sudanese counterparts. This made the Southern Sudanese withdraw into their ethnicities, their parochial agendas, negative attitudes and behaviours, which tended to block positive thinking about the country to which they all belonged. The peculiarity of Southern Sudan and its people played out as a tendency towards separateness and of being treated as a special consideration. Over the course of time, South Sudanese began to internalize the perceptions of inferiority, of having a minority status, of being outside the "norm" of Sudanese culture and history.

This negative attitude, or sociopolitical duplicity, hampered and stymied the development of a legitimate concept of a South Sudan national consciousness. The idea of South Sudan as a nation and the struggle to achieve its independence were defined from a negative point: the South's antagonism towards north Sudan as an enemy. The enemy became the common denominator of the sense of nation shared by all of its 64 ethnicities. Thus, once the people had removed the denominator by achieving independence, the lack of a positive point of departure to form and inform the nation has bred only further sociopolitical duplicities in the form of ethnic-based political and economic hegemony and dominance of one ethnicity over all the others, which have culminated in the civil war. The corresponding attitude and behaviour of the Equatorian elite and their tendency to separate from the rest of South Sudan because they imagine that they cannot defeat Dinka hegemony and domination, as happened in the 1980s in the form of *kokora,* resonates with this analysis. It is now the main driver of "federalism" in the political discourse of the opposition and non-Dinka ethnic groups.

Federalism is not a panacea for the political ailments of South Sudan. Political exclusion, social discrimination, and economic marginalization and neglect have grown because of the oppressive system in place. The people of South Sudan will not combat and transform these ills by federating the country into three, ten, or more states. This would be tantamount to broadcasting the oppressive system to every village and hamlet in South Sudan. The way to go about this is to mobilize, organize, and unite the people to destroy the regime and transform the condition of oppression to build justice, freedom, fraternity and prosperity for all. This thinking underscored the concept and vision of the New Sudan.

Without a paradigm shift, South Sudanese do not have the possibility of transforming oppression and entrenching the unity of the Sudan and its people. The tendency to create more states in South Sudan only enables the oppressive regime to buy allegiances and reproduce itself. This profusion of states now serves as a big obstacle to a transition to statehood and nationhood.

The formation of the SPLM/A, chanting the slogan of a united socialist New Sudan, is something many people on the political left took with a pinch of salt. This is not because a socialist movement cannot emerge from southern Sudan. It is just that society is southern Sudan was still backward and the level of social awareness and political consciousness still low as its productive forces remained underdeveloped. The ideological shift from the revolution (liberation) to liberal and right-wing ideologies, coinciding with the collapse of the socialist camp, led to a political shift from the vision and concept of New Sudan to a demand for the right of self-determination for southern Sudan. This opened the way for liberal peacemaking, culminating in the Comprehensive Peace Agreement (CPA) in 2005, and independence and the birth of the Republic of South Sudan in 2011.

Chapter Two describes and discusses the SPLM/A as a revolution that never was. Its leaders imagined it as a revolution but their practice was contrary to the revolutionary ethos. It lacked a political ideology; its leaders shunned ideological training, political enlightenment of the masses, and organization of institutions and instruments of people's power. It therefore boiled down to a military and militaristic organization. It was not a liberation enterprise because it employed militarism as a tool for suppression and the dampening of people's social awareness and political consciousness. The excessive reliance on militarism supported a leader's cult of personality, leading to personification rather than institutionalization of the SPLM/A power and public authority. The militarism, dampening of consciousness, and the leader's cult of personality led to an upsurge of Dinka ethnic nationalism and the evolution of an elitist class completely alienated from the liberation ethos and the masses. The questions of power and the struggle to wield it distracted the movement from the issues of social and economic development of the areas that came under its military control — this control being its raison d'être — and became the main driver of the internal political contradictions that triggered splits and internecine fighting within the SPLM/A throughout the entire period of war. This overshadowed the liberation process and prevented the evolution of a national agenda that would overcome ethnic and provincial tendencies.

The manner in which the SPLM/A managed the war of national liberation continued after the CPA, precipitating conditions for the start of a civil war. The current conflict is, in essence, a reflection of the political and economic failure of the SPLM/A as a revolutionary force in South Sudan. The CPA thrust the SPLM/A onto the unfamiliar ground of government and managing a state. In Chapter Three, I have attempted to analyse the causes and triggers of the civil war, which erupted in 2013, examining the internal power struggle driven by ethnic ideologies. It is worth saying that the failure to build strong political and state institutions and instruments of power during the war of national liberation entrenched the personification of power and this now drives the power struggle in the SPLM. The links between state power, ethnic ideologies and the primitive accumulation of wealth combined into an explosive alloy that transformed the regime into an ethnocentric, kleptocratic, and totalitarian dictatorship. This dictatorship was supported by regional and international comprador capitalism in the context of the extraction and plunder of South Sudan's natural resources.

The war could have been avoided but President Salva Kiir had emasculated the state and political institutions that would have intervened, on account of their constitutional functions, to stop the president from escalating the political crisis in the SPLM in order to unleash war. As SPLM chair, Kiir paralyzed the political functions of the SPLM and rendered irrelevant the organs that make up the ruling party. The Legislative Assembly abdicated its oversight functions; ethnic politics made the august house a rubber stamp of the executive. The judiciary lost its independence because the chief justice was a member of the JCE, being the chairperson of the Agwok community in Kiir's home area. The judiciary, therefore, could not challenge the unconstitutional decisions the president enacted into law. I also explain how the president blackmailed the SPLA generals, allowing them to steal money to the point that they could not face him when he recruited and armed a private army, Dotku Beny, separate and parallel to the SPLA he is commander in chief of. The army had the capacity to prevent the war by arresting and allowing the impeachment of the president for treason. The IGAD-mediated peace agreement (ARCISS) was flawed from its inception because of its negotiation modality. The division within the mediation created loopholes for non-implementation and this created conditions for rekindling the conflict, leading to the collapse of the TGoNU and the ARCISS. It is not clear whether the attempts to revitalize ARCISS will ever bear fruit, given the weakness of the opposition and the intransigence of President Kiir and the hawkish elements in his regime.

The IGAD High Level Revitalization Forum (HLRF) can only result in cosmetic changes in the power-sharing agreement. This leaves the conflict elements energized and combustible. In the absence of radical changes in the oppressive nature of the regime, it means that the proposed elections at the end of the interim or transitional period may trigger the conflict again, bringing the country back to square one. In view of these dilemmas of vicious cycles of war and peace, the question remains: What is the alternative?

In Chapter Four, I discuss national democratic revolution (NDR) as the only viable option for fixing the social, economic, and political crisis in South Sudan. NDR builds on the concept that the fundamental contradiction in South Sudan is the centuries-old condition of socioeconomic and cultural backwardness of its people, characterized by poverty, ignorance, illiteracy, and superstition. This condition submerges their consciousness and prevents a correct perception of reality. I discuss the programmatic platform on which NDR is anchored, a platform that addresses the myriad of problems that the right-wing and traditional leaders have failed to grasp.

South Sudan has enormous natural resource potential. The main task of the NDR is to develop and free the national productive forces from all kinds of foreign control and domination. However, to spark the national democratic revolution, all the progressive democratic social and political forces must coalesce into an alliance united by a common desire to construct a national democratic developmental state in South Sudan, one that addresses the condition of socioeconomic and cultural underdevelopment. The national democratic programme, therefore, is a tool to address poverty, ignorance, and illiteracy in society, and to address the question of ethnicity, which the political elite has exploited to maintain themselves in power. The NDR is a socioeconomic and political development paradigm, which is appropriate for this historical stage of development in South Sudan.

The purpose of this book is to stimulate critical debate and political discourse both at home and among the South Sudan diaspora on the future of South Sudan and the destiny of its people. The people of South Sudan love their country, despite the difficulties caused by the political elite in pursuit of their selfish ambitions for power and wealth. They are resilient, tenacious and forgiving. With a responsible government and just system, they could one day rebuild their lives.

The collective weakness is our inability to liberate ourselves from the claws of negative ethnicity. This is evident among the South Sudanese who have migrated in sizeable numbers to other lands, to the USA, Canada, and Australia. They have carried the ethnicity virus to form into communities based on ethnicity and clans, and interact based on prejudices and animosities communicated from relatives back home. The divisions in the South Sudan diaspora reinforce the conflicts back home, creating a vicious circle of self-destruction. I would advise those in the diaspora to integrate into and benefit from the host society in terms of knowledge and technology, as the Asians and Europeans have done. It will be in this way that sons and daughters living abroad could benefit the Republic of South Sudan in the future.

CHAPTER ONE

Elites, Ethnic Politics, and the Stunted State

The unprecedented, even hysteric, euphoria that accompanied South Sudan's independence celebration on 9 July 2011 can only be explained by the collective struggle that spanned nearly six decades. The people of South Sudan had every right to be euphoric. Many shed tears at the raising of the SPLM colours and the simultaneous lowering of the Sudanese flag that had flown over Southern Sudan soil since 1 January 1956. The South Sudanese had traversed a turbulent path to independence. Their relentless struggle, inspired by dreams of freedom, justice, fraternity, and prosperity, had paid off at last, giving them full control over their destiny. The birth of the Republic of South Sudan had the goodwill of its people, the members of the international community who assisted the struggle through massive international humanitarian intervention, as well as the regional and African friends of the people of South Sudan who provided logistics for the war of liberation.[3]

But it would be with great difficulty that a region like South Sudan, emerging from decades of war and conflict, could undertake the task of statehood and nationhood. The spectre of fragility still afflicted and affected every aspect of human life in post-war South Sudan. The liberation leaders still suffered from the war hangover. The culture of peace and state formation, in terms of institutions and instruments of

---

[3] The first benefactors of the SPLM/A were the government and the people of Ethiopia, Libya's Col. Muammer Gadhafi and South Yemen.

power, had yet to permeate and influence the management skills of the new state. Moreover, the art of government and good governance for that matter was a challenge for many of the SPLM leaders and cadres. Some of them had entered the war of national liberation at a tender age, politically speaking. This would not have been a problem if the SPLM/A had organized in a manner that gave knowledge and experience to its leaders and cadres. In terms of patriotism and respect for the people, some of the leaders who were now to govern the nascent state were worse off than when they joined the SPLM/A in 1983. The immediate task in front of them required skills and morals completely different from the ones they had employed to conduct the war of national liberation. Peacetime sensibilities were different, creating a sociopolitical disconnect when the leaders tried to manage the fragile state in the same way they had led the war of national liberation. This triggered a spark and the resultant conflagration brought a quick end to the independence euphoria. Less than two years into its independence, the Republic of South Sudan had slid into a situation of war, vindicating those who had doubted the ability of South Sudanese to govern themselves.

Academics, researchers, and politicians may spend time splitting hairs on this issue. I am convinced that it was not about the people of South Sudan failing to govern themselves; rather, it was the political leadership in Southern Sudan failing to meet the aspirations of the people. The art of government is something acquired through learning and unlearning. However, the failure of the political elite to meet people's aspirations for socioeconomic development stemmed from two fundamental factors.

The first factor was the lack of political ideology that would have enabled an understanding of the nature of the socioeconomic and cultural backwardness of the country and methods for its transformation. Linked to this was the refusal to organize and construct the democratic political institutions and instruments of power necessary for managing the liberation processes. These factors rolled into an explosive alloy, the domino effect of which transformed into the drivers of social and political unrest in South Sudan. In this respect leadership is not just about the individual at the helm but also about the national liberation movement. It is about the ruling party: its ideology, political objectives, institutions, and instruments of public authority and power that leaders constructed or did not construct in the course of two decades of struggle. In this respect, therefore, there was a failure to transform the SPLM/A from a spontaneous mass movement driven by individuals, in the context of struggle for struggle, into a genuine national liberation movement with defined strategic political objectives to transform the conditions of socioeconomic and cultural backwardness of South Sudan.

We believed that the revolutionary war of national liberation was a negation of the established system of political exclusion, economic marginalization and social discrimination practiced in the Sudan consequent to its historical development. The SPLM/A was to be a revolutionary solution to the contradiction inherent in Sudan's colonial history and after. This meant that the SPLM/A should have built a socioeconomic and political system completely different and antagonistic to the National Congress Party (NCP), as well as the regimes that preceded it in governing the Sudan. This is where the political failure lies, which now plays out as the civil war and the deepening social, economic, and political crisis of the regime. These crises are the outcome of attempts by the political leadership to replay the politics of earlier regimes.

The Sudan, and for that matter South Sudan, was a colonial construct under conditions of extreme violence, the relics of which to this date still inform and condition the attitudes, behaviours and relations of the Sudanese people, whether in its southern, western, central, eastern, or northern parts. As a colonial construct it suggests that the evolution of the Sudan both physically and in the social consciousness of its people is intrinsically linked to the colonial policy, the then-dominant sociopolitical engineering processes at work and the psychological effects they produced. It therefore requires on every scholar who investigates the current context of South Sudan to study the recent and contemporary history of the Sudan. This is precisely because, until 2011, South Sudan was an integral part of the Sudan. The struggles in southern Sudan that eventually culminated in its secession from the Sudan are closely linked to the socioeconomic and political developments of the Sudan from 1821, following the Turco-Egyptian invasion of northern Sudan. The sociocultural and political attitudes and behaviours in South Sudan today can be traced back to this history. The evolution of the southern Sudan as a political concept and its eventual secession as an independent country should be seen in the context of British colonial policy.

In this connection it is necessary from the outset to review certain concepts and perceptions that inform the evolution of social consciousness in Southern Sudan as a subset different from and antagonistic to the Sudanese national consciousness prevalent in

Arab and Islam-dominated northern Sudan. Both the southern and northern elite would agree that this subnational characterization, referred to as "the problem of southern Sudan", dominated relations between southern Sudan and the Sudan after independence in 1956. The very concept of "the problem of southern Sudan" is a right-wing construct arising from their inability to conceptualise or understand the socioeconomic and political character of the Sudan. It was an incorrect reading of the socioeconomic and political reality of the Anglo-Egyptian Sudan. The fundamental contradiction that continues to afflict the Sudans (both the Republic of the Sudan and the Republic of South Sudan) is the general problem of socioeconomic and cultural underdevelopment of the Sudanese people.

This condition of socioeconomic and cultural backwardness is a general situation throughout the peripheral Sudan. However, this condition was particularly extreme in southern Sudan because of the colonial administration politics of uneven socio-economic development, dictated by extraction and the pursuit of profit. There was some measure of investment in some parts of northern Sudan, particularly in Gezira and Khartoum. This selective development to satisfy colonial economic interests led to the emergence of a small, modern economic sector linked to the colonial state, what was later categorized as the Hamdi triangle, leaving the rest of the country as a source of cheap labour for the Gezira and other large-scale mechanized agricultural schemes in the White Nile and Gedaref areas.[4] It is worth remembering that the British reconquest of the Sudan came in the context of the European scramble for Africa. The Sudan was governed by a condominium of the British and Egyptian crowns vide the Anglo-Egyptian Condominium Treaty (1899). It is also important to note that three major political objectives prompted the British decision to reconquer the Sudan from the Mahdiyya.[5] These were, first, to defeat and punish the Mahdists for the death of Charles Gordon, the governor-general of the Turco-Egyptian state; second, to restore the Sudan to the Egyptian Crown; and third, to abolish and stamp out the Nile Valley and Red Sea slavery and slave trade in the Sudan. The British achieved

---

[4] Named after the former NCP economist and minister of finance and national economy. Hamdi believed that the *kayan al shamal* ruling elite should just concentrate on the triangular area bordered by Atbara in the north; El Obeid in the west; Sennar in the south; Gedaref, Kassala, and Port Sudan in the east; and forget about Southern Sudan, Dar Fur, and northern Sudan.

[5] The state and system of government established in the Sudan after the Mahdist nationalist revolution defeated the Turco-Egyptian state in 1885.

their objectives but refused to restore the Sudan to the Egyptian Crown. The Anglo-Egyptian Sudan was essentially British-administered while the Egyptians footed the bill for this administration. This generated political ripples between the two powers in the execution of the condominium treaty. The upshot of the poor relations was the White Flag Revolution, staged by Sudanese elements in the Egyptian Army of occupation in the Sudan.

The British reaction to the White Flag Revolution was typical: collective punishment of the people who had challenged the power and authority of the occupying power. The British colonial authority correctly read the threat that Africans inspired by Islam and Arab culture posed to its colonial interests. Suffice to say that the leaders of the White Flag Revolution — Lt. Ali Abdel Latif and Abdel Fadhil el Mahz — were black African Sudanese in the Egyptian Army. The British administration decided to insulate and isolate southern Sudan, Nuba Mountains and Southern Blue Nile — areas inhabited by non-Muslim African people — from the rest of the country and the civilized world. It enacted the Closed Districts Ordinance and instituted the "policy of southern provinces" which saw the southern provinces of Bahr el Ghazal, Equatoria and Upper Nile administered differently and separately from the rest of the country. Special travel permits were required to cross their common borders.

The strikingly negative aspect of the British policy of southern provinces, apart from the neglect of socioeconomic development, was its surrender to the Christian missionaries the provision of education in southern Sudan. The Christian missionaries did not have any other capacity apart from proselytization. The objective of the limited, substandard education the missionaries offered was to produce junior clerks, bookkeepers, dressers, village-school teachers, and timekeepers to serve the colonial administration. It was an education deliberately tailored to instil in southern Sudanese extreme hatred of the northern Sudan in general, and the Arabs and Islam in particular. It also instilled in southern Sudanese an inferiority complex and a fear of authority. This rendered them apolitical, while their pathetic socioeconomic and cultural backwardness could neither stir in them anti-colonial passions nor inspire nationalist instincts. This substandard education efficaciously diverted their attention from their backwardness to a hatred of the northern Sudanese. Thus, in matters of national liberation, southern Sudanese unconsciously found themselves on the same side as the British colonialism, in the false belief that the British would develop southern Sudan to the level it could one day govern itself.

The situation in northern Sudan was completely different. Its proximity to Egypt and the Middle East enabled its people to access modern education facilities up to the university level; there was a social and political awareness linked to the Islamic faith, which enabled social clubs and civil institutions to sprout in northern Sudan, laying down the sociopolitical foundations of the nationalist anti-colonial movement.[6] Social awareness and political consciousness, foundation stones of nationalist anti-colonial movements, are functions of the development of national productive forces and therefore reflect the level of socioeconomic, cultural and political development. Education and knowledge of social and political processes play a pivotal role in the evolution of social awareness and political consciousness. Therefore, the British colonial policy surrounding the Closed Districts Ordinance and the "policy of southern provinces" — imposed on the southern provinces, Nuba Mountains, and Southern Blue Nile provinces — condemned the people of southern Sudan to ignorance, illiteracy and the superstition inherent in ethnic autochthony and exclusive tribal life.

The other aspect of the British policy of southern provinces linked to reconquest objectives of Christian proselytization was the undeclared intention to separate off the southern provinces of the Sudan and annex the area to British East Africa. This ostensibly was to stop Islamic penetration into central Africa. This policy could not have been more misguided: Islam had reached Central Africa from the Indian Ocean coast long before the European occupation of the Sudan. However, political realities stirred by post-war anti-colonial movements in the world forced a reversal of this policy to allow for reunification of the hitherto separately administered parts of the Sudan. This policy reversal, coming after nearly three decades of separate and uneven socioeconomic and political evolution of northern and southern Sudan, suggestive of different idiosyncrasies and political sensibilities, inevitably led to social and political problems in their relations. Moreover, the British administration did little in terms of socioeconomic development to improve living conditions and, therefore, allay southern Sudanese fears of the anticipated symmetrical relations with their northern Sudanese compatriots. The Azande development scheme came too little too late.

---

[6] Islam is state, religion, and culture, all embedded together and therefore influencing social and political consciousness.

In northern Sudan, unlike in the southern region, there were social and political formations. There were organized and authentic political parties linked to theocratic sects and a secular intellectual formation, the Graduates' Congress, which led the nationalist anti-colonial movement in northern Sudan. This reflected a high level of social awareness and political consciousness. In the southern provinces, however, colonial policy entrenched sociocultural conditions, which prevented the evolution of a shared national awareness and political consciousness among southern Sudanese. Since there were no organized political parties, the politicians who rose up to represent the people of southern Sudan were unable to pull the masses into a democratic and political programme linked to the nationalist anti-colonial movement in northern Sudan. The Welfare Committee Movement that fronted for southern Sudanese social and economic demands, and tried to put pressure on the colonial administration, was formed only after the Juba Conference in 1947.

The terrible social, economic, and cultural backwardness of southern Sudan, the tribal autochthony and its exclusiveness, and the complete absence of a working or bourgeois nationalist class remain to date impediments to authentic national state formation, national cohesion, and stability. This was so even after Sudan gained independence in the 1950s. This stemmed partly from the faith the burgeoning Southern Sudan political leaders put in elements of the colonial administration to protect the South from the North. In the end, northerners came to see southerners as agents or puppets of the colonial power. This condition of poor social awareness and political consciousness created the breeding ground for ethnic nationalism and its ideology of ethnic supremacy, trumping attempts to form a progressive national liberation ideology that would unite all the ethnic communities in southern Sudan, as I describe in Chapter Two.

Evolution of Political Action in Southern Sudan

The British colonial administration's frenetic efforts to unite the two parts of the Sudan as it edged towards independence came in the form of a conference. Although it appeared to be a forum for southern opinion about the proposed unity with the north, the Juba Conference of 1947 came in the wake of the reversal of British policy on the southern provinces (1946). The colonial civil secretary, Sir James Robertson, convened the Juba Conference in Juba to underscore this change of policy, which had kept apart for three decades northern and southern

Sudan. If anything, the conference was used to manipulate the southern representatives into accepting unity with northern Sudan. Sir James Robertson later admitted,

> I looked upon the conference solely as a means of finding out the capabilities of the Southerners, and it was quite inaccurate for some people to say later that at the Juba conference the southern representatives agreed to come in with the north. No decision could be made at the conference, since members had received no mandate from their peoples ... the only decision resulting from the conference was taken by myself.[7]

Indeed, the Juba conference exposed the extent to which the British southern policy had disadvantaged the people of southern Sudan, leaving them socioeconomically and culturally backward compared to northern Sudanese.

Thus, when some southern Sudanese conferees requested that the colonial government let southern Sudan remain under British rule until such time as it was ready to govern itself they appeared to be driven by genuine concerns over this social and political disparity. It was also a sign of desperation triggered by the southerners' sense of inferiority and alienation from their northern compatriots. It is, therefore, difficult to view the request as an authentic wish or will of the people of southern Sudan, regardless of the recommendations that came out of the Juba Conference. This is precisely because, while graduates of law, economics and other humanities represented northern Sudan, the people of southern Sudan were represented by tribal chiefs, junior clerks, and other colonial officials, who by virtue of their jobs would not express a political opinion. It was in this vein that Sayyed Edward Odhok Didigo made sure that the minutes noted that he did not represent the Shilluk people because that was the prerogative of the Shilluk king.

The Juba Conference achieved the desired objective of the colonial administration to placate British Southern administrators. They were opposed to the 1946 Aministrative Conference for Southerners to send members to the Legislation Assembly in Khartoum, thereby bringing the Sudan into independence as one country. This was notwithstanding the fact that the conference entrenched the suspicions of southern Sudanese towards the north, particularly in in view of the overtly racist attitudes of some of the northern political elite. The conference alerted the southern Sudanese to a process that had never before crossed their

---

[7] This was in a conversation with Walter Kunijwok Ayoker, a PhD Student at Oxford University in the 1970s, quoted by Douglas H. Johnson in *South Sudan Past Notes and Records* (2015).

minds. It made them aware and hooked their hopes to the process leading to independence. This heralded the beginning of politics in southern Sudan. This awareness, which was not supported by a clear understanding of the nature of politics, made it difficult to combine and unify this nascent political movement in southern Sudan with the nationalist anti-colonial movement in northern Sudan, regardless of the fact that Sudan would soon become independent as one country.

Nationalist and political developments in Egyptian accelerated the Sudanese independence process. It is worth mentioning that the overthrow of the feudal regime had a profound impact on the condominium powers in the Sudan. The nationalist government in Cairo wanted the Sudan to become independent within the context of the unity of the Nile Basin. The Anglo-Egyptian Cairo Agreement of February 1953 provided for self-determination for the Sudanese people and accelerated the process of self-rule and formation of a government to lead the country to independence. The northern political elite harboured condescending and paternalistic attitudes towards their counterparts in southern Sudan (as reflected in their agreement with the new Egyptian regime, without involving southerners). This conditioned and influenced the south Sudanese views toward the post-independence unity of the Sudan, and strengthened the resolve for a federation with the north.

The prevalent socioeconomic and cultural backwardness and the exclusive tribal and rural life in southern Sudan are conditions under which evolution of people's social awareness and political consciousness, as well as the cultivation of a culture of organized political activity, can never emerge. Social awareness, political consciousness, and organized political activity trigger and promote critical thinking and increased political activity, leading to more refined organizational skills. Politics in southern Sudan, mainly in the context of the struggle for rights, started as late as the 1950s. As earlier mentioned, the British policy of southern provinces surrendered the provision of education to Christian missionaries, who suppressed political awareness and, therefore, rendered southerners incapable of organizing politically. The first authentic political party southern Sudanese created was the Liberal Party (1954–1958). Without exception, the big names that pop up in the history of political struggle in southern Sudan, beginning with the Juba Conference in 1947, were all right wing, liberals, or conservative traditionalists whose beliefs were anchored in exclusive tribal life.

The problem of the right-wing and the traditionalist politicians in southern Sudan, like everywhere, is their lack of scientific understanding of the underpinnings of society's development. This explains why they ignored the fundamental contradiction between the Sudanese people and imperialism, which necessitated a joint concerted social and political struggle for independence and sovereignty. Instead, they projected and heightened the secondary contradictions between southerners and northerners in order to promote secessionist tendencies in their political work. This created a political environment of mutual mistrust, suspicion, manipulation, trickery, and chicanery in the Sudanese body politics, characterized by extreme asymmetry in the distribution of power and wealth.

The Genesis of Sociopolitical Duplicity

Sociopolitical duplicity includes the attitudes, behaviours, and psychological syndromes that emerge in a political environment characterized by conditions of extreme power asymmetry. Power defines, in both political and economic conditions, the relations between social and political groups, and therefore determines social and political stability in the country. Sociopolitical duplicity plays out in political chicanery, backtracking on promises, political exclusion, economic marginalisation, and social discrimination based on race, ethnicity, religion, language, or gender; as well as in syndromes of inferiority, superiority, hegemony, domination, and such attitudes as "born to rule."

The syndrome of sociopolitical duplicity we observe among the South Sudanese political elite is a product of the relationships in the Sudan that triggered the two civil wars, leading eventually to the independence of South Sudan in 2011. It is typical of oppressed people, as studies by Frantz Fanon in the *Wretched of the Earth* (1963) and Paulo Freire in the *Pedagogy of the Oppressed* (1975), showed. These syndromes underpin South Sudan's current traumatising predicament. They play out in the form of pretension, dishonesty, double-talking, dual and incoherent national identity, displays of superiority over other citizens by treating them as second-class citizens to engender a corresponding sense of inferiority, and many other serious political obfuscations in the southern Sudanese political thought and practice.

These sociopsychological and political factors are congenital with colonial state formation in the Sudan. They therefore are sociopolitical constructs located in the violence linked to the state formation and the subsequent uneven socioeconomic and political development of the

Sudan. The two parts of the same country were at different and varying levels of socioeconomic and cultural development when the British colonial administration reversed its policy of southern provinces in order to unite the country before independence.

The apparent weakness of the left-wing forces in the nationalist movement in northern Sudan entrenched the dominance of right-wing and sectarian religious political forces in the body politics of the emerging Sudanese state. The minor role assigned to southern politicians, informed by northern Sudan's condescending attitudes towards southern Sudanese in general, calling them *abeed* (slave), "missionary boys", among other derogatory words, weakened the nationalist agenda for the unity of the Sudanese people and heightened southern Sudanese determination to federate the country. The question of which sectarian party, between the Ansar sect's Umma Party (UP) and the Khatmiyya sect's National Unionist Party (NUP), would raise the flag of independence was a factor in the elections for the Constituent Assembly (1954), leading to self-government. Ismael el Azhari's NUP won the largest number of seats, making him the prime minister. This was the result of an alliance with southern Sudanese, whom he promised positions in government. Because they had no organized political outfit, the southern politicians played a secondary role in the power scrimmage, which was dominated by the Umma Party, NUP and People's Democratic Party (PDP), collectively known as *kayan al shamal*.[8]

Members of the *kayan al shamal* did not treat the southern politicians as equals, heightening the mutual suspicion, which spiralled into political adventurism on both sides in the Sudanization of the colonial state. The politics of double-talk and empty promises culminated in the military action undertaken by the officers and soldiers of the Southern Corps in Torit on 18 August 1955. In fact, had the *kayan al shamal* acted wisely and sensitively to southern Sudanese sensitivities as they managed the Sudanization, it would have been possible to defeat the conspiracy to split the country. Their attempt to stifle the workers' dissent in Nzara and the forceful transfer of the Southern Corps of the Sudan Defence Forces (SDF) to northern Sudan rendered inevitable the mutiny in Torit and the outbreak of the "southern disturbances" in August 1955.

---

[8] No Southern Sudanese leader participated in the 1952 Cairo Agreement talks. The only participants were northern political parties and the new Egyptian regime. This agreement provided for the exercise of the right of self-determination. This became the basis of the SPLM's contention during the CPA negotiations that the people of Southern Sudan, unlike their compatriots in northern Sudan, had never exercised their inalienable right to self-determination.

The dominance of right-wing and neo-liberal ideologies in the body politics of the nascent state not only distorted and dichotomized the nationalist anti-colonial movement but also played out clearly in the political events that led to the Torit mutiny and the subsequent repercussions and revenge campaign. In fact, the mutiny was a reflection of the lack of political sophistication among southern Sudanese political groups and their manipulation by elements of the British colonial establishment. Although the people of the Republic of South Sudan celebrate 18 August 1955 as marking the beginning of the armed resistance to northern Sudan's political establishment, this came as an afterthought and falsehood peddled by the SPLM/A in the wake of the war of national liberation.

The objectives of the mutiny were not linked to the nationalist anti-colonial movement in terms of accelerating the independence process. The mutiny was indeed independence's antithesis and was the result of a confused power struggle between the competing political groups in southern Sudan (Garang, 1961) and the obfuscations interjected by elements in the British colonial administration who wanted to continue colonial rule in the guise of separating and annexing southern Sudan to British East Africa. These British elements had no way of coming to their aid on the D-day, forcing them to surrender to the forces airlifted from northern Sudan. The mutiny (and the subsequent politicking) not only further polluted north-south relations, it also denied the people of Southern Sudan the benefit of the patriotic role they had played in the unanimous vote for Sudan's independence in the Constituent Assembly on 19 December 1955. The *kayan al shamal*, now fully in control of the state, treated the southern Sudanese as second-class citizens in the country of their birth. The mutiny and the disturbances in southern provinces, as the political establishment categorized the mutiny as it engulfed all of southern Sudan, worsened the already poor relations between northern and southern Sudan as the country edged towards independence.

The *kayan al shamal*, representing the social, economic, and political interests of the Arabs in the Sudan, notwithstanding their demographic minority status, took full control of the state. Not only did they monopolize the political and economic powers of the nascent state, they also defined the Sudan along the two parameters of Islam and Arab culture, considering the Sudanese nationality in transition to full integration of the Africans in the Sudan into Arab nationhood. This definition of the Sudan along Arab and Islamic parameters created a false socioeconomic and political reality that, as will become apparent later, the dominant South Sudan political elite failed to politically resist but instead belaboured to join their system. This rendered the Arabized riverine nationalities (Danagalla, Shaigiya, and Jaalieen), collectively referred to as *kayan al shamal*, the de facto rulers of the Sudan, to the chagrin of African Sudanese, whom they categorized according to their respective regions as *Garaba* (westerners), Sharqieen (easterners) and Jinubieen (southerners).

The northern Sudanese claim to being Arab links to the Islamic history of the area. Traditionally, the rulers were portrayed as the direct blood relatives or descendants of the Prophet. This suggests that those in the Sudan who have Arab blood in their veins would automatically claim power, thus reinforcing the fallacious assumption that Islam and Arab culture were the dominant features of the Sudan. In this social and political configuration of the Sudan it was difficult for non-Arab Muslims, particularly people from Dar Fur and Eastern Sudan, to contradict this falsehood. It fell to the southerners alone, including Muslims, to contest and combat this falsehood in the form of the two civil wars. It is always difficult, if not impossible, to engineer solidarity and unity among the politically excluded, the economically neglected and socially discriminated; religious fraternity and fellowship poses a stronger counterforce than class solidarity. As a result, support for southern Sudan federation among the African bloc (Beja and Nuba) in the Constituent Assembly (1956) fizzled out quickly.

In this respect, it was easier for the *kayan al shamal* to mobilize and turn against the South the Muslim African ethnicities in northern Sudan (including Fur, Zagahwa, Masaalit, Nuba, and Funj) on the basis of religious solidarity. Indeed, submerged by poverty and ignorance these Africans could not recognise the similarity of their socioeconomic condition to that of the southern provinces. They therefore fought the war (1955–1972) in southern Sudan as foot soldiers commanded by officer corps hailing from the *kayan al shamal* in what the Arabs designed as "*aktul el abeed b'abeed*" (kill a slave with a slave), suggesting that the riverine Arabs have never trusted the African Muslims in the North.[9] This attitude takes on another connotation — of the *garaba* versus *awlad al bahr* — in the context of the violent contradiction that

---

[9] After the war and following the Addis Ababa Agreement (1972), Southern Sudan won regional autonomy while the foot soldiers from Dar Fur, Nuba Mountains, and Southern Blue Nile who fought the war zealously and enthusiastically, razing villages, raping, and killing southerners indiscriminately and mercilessly, went back to their villages, bitter with the *kayan al shamal*. When the war erupted again in 1983, these Africans took up arms to fight for their rights. The

emerged between Khalifa Abdullai el Taisha and the *Ashraf* (relatives of the Mahdi) following the death of Mohammed Ahmed el Mahdi in 1885, leading to their rebellion against Khalifa's rule in the northern province.[10]

The post-colonial Sudanese identity and national consciousness fragmented along many lines. On the one hand, there was the Arab-Muslim identity and concentration of political and economic wealth in the hands of the *kayan al shamal*, now in control of the centre and, on the other, the oppressed, poverty-ridden and politically excluded African masses in the west, south, and east. The national politics of sustaining such a sociopolitical configuration must, of necessity, be based on an extreme power asymmetry. This created divisions between the rulers and the ruled along clear racial lines. The Arabs were the rulers and Africans the ruled, spurring images of superiority and inferiority respectively in the psyche and social consciousness of the rulers and the ruled. This prevented or indeed blocked evolution among the oppressors and the oppressed of shared values like a unified national consciousness and commitment to a national identity. This dichotomized identity was very clear to southern Sudanese, unlike their other African compatriots where the factor of Islamic religion lingered to explain some of their attitudes and behaviours.

A cursory review of the period from independence in 1956 and the leftist military coup of May 1969 shows a pattern of attitudes and behaviour among the southern Sudanese political class and intellectuals in general that affirmed the power asymmetry between northern and southern Sudan, between the Arabs and Africans in the Sudan. Similar features were evident in the socioeconomic and political development of the independent Republic of South Sudan, which supports a theoretical generalization of the sociopolitical duplicity in the political thought of South Sudan's political elite. The factors of sociopolitical duplicity that triggered the north-south Sudan standoff and perpetual civil strife, which culminated in its dismemberment, are now at work in South Sudan, blocking its transition to statehood and nationhood.

---

war that erupted in Dar Fur in 2003 was part of the awakening of the Muslim Africans to their predicament under the dominance of the *kayan al shamal*.

[10] In this context, the riverine Arabs, the Ashraf, saw themselves as the rightful inheritors of the Mahdist state in terms of power and wealth. This contradiction played out in the consolidation of western Sudan as the stronghold of the Ansar, while eastern Sudan was the stronghold of the Khatmiyya. With the rise of the elitist Islamic fundamentalist movement, the social base of which was in Dar Fur and Kordofan while its leadership came from *awlad al bahr*, this contradiction flared up against in the form of war in Dar Fur.

It is worth saying that the first generation of southern Sudanese politicians (1940s–1965) had high ambitions, in terms of their political consciousness, organization, and mobilization of the masses for political purposes. They were the architects and engineers of southern Sudanese nationalist sentiments, for lack of a better expression to describe the rudimentary, subconscious feelings that evolved among southern Sudanese consequent to the implementation of the British colonial policy of southern provinces. These instincts united the people of southern Sudan, particularly among the educated class. The schools were the avenues for enriching those sentiments, leading to the emergence of the second and third generation of political leaders and activists. The striking feature of these early politicians was the apparent lack of ethnic tendency in their political dealings, which emerged much later in the context of political party organization and mobilization.

In the sense of political development and the sophistication of political work, southern Sudan produced second-generation (1956–1983) and third-generation (1983–) political leaders without clear distinction, even though they had access to better education facilities and opportunities to develop their political and organizational skills. For whatever reason, these emerging political leaders, although operating in a better national and international political and diplomatic environment, were not able enough to benefit from that environment. The reason for this anomaly is simple. The negativities inherent in the extreme condition of power asymmetry in their relations with the *kayan al shamal* submerged their consciousness and blocked critical and strategic thinking, disposing them to parochial agendas and sensibilities. One such negativity is the sociopolitical duplicity that hampered and stymied the engineering of a scientific concept of a South Sudan national consciousness from a positive vantage point, and also prevented a liberation-led concept and vision of the new Sudan. Instead, the concept of South Sudan as a national state was defined from a negative reference point, informed by the years of struggle and antagonism towards the "enemy." The enemy became the common denominator for the sense of nation, comprising all the ethnicities and largely informed by social and political duplicity. Thus, once that common denominator disappeared — whether by defeat or independence from it — the lack of a positive point of departure to form and inform the nation bred only further sociopolitical duplicities.

In an effort to illustrate these recurrent phenomena, let us examine the Turco-Egyptian occupation of northern Sudan and the establishment of a corrupt and oppressive regime centred in Khartoum. This united the Sudanese people against the regime in a revolution under the leadership of Mohammed Ahmed el Mahdi. The defeat of the Turkiyya did not produce a just and democratic Mahdist state in the Sudan to reflect the aspirations of the Sudanese people who had united against oppression and the plunder of their natural resources. The Mahdist state (1881–1898) reproduced an oppressive regime, leading to the rebellion of riverine Arabs against the rule of Khalifa Abdullai. The rebellion and discord within the Khalifa's regime facilitated and accelerated the defeat of the Mahdiyya and the reconquest of the Sudan, leading to the establishment of the Anglo-Egyptian state in the Sudan (1898–1956).

The nationalist anti-colonial movement emerged first in northern Sudan, where social awareness and political consciousness had evolved, benefiting from the colonial system of uneven socioeconomic and political development, as well as northern Sudan's proximity to Egypt and the Middle East. However, the Arab-dominated northern political elite exploited this to disadvantage southern Sudan. The disparaging and condescending arm's length posture northerners adopted towards their southern compatriots invoked secessionist tendencies in southern Sudan. However, these secessionist movements in southern Sudan did not encourage, as would have been expected, the type of social awareness and political consciousness that could be used to form and inform the foundation of an emerging South Sudan nation. Instead, subconscious subjectivities and sensibilities were stirred, which triggered civil strife and stymied the process of state formation and nation building.

The nearly three decades' long (1956–1983) experience with state formation and nation building in the Sudan demonstrated how difficult it was to erase the negative images of slavery and slave trade from the Arab elite subconscious, which their ancestors carried out on the Africans in the nineteenth century. The commonplace use of the word *abeed*, meant to remind the southerners of their inferiority, widened the rift between the northern and southern Sudanese throughout this period. The Liberal Party, the main southern political outfit, carried out most of its political activities in Khartoum and other northern Sudanese towns and cities because of the existing state of emergency in southern Sudan. The military coup on 17 November 1958 ended political work in the country and heightened the state of emergency in the southern provinces. The Liberal Party dissolved and most of its leaders went into exile to continue the struggle outside, unlike the northern political parties, which continued the struggle inside the country, albeit clandestinely.

The inability of southerners to work clandestinely stemmed from their lack of political organization. This made it impossible for southerners to mobilize and organize political activities in southern Sudan except through tightly closed, exclusive circles of acquaintances defined by blood, ethnicity, or provincial relations, which inspires confidence to communicate within the secured circle.

The lack of organized and established political parties in southern Sudan made it impossible to carry out a programme of political education, organization, mobilization, and the training of younger political leaders and cadres. This was not the case in northern Sudan: organized and established political parties had existed for a long time, before the beginning of the nationalist anti-colonial movement, due to factors mentioned earlier. In fact, the Mahdist revolution that defeated the Turco-Egyptian state was part of this political consciousness. The political parties turned the schools into their hunting grounds for recruits and development of their cadres and political activists. One of the negative and indeed detrimental aspects of the British policy was that it promoted apoliticism, which meant that southern Sudanese only aspired to finding work within the civil services, where they concentrated on showing diligence in order to be promoted within its ranks. As a result, southerners engaged in political work only after they had completed their careers and become pensioners.

This is usually too late to catch up with those who would have started political work at an earlier age. Politics and active political struggle are perfected through practice, without which Southerners found themselves often on the receiving end in the relations with their northern compatriots. People acquire political knowledge and skills by a dedication to learning and practice. It cannot be otherwise, and this explains why northern Sudanese were more politically organized and skilful in the art. It therefore took until the May Revolution of 1969, when the older generation of southern Sudanese politicians was phased out, partly because of age and partly because of the complexity of the state social and political engineering processes, which required younger and more educated politicians.

In such an environment of fear of state police and security agents obtaining in the southern provinces, it was difficult to build on the experience of the older generation of political leaders through political rallies, party conferences, or formal meetings. It was therefore much easier to mobilize for rebellion and military work than for political protests and demonstrations. Most of the second- and third-generation southern Sudanese political leaders and activists, excluding those who had enrolled in northern schools and the student movement, grew up and developed in this oppressive political environment, forcing many to join the Anya-nya Land Freedom Army. This phenomenon of retarded evolution of the culture of organized political work, started by the British in the guise of substandard education and other procedures, had impacted negatively on the evolution of social awareness, political, and ideological consciousness, as well as the development of political skills in southern Sudanese intellectuals, putting them at disadvantage compared to their northern Sudanese counterparts.

The general poverty and inability to raise the necessary financial resources to undertake political work and represent their people put them at disadvantage and left them prone to manipulation and blackmail by the northern political class. It was a typical case of gaining political freedom and independence but having no corresponding economic power. In fact, the *kayan al shamal* never acknowledged southern Sudanese as equal citizens; they frequently referred to southern Sudanese as *abeed* (slave) to remind them of their inferiority and, hence, should not claim equality in matters related to the governing of Sudan. This was to alienate the southern Sudanese, rendering them unequal partners in the emergent independent Sudan and compounding their sense of inferiority, which was played out in the many cases when they were tricked by northern politicians (Abel Alier, 1990).

This political chicanery became a characteristic feature of north-south relations, particularly during periods of democratic dispensations that intermittently intervened between 1956 and 1989. The southern Sudanese politicians, because of their unequal economic and political power, more often than not found themselves treated as second-class citizens when it came to power and governing the country. It was only in the brief period of the transitional government following October 1964 that the *kayan al shamal* treated southern Sudan fairly in the allocation of ministerial portfolios. For the first time a southern Sudanese occupied a sovereignty portfolio (Ministry of Interior) and two other services portfolios, in addition to membership in the Supreme Council of the State. It was also the first time a Southern Sudanese member of the Supreme Council of the State, Sayyed Luigi Adwok, occupied the rotating chair of the Council (March 1965).[11] Hitherto, and thereafter,

---

[11] During his one-month tenure as chair of the Supreme Council, Sayyed Luigi Adwok welcomed Queen Elizabeth on a reciprocal visit to the Sudan. That a Southern Sudanese, as head of state, received the Queen infuriated the northern Sudanese political establishment, prompting a

southern Sudanese served in the less luminous ministries of labour or animal resources.

It was only in the aftermath of May regime's demise in 1985 that southerners, mainly youthful graduate politicians, managed to rub shoulders with their northern compatriots in the power scrimmage. Even so, during the negotiation of the transition to multiparty dispensation in April 1985, in a spectacular move to assert their presence, the older politicians, who accepted only what their northern masters offered them, sprouted from nowhere to short-circuit the younger politicians with a modest demand from the political coordinator in the Military Council. The younger intellectual politicians had wanted the prime minister's portfolio for southern Sudan, given that a northerner was already the head of state as the chairman of the Military Council. However, faced with a divided southern position, the military coordinator granted the request by the South Sudan Political Association (SSPA) for creation of the hitherto non-existent position of deputy prime minister, which would be occupied alongside a ministerial portfolio.[12] This resolved the struggle among the northern contenders for the prime minister's position.

Owing to their high level of political organization and a measure of economic strength, the *kayan al shamal* emerged as the dominant political force in the country and inherited the colonial state. Sudanese from the south, west, centre, and east had only a marginal participation and hence were given only a second-class role in the social, economic, and political engineering of the state. The southern Sudanese had *abeed* indelibly stamped on them no matter their social, economic, and political status, leaving them worse off than all the others. They had been conquered, in all meanings of the word, in terms of their relations with their northern compatriots in matters to do with decision and policy making, further revealing the apparent power asymmetry.

In the public service, a northerner was likely to progress faster to become his southern colleague's senior in the hierarchy, although as students in the university they may have graduated at the same time.

---

constitutional amendment to abolish the monthly rotation of chair of the Supreme Council, making Ismael el Azhari the permanent head of state.

[12] This was an ad hoc political outfit, a group of former Southern Region politicians, formed to enable their participation in the new system. It was reminiscent of the formation of the Southern Front (SF), instead of resuscitating the Liberal Party following the overthrow of the military regime, which banned it. Unlike the northern political parties, which continued to operate clandestinely under dictatorial and totalitarian regimes, southern political parties voluntarily dissolved to enable their incorporation into the new regime.

In some professions and services, southern Sudanese would be given technical tasks while northerners engaged in the administrative aspects of the profession, giving them opportunities for gaining policy and decision-making skills. This imprints a psychological image of northern Sudanese as superior and leaders in every aspect of life, whether in commerce, trade, industry, administration, or the politics of the state. In reality, relations built on such misconceptions or distorted social constructions were deliberately and efficaciously promoted to generate in the southerners syndromes of inferiority, ineptitude, self-hatred, non-commitment, alienation, double-talking, dishonesty, rebelliousness, and, in a nutshell, sociopolitical duplicity, which encapsulates all these behaviours and attitudes.

The greatest weakness of southern Sudanese intellectuals in general has been their inability to organize or engage in organized political activities that could unite their struggle across ethnic and provincial lines, although this is a colonial legacy more specifically linked to the Christian missionary education.[13] This education system frowned on politics in general and inculcated subservience to officialdom. As a result, and coupled with the government's suppression of political activities in southern provinces, it has not been easy for the present generation of southern politicians to emancipate themselves from this legacy. Instead, political agitation and mobilization to resist government policies of Arabization and Islamization (1958–1964) took the form of clandestine, ethnic-based groupings, where communication was conducted in local languages to avoid the usually northern-origin secret police informers and security agents.

Ethnic and provincial associations in schools began initially as a precaution against the security agents and police informers; nevertheless, these became entrenched, as a security precaution, in the attitudes and behaviours of southern Sudanese intelligentsia. It became, as I note in the following sections, their only means of organization and disrupted their unity of purpose. The intrusion of ethnicity and provincialism into southern Sudanese politics of struggle against the different Sudanese regimes came in the wake of the split in 1964 of the

---

[13] The education systems in southern and northern Sudan were unified only in 1970 with the introduction of the new curriculum. Hitherto, the southern curriculum differed in content and scope from the national curriculum; it for instance did not offer subjects like the history of the Sudan and civic education, which had the potential to raise social awareness and political consciousness in the students. Instead, it offered more neutral subjects like geography and European history.

Sudan African National Union (SANU), and the return to the country of William Deng Nhial to engage politics under the same name. This action paralleled the bitter battles in the bush of southern Sudan among the Anya-nya freedom fighters, which Rolf Steiner succinctly described as behaving "cowardly" when it came to facing government troops, but fiercely among themselves, forgetting that they had a common cause.[14] The struggle against each other, in the face of a common enemy, was typical of southern Sudan's political elite and comes from a perspective that prioritises secondary over primary contradictions and distorts or suppresses their perception of the common enemy.

The inability to organize political activity in the face of growing government repression back home invoked in southerners apathy and despair, and led to a complete rejection of anything political. I vividly recall those evenings at the University of Khartoum Student Club, when southern Sudanese students would be playing cards while their colleagues — like them, future political leaders — were engaged in political debates on the situation in the country. It was a bitter struggle to change the name of the Student Welfare Front (SWF) to the African National Front (ANF), ostensibly to give it a political content and link it to the political and armed struggle the Anya-nya was waging in the forests of southern Sudan. But even with high-sounding, pan-African political idiosyncrasies invoked, this did not influence the dominant right-wing political thought in the organization. It did not take long before reactionary elements in the ANF leadership conspired to elbow the progressives out of the party. They had to form the Southern Sudan Progressives, an alternative group, to challenge the High Executive Council-sponsored ANF leadership in the politics of the Southern Sudanese student movement.

Many of the current political and military leaders in South Sudan are products of that era of the political evolution of South Sudan. They received better educations than their independence-era political leaders and politicians. They had the opportunity to mingle and interact on equal terms with their northern Sudanese colleagues; they had no cause for feeling inferior. In fact, many of them did well academically, scoring high grades, attending university, and even becoming part of the university faculty. They pursued politics within the existing totalitarian political system — the Sudan Socialist Union (SSU) — but without fully

---

[14] Steiner was a German mercenary who helped train the Anya-nya in Equatoria. The agents of the Sudan government captured him in Uganda and flew him to Khartoum for trial. They later released him, presumably after the intervention of the West German government.

integrating into pro-Arab or pan-Arab sensibilities. Because of these constraints, they could not chart an authentic Pan-African ideological or political path. In the end, they endorsed politics and policies that they were completely at odds with.

This socioeconomic and political development of southern Sudan deprived it of left-wing and revolutionary politics. The social and political environment in southern Sudan was by no means conducive to their activities. The few Marxists and revolutionary democrats in southern Sudan evolved and developed within the workers' trade union and student movements in northern Sudan, and never had an opportunity to influence events in the south. The opportunity for left-wing politics in southern Sudan arrived only with the 1969 military coup in Khartoum that ushered in the May regime. This transformed the political landscape in southern Sudan. It proscribed right-wing liberal democracy and enabled left-wing politicians and political activists to stand on the political stage.

In a declaration, the Revolutionary Council recognized the socioeconomic and cultural disparity between southern and northern Sudan and called for a political programme to bridge the gap. This created an environment for southern Sudanese left-wing and democratic social forces to organize and engage in political action. Even though the war raged, the creation of the Ministry of Southern Affairs and appointment of Joseph U. Garang to head it completely transformed political life in the southern Sudan. But the brief period between May 1969 and July 1971 witnessed political and ideological turbulence in the revolutionary camp that reversed the revolutionary tide in southern Sudan. A split occurred within the Communist Party of the Sudan in 1970, with a faction demanding it be dissolved into a mass-democratic movement including the Pan-Arabists and other leftist groups. The members of this faction became the core of the May regime and ideologues of the SSU. What followed was a counter-revolutionary alliance of the political right wing into the National Front and armed resistance in Omdurman and Abba Island in March 1970 and, only a year later, the left-wing, anti-Nimeri coup and its counter-coup on July 19 and 21, 1971, respectively.[15] These

---

[15] Events over the three days were dramatic in both their national and international dimensions. On 19 July, Maj. Hashem el Atta led a daytime bloodless coup, arresting Nimeri and many of his officer corps, and declaring a national democratic revolution. In an imperialist conspiracy hatched in London, Libya's Col. Muammer Gadhafi ordered the landing of a British Airways plane and arrested Lt. Col. Babiker el Nur and Maj. Farouk Osman Hamadalla. This action triggered the counter-coup in Khartoum and restoration of Gaafar Mohammed Nimeri as president.

political developments culminated in a total reversal of the revolution, putting the Sudan under President Gaafar Mohammed Nimeri in the imperialist camp.

The events of July 1971 were an irreparable disaster to the democratic and revolutionary forces of the Sudan. Nimeri's execution of the Communist Party's top leaders — Abdel Khaliq Mahgoub, the secretary-general; Shafie Ahmed el Sheikh, vice president of the International Federation of Workers' Trade Union; and Joseph Ukel Garang, lawyer and southern member of the party's Central Committee — left the Communist Party and the entire revolutionary and democratic movement in the country in total shock and disorientation. The execution of Garang had an atrophying effect on the evolution and development of the nascent democratic and revolutionary movement in southern Sudan. The clampdown on left-wing political activities coincided with the regime's ideological shift to the political right, which pushed it into an agreement with the separatist Southern Sudan Liberation Movement (SSLM), the political wing of the Anya-nya, in March 1972. The Addis Ababa Agreement created a political environment in southern Sudan conducive for implementing the distorted version of the 9 June Declaration that provided for regional self-government.

It was clear from the nature of the forces that brokered the Addis Ababa Agreement that the Southern Region would be in the grip of reactionary and counter-revolutionary forces. It was a choice opportunity for the formerly defunct right-wing southern politicians, who had thronged to the newly established SSU to reorganize politically and manage the regional self-government. There was nothing socialist about the SSU in terms of ideology or political programme save the name. Nimeri denationalized businesses and industries and embarked on a capitalist path of socioeconomic and political development under the tutelage of the World Bank and the IMF.

The Addis Ababa Agreement ended the 17-year war but it did not address the fundamental contradictions that underpinned the war. With the social and economic development of the Sudan tied to the dictates of the IMF and the World Bank, particularly the imposition of their dreaded structural adjustment programme (SAP), it was lost on the Southern Region and the SSU to address the socioeconomic and cultural backwardness of southern Sudan. The essence of the regional self-rule was to enable the people of southern Sudan to transform the centuries-old condition of poverty, ignorance, illiteracy, and superstition under the leadership of the democratic and revolutionary forces implementing the programme of the national democratic revolution. Thus, with the slogan of "national unity", the May regime and its subset in the Southern Region so hypnotized the people that they did not recognize the oppressive and manipulative character of the regime.

History has shown that the right-wing section of the petty bourgeoisie has never been faithful to the masses. They instead exploit for their selfish political ends people's yearning for emancipation from poverty and ignorance. Amílcar Cabral (1966) concluded that for the petty bourgeoisie to lead the masses in the struggle for liberation it must commit class suicide in order to rise up in the guise of revolutionary peasant or intellectual. Short of that ideological transformation, this class reverts to pursuing its parochial economic and political interests. In this respect, we could assume that the dictates of socioeconomic and political class interests forced the political elite, who had fought the 17-year first civil war in southern Sudan, would betray the masses by abdicating the responsibility to bring social and economic development. The old regime politicians and the former SSLM leaders conjoined in the SSU, which was a canopy under which they nurtured and cultivated parochial ethnic and provincial interests as they engaged in a cutthroat power struggle. They could not envision addressing those parochial interests in the totality of Southern Region without necessarily fragmenting the people along ethnic and provincial lines. This power struggle eventually led to the destruction of the Southern Region itself. It was typical right-wing politicking, which projects parochial or secondary contradictions to dangerous heights, rendering impossible compromise for the higher common or national interest.

The regional self-rule, in the guise of the Southern Region, encompassed the executive organ, the High Executive Council (HEC), and the legislative organ, the People's Regional Assembly (PRA). The establishment of these offices was a major victory for the people of southern Sudan. This victory, notwithstanding the undemocratic and totalitarian nature of the May regime that consummated it, were concrete foundations upon which the people of Southern Region would have scored more socioeconomic and political gains. However, the dominance of the right-wing elements in the political economy of the regions made it impossible to transform these political gains into socioeconomic gains for the people. Instead, they made it a struggle for power and dominance. The formation of ethnic-based associations like the Dinka Unity, the Luo Union, and provincial groups like the Equatoria Central Committee (ECC) as drivers of this power struggle within the precincts of the SSU gave the national party a semblance of legitimacy. Nimeri exploited these unprincipled differences not only to divide these politicians further and weaken their common stand on the issues of borders and the placement of the oil refinery, but also to dismantle the Southern Region by abrogating the Addis Ababa Agreement.[16]

Every social situation carries within it the seeds of its destruction or transformation. The colonial system produced social and political forces in the Sudan that expelled the colonial administration. The politics of political exclusion, economic marginalization, and social discrimination of the non-Arabs and non-Muslims in the independent Sudan triggered the emergence of forces in the peripheral Sudan that led to its dismemberment in 2011. The present situation in South Sudan is a case of negation of negation. The Republic of South Sudan is pregnant with social and political contradictions, the resolution of which will either fragment or fix South Sudan, so it can become a stable, peaceful, and prosperous country. The situation is characteristically developmental in that it is bound to trigger the emergence of new mode, and/or relations of production incompatible with the prevailing conditions.

There has never been appreciable development of southern Sudan's productive forces. The country remained sunk in socioeconomic and cultural backwardness, notwithstanding its enormous natural resource potential. The civil war made it difficult to invest in and develop these natural resources. The northern Sudanese suspicion of southern Sudanese intentions to secede became their main reason to shift away from the funding of projects that feasibility studies had shown to be economical. These included the Equatoria Project Board, Mangalla Sugar, Malakal Paper and Pulp, fisheries, and fruit-canning industries. The logic was so parochial and self-defeating: no development because then southerners will secede. But the very lack of development was the driver of secessionist movements in southern Sudan. Fifty-five years after Sudan's independence, the Republic of South Sudan was born. Alas! In 50 years of conflicts and war, so much has been lost: energy, resources, and lives. But sadly, the failure of nascent South Sudan to transit to statehood and nationhood now parallels the collapse of the post-colonial Sudanese state.

What followed 1 June 1983 constitutes the subject matter of this discourse: the sociopolitical duplicity in South Sudanese political

---

[16] The HEC and the PRA stood firmly against Nimeri's decisions to build the oil refinery in Kosti and to change the borders of the Southern Region in order to locate the oil fields within Kordofan Province.

thought and action. The sociopolitical duplicity arose from the lack of a true commitment to any course, whether for the country, people, or land, while exploiting that cause for personal gain in the scramble for power and wealth. Southern politicians had played this political game with the northern political establishment since the 1950s, when they exalted the unity of the Sudan in order to buy personal political favours while promoting a southern Sudan cause for which they were not truly committed.[17] There was ambivalence and oscillation, without embarrassment or guilt, between the two extremes of a southern Sudanese identity that is African and, at the same time, a Sudanese culture that is defined as Islamic and Arab.

In less than ten years (1972–1981) the southern political elite that governed the Southern Region had fragmented into hostile power groups that were based not on ideology but on personalities and, by extension, ethnicity and provincialism. They were completely oblivious of the danger lurking behind their divisive politics and could not recognize Nimeri's manipulation of their differences. The radical southern politicians viewed Abel Alier as a weak leader who would not express southern frustration with Nimeri's lack of social and economic development for the south. The struggle, centred on removing Abel Alier as president of the HEC, started with the 1978 elections that returned Gen. Joseph Lagu as president of the HEC, in what was popularly called the "wind of change." This immediately prompted Nimeri's direct interference in the democratic process in the Southern Region, and this coincided with Chevron's discovery of huge petroleum deposits in Western Upper Nile. This discovery and the process of petrodollars shifted the focus of southerners to social and economic development.

Nimeri and his regime represented the social, economic, and political interests of *kayan al shamal*, whose unwritten rule was to keep southern Sudan absolutely dependent on the north, ostensibly to prevent its secession. The discovery of oil in southern Sudan definitely spurred ideas of socioeconomic development and was, therefore, antithetic to this unwritten rule. Indeed, Nimeri's idea of locating the oil refinery in Kosti, as dictated by Chevron's economic interests, resonated with the *kayan al shamal*'s objectives. However, this drew swords in the Southern Region: both the HEC and the People's Regional Assembly (PRA) united against the plan to relocate the proposed oil refinery from Bentiu

---

[17] Nimeri appointed a Southern Sudanese minister of information and culture to propagate the unity of the country and to promote Arab culture at a time when the Southern Region projected an African identity for Southern Sudanese.

to Kosti, triggering a political standoff with Nimeri and the central government. Nimeri, in a clever strategy, shifted this political standoff by dividing the southern opposition, exploiting the power struggle in the Southern Region between the Equatorians, led by Gen. Joseph Lagu, and the Dinka group led by Abel Alier.

By the end of 1980, Gen. Joseph Lagu had scuttled the "wind of change" in the SSU that had ushered him into the presidency of the HEC. Indeed, he came from outside the southern Sudan realpolitick. His attempts to incorporate members of Abel Alier's camp precipitated a political crisis, prompting his impeachment on trumped-up charges. Once more, the PRA elected Abel Alier president of the HEC but on the ticket of Dinka unity; the Equatorian block refused to vote for a Dinka. The impeachment of Lagu and the re-election of Abel Alier as president of the HEC marked a turning point in social and political relations in the Southern Region. This played well with Nimeri's political objectives and strategies for the development and exploitation of the oil fields in western Upper Nile Province, which he renamed Unity Province to underscore his strong message against southern secessionist tendencies.

The virulent power struggle among southerner politicians hinged on its political stability and Sudan's national security could automatically invoke Nimeri's direct intervention in the Southern Region through a constitutional edict. Thus, when the power struggle spilled over to the oil-refinery issue, the HEC and PRA were united in solidarity against the relocation of the refinery from Bentiu. President Nimeri exploited the political cleavages wrought by the election of Abel Alier as president of the HEC to win over the Equatorians. He decreed the dissolution of the HEC and appointed a caretaker military administration to prepare the region for snap elections. Democratic practice in a totalitarian setting torn apart by ethnic and provincial sensibilities can be tricky. It is not a straightforward affair because the issues are not clearly defined. The situation had all the negative elements of southern secessionism: rivalries for personal power ensheathed in ethnicity and provincialism, and a dictator who had shifted to the imperialist camp in the context of ideological and superpower rivalry in the Horn of Africa.

Amid this complex situation, two antagonistic camps emerged in the Southern Region to contest the elections for the PRA in early 1982. They were the Council for Unity of Southern Sudan (CUSS), incorporating all the elites of the Southern Front led by Abel Alier, and the Re-division Camp, incorporating the Equatoria Central Committee (ECC), the SANU members, and other floaters. The alliance between the ECC and SANU, which returned Engineer Joseph James Tambura as president of the HEC, was shrouded in political chicanery and doublecrossing within SANU, which saw Dhol Acuil Aleu named as deputy to Tambura. The SANU leadership of Samuel Aru Bol never countenanced the dismantling of the Southern Region. It appeared that Dhol Acuil and Matthew Obur Ayang voted for Tambura in return for personal positions. There were no ideological or longterm interests to bind them in the alliance. The fissures started to appear in the alliance when the ECC insisted, through the agency of Gen. Joseph Lagu, on implementation of the re-division of the Southern Region agenda. This led to the arrest and detention of CUSS leaders and, surprisingly, Hon. Matthew Obur Ayang, speaker of the PRA, and Hon. Dhol Acuil Aleu, the vice president of the HEC. This added to the total confusion among the politicians and the complexity of the situation. President Nimeri not only possessed the political initiative, he was the master puppeteer; he pulled all the strings that tied southern Sudanese factions to his strategic political objective for remaining in power.

Blinded by parochial self-interests and ambitions for power, the southern political elite — whether Dinka, Equatorian, or others, which combined the Nuer and smaller ethnicities — inadvertently played into Nimeri's political tricks to destroy the hard-won regional self-rule. Had they stood firm and focused on the issue of social and economic development of the Southern Region, the chances were that Nimeri would have backed down in return for the Southern Region's political support against his detractors in the North, notwithstanding his new alliance with Dr. Hassan el Turabi of the National Islamic Front (NIF). The southern political elite could have reminded President Nimeri of Fr. Saturnino's famous speech to the Parliament in 1958 to forestall hair splitting over "re-division" or "unity" of the region, and focus the debate on the social and economic backwardness of the Southern Region.[18]

The social and political situation in southern Sudan on the eve of Nimeri's decision to abrogate the constitutional basis of the regional self-rule in southern Sudan shows a complete lack of shared values among the southern political elite. They had shamelessly drawn swords against each other and only Nimeri was their arbiter in whatever linked

---

[18] "The South has no intention of separating from the North, for had that been the case nothing on earth could have prevented the demand for separation as a right accorded to free people to self-determination. The South will at any moment separate from the North if and when the North so decides, directly or indirectly, through social, economic and political subjugation of the South." From the proceedings of Parliament, March 1958.

them as southern Sudanese. They quickly forgot their common cause and the 17-year war the people had fought to achieve the self-rule. In their anger with each other they overlooked the danger Nimeri and the Arab establishment posed to their existence as a people. They were ready to cocoon themselves in their weak subregions of Bahr el Ghazal, Equatoria, and Upper Nile. The strongest provincial voices came predominantly from Equatoria, which agitated vehemently for *kokora* (loosely translated as "decentralisation" or "federalism"). An overzealous politician from Upper Nile went to the extreme of demanding "Upper Nile region without Bor Dinka."

It is possible that the events that triggered the army mutiny in Bor could have precipitated Nimeri's abrogation of the Addis Ababa Agreement. However, it is also possible that he could have engineered these events through the agency of Gen. Sadeek el Banna, the commander of the Southern Division of SAF; for instance, through the misappropriation of money to create conditions for dismantling the Southern Region. This renders incredulous the claim in the SPLM Manifesto (1983) that an underground organization of the former Anya-nya officers existed and planned the mutiny as the prelude for an armed insurrection against Arab-dominated northern Sudan. Nimeri achieved the objective of splitting the Southern Region, though at a steep cost. He was able to crush the mutinies in Bor, Pochalla, and Ayod but he did not anticipate the formation of the SPLM/A as a formidable force until the Anya-nya II disrupted the Chevron activities in the oil fields in February 1984. The SSU politicians of the defunct Southern Region shifted to Khartoum to re-enact the political games of the 1960s, playing each against the other.

The war in southern Sudan contributed to the demise of the May regime on 6 April 1985 in what appeared like a replay of the 1964 overthrow of the Abboud military regime, in all its social and political dimensions. An insurgency in southern Sudan and a popular uprising in Khartoum and other northern cities had led to the capitulation of a military dictatorship. It is necessary to note the shifting role of the southern political elite in the situation of resurgent political party's activities in the new liberal democratic political dispensation following the demise of the May regime. The southern political elite was disposed to replay the same role as in 1965, notwithstanding the changed character of the southern insurgency. From within their poverty-stricken political outfits, these southern politicians outdid themselves jostling to win favour with the different elements of the *kayan al shamal*. However, in a rare display of integrity and principle, the Sudan African Congress (SAC) pulled out of Sadiq el Mahdi's government in protest against the burning of villages in Upper Nile and the killing of southerners in El Dhaien in southern Dar Fur. The other political parties continued in government, unperturbed by the heinous crimes the government forces had committed in their constituencies. Some of them would later feign SPLM/A membership as clandestine operators, providing information to the SPLA general headquarters while serving in the governments of Sadiq el Mahdi and Omar el Beshir.

The immediate post-Nimeri era witnessed very interesting political developments. The southern Sudanese political elite on both sides of the political divide for the first time struggled, albeit duplicitously, for Sudan's unity. No political party, whether in the coalition government Sadiq el Mahdi pieced together (1986–1989) or in the opposition, raised the issue of the "problem of southern Sudan", as it had been referred to during the second republic. The semblance of unity among the politicians who had been part of the creation of the Southern Region was broken and beyond repair. They remained suspicious of each other. This played into the hands of the *kayan al shamal*, enabling Sadiq el Mahdi to procrastinate on the constitutional conference agreed at Koka Dam until the NIF struck in a coup that overthrew his government on 30 June 1989.[19] The SPLM/A, although presumed a national liberation movement, was predominantly southern Sudanese in composition and leadership. Nevertheless, it called for a united socialist New Sudan based on freedom, justice, fraternity, and democracy. This suggested that the SPLM/A, like the other southern Sudan-based political parties, had eschewed southern Sudan secessionism in favour of the unity of Sudan. This necessitates a discussion in view of the paradigm shift from the concept and vision of a New Sudan to self-determination and secession of South Sudan provided for in the CPA 2005.

The discourse is about the political attitudes and behaviours of the southern Sudanese political elite in the different political circumstances in the Sudan and after independence in 2011. A question keeps nagging as to whether or not the SPLM/A leadership, which was predominantly southern and particularly Dinka in composition, genuinely desired unity of the Sudan. If so, when and why did it change to the extreme of calling for the people of southern Sudan to exercise their inalienable

---

[19] The SPLM/A and the social and political forces of the popular uprising that overthrew Nimeri convened a conference to discuss the future of the country in March 1986 at Koka Dam, Ethiopia. One of the resolutions was to convene a constitutional conference.

right to self-determination? Did the collapse of the Derg and the Nasir Declaration trigger this change of heart?[20] How is it that the political parties which had formed tribal militias to support Khartoum's war against the SPLA later came around to support the SPLM/A bid for the exercise of the right of self-determination, so much so that the vote in the referendum on self-determination registered 98.7 per cent in favour of secession? One expected that the NCP and other northern Sudan-based parties would have voted for unity of the Sudan. How can we explain the new civil war that is now tearing apart South Sudan and its people instead of consolidating the new nation's freedom and independence? Far from the sovereignty that people fought for over six decades, South Sudan is now dependent on international humanitarian beneficence and serves as an economic colony of both Uganda and Kenya. This is a serious contradiction and has arisen from an attitude of sociopolitical duplicity — of saying one thing that purports to serve wider interests but doing another different thing that is of parochial and personal interest.

The SPLM/A was a political construct of the second- and third-generation southern Sudanese political elite, who themselves are the product of the culture of sociopolitical duplicity that characterized politics throughout the three decades of post-independent Sudan. Many of these politicians learned and practiced its elements as tools for personal and social survival. It is a fact that snobbery, cleverness, and trickery can be useful survival strategies in situations of power asymmetry. In a situation where politics are organized and exercised based on parameters that exclude or discriminate other citizens, people will resort to practices that camouflage their reality. However, these practices can only be effective at the personal level or for very limited objectives; extending them to wider sociopolitical engineering processes, as in a national liberation movement, can have devastating consequences.

Many people in northern Sudan, particularly the political left, took with a pinch of salt the emergence from southern Sudan of the SPLM/A projecting the slogan of a united socialist Sudan. The decision by some of us, members of the Communist Party of the Sudan (CPS), to join the ranks of the SPLM/A was a matter of serious internal ideological self-struggle. The CPS, in its clandestine and published literature, eulogized and encouraged its members and other democratic forces to support

---

[20] In most of Col. John Garang's recorded speeches he boasted that his first bullet was against those who wanted the SPLM/A to fight for the secession of South Sudan.

the SPLM/A. However, this was a case of the enemy of your enemy is a friend, nothing more or less. Hailing from backward parts of the Sudan, where no industrial working class was mobilised to build socialism, the chance of a revolution taking root in southern Sudan was a farfetched possibility. The CPS leadership could not envisage, even from a theoretical perspective, that the peasants and nomads could politically mobilize and organize to start a revolution. The Chinese, Cuban, and Vietnamese revolutions were all peasant revolutions.

However, those of us from the CPS who joined the SPLM/A's ranks were wrong: the "movement" was not a revolution. It turned out to be an expression of the sociopolitical duplicity of southern Sudan's political elite. In fact, this elite paid back the northern Sudanese compatriots in the same coins of political snobbery and trickery. The slogan of a united socialist Sudan was a political gimmick. The SPLM/A leadership failed to transform the slogan into a social and political reality in the form of a political programme. This explains the collapse of the National Democratic Alliance (NDA), which in essence would have been the expression of this unity. How could the SPLM/A construct unity and socialism without the equal participation of corresponding social and political forces from other parts of the Sudan? In fact, the elements of the petty bourgeoisie in both southern and northern Sudan were equals in the political snobbery game.

Political leadership in any situation is a product of a particular socioeconomic and political context. Revolutionary leadership emerges in the context of a revolutionary situation. However, some leaders imbued with revolutionary thinking emerge before the revolutionary situation has matured and therefore act in such a manner that aborts or subverts the revolution. In most cases the objective reality overwhelms, submerges, and forces them to relinquish the revolution along the lines of "Join them if you cannot defeat or win them over." The upsurge of Jieng (Dinka) ethnic nationalism in the context of the SPLM/A-led war of national liberation can only find explanation in this aborted or subverted revolutionary situation in southern Sudan. Thus, by shunning political and ideological awareness the SPLM/A leadership inadvertently, or advertently, promoted the emergence of ethnic ideologies, which fettered the development of the revolution.

Ethnic ideologies of hegemony and domination are the very negation of liberation and social emancipation. Indeed, as an expression of the elite's sociopolitical duplicity, some elements from Bahr el Ghazal started chanting the Dinka slogan of *"Awich ku aɲich ku"* (We know what we want) in the final days of the war of national liberation, it was obvious that a betrayal had occurred. A betrayal of the liberation, which suggested that only the Dinka — of all the other 64 ethnicities involved in the liberation process — knew what it was all about. This resulted in the formation of Bahr el Ghazal Elders (BGE), precursor of the Jieng Council of Elders (JCE) to prop up Kiir's leadership of southern Sudan immediately he ascended to the helm after the death of Dr. John Garang de Mabior in July 2005. This transformed the SPLM/A politics into an avaricious scrimmage for power and wealth, culminating in the eruption of violence in December 2013.

The Elite's Sociopolitical Duplicity and the Challenge of South Sudan's Transition

South Sudan is in the middle of a civil war that has shattered the hopes of a transition from war to peace. If there is a singular factor that contributed immensely to the failure to move from war to peace and to statehood and nationhood, it is South Sudan's political elite and its attitude towards power and wealth. The political elite comprises the leaders on both sides of the war of national liberation who congregated in Juba upon the conclusion of the CPA. It is the attitude of mindless greed expressed in the form of "either me, my clan/ethnicity or nothing" that quickly trumps the national agenda. This underscores the behaviour of some of these leaders, which sparked the current civil war.

This attitude is a product of two processes linked to the war of national liberation: the SPLM/A process in the forests of southern Sudan and what I call the Ingaz process, the outcome of the 1989 Al Ingaz Revolution, in Khartoum and garrisoned towns in southern Sudan. It evolved in the context of dogmatic loyalty and instantaneous obedience to authority, which was manifest in allegiance to a person rather than cause, a lust for wealth and power, and political and moral corruption. These misdemeanours rolled into a culture that stripped the political, military, and business elite of their nationalistic instincts and patriotism, leading to destruction of the societal core values of integrity and respect for public property.

The strategic political objective of the war of national liberation was, apart from independence and sovereignty, to develop the national productive forces and to free them from any form of foreign control and domination. This was contingent on a national political leadership liberated from the colonial legacy and emancipated from ethnic/tribal bondage. These attributes do not evolve by themselves but are inculcated in the process of learning and practice. The SPLM/A's failure to build a liberation culture that placed the masses at the centre of socioeconomic and political engineering processes lies at the root of South Sudan's inability to jump the critical border between war and peace.

Definitely, after prosecuting a scorched-earth war, there was nothing good the people of southern Sudan would have expected from the elements of the Ingaz system. Those southern political leaders returning from the Ingaz institutions to join the SPLM worked to ensure its failure. The SPLM/A had not built strong revolutionary or ethical firewalls to protect its systems from the Ingaz viruses. In fact, the two systems dovetailed and coiled into the most corrupt regime unprecedented in the history of southern Sudan, a regime that ignores or rather overlooks merits, qualifications, and experience in favour of political loyalty and the ethnic ideology. As a result, a generation of functionally illiterate and corrupt, power-hungry youthful leaders have joined the political theatre, consigning to the dustbin of history the most seasoned, experienced, and decent leaders Sudan had produced in the realm of politics and in public service.

The political elite that has emerged at the pinnacle of power in the young Republic of South Sudan controls no means of production. Their power derives from the control of the state and its institutions. It manages a consumption- rather than production-based economy lubricated by the oil revenues. The power and influence of this class derives from its parasitic relation with the state apparatus as ministers, legislators, contractors, rent-seekers, commission agents, and other intermediary functions. The control of the state and its resources has enabled this parasitic class to reproduce itself in different parts of South Sudan. It is ideologically bankrupt and, as a result, cannot conceptualise transforming the socioeconomic and cultural backwardness of South Sudan.

A large section of those within the political elite would appear to be highly educated; many of them hold academic degrees in economics, law, government, medicine, engineering, and arts, but are nevertheless backward and primeval in their political thought. Many, particularly those hailing from the pastoral communities, have hardly emancipated themselves from the exclusive tribal life and its attendant parochialism and chauvinism. This comes out clearly in the way they have managed the nascent state as if it were a village system in which all that matters is social relations. They make appointments to state institutions based on clan, ethnicity, or province in a manner that overlooks educational merit, qualifications, and/or experience and diligence. In this connection, some individuals with intellectual horizons limited to their village setting have found themselves handling national, regional, and international dossiers in the corridors of state power. Some of those returning home from the diaspora in the United States, Canada, Australia, and Europe — where they worked as street cleaners, waiters, porters, and gas station attendants — became ministers in GoSS and state governments soon after the 2005 peace agreement.

Many came back with forged academic papers yet their tribesmen appointed them to senior positions in the civil service, where they messed up the already declining bureaucratic standards. The foundation of the state is a bureaucracy comprising highly educated, trained, and efficient personnel appointed based on diligence and merit. The bureaucrats are the institutional memory kits of the government ministries and departments. Any political interference in the bureaucracy that affects the personnel renders it unprofessional, inefficient, and ineffective. In this situation, government policies remain unimplemented and the system slowly grinds to a halt. Bureaucratic decision builds from the bottom to the top by individuals trained to make decisions. Any upstart, in terms of a lack of training or political imposition, disrupts and creates an imbalance in the system. When GoSS formed in 2005 most of the ministers, particularly coming from the army and a civil society background, had little prior experience in government.

The Ingaz system had neglected and eroded the bureaucracy in the southern states. The Council of Southern Sudan, which was formed after the Khartoum Agreement, was a farcical replica of the defunct HEC. Thus, the government of Southern Sudan (GoSS) virtually started from scratch, with little or no reference point, since the SPLM brought in no system of its own. This might explain why GoSS never had a policy on anything, although the SPLM operatives bragged of the existence of a "Strategic Framework from War to Peace Transition," a social and economic document hurriedly thrown together following the 9 January 2005 signing ceremony of the CPA. The SPLM had no difficulty generating ideas and a programme; its real difficulty was the lack of bureaucratic institutions and instruments to implement those policy statements, speaking to the obstinate refusal to organize and build institutions within the liberation movement.

The same inaction in the executive paralleled that in the legislative arm of the government, the Southern Sudan Legislative Assembly

(SSLA), tasked with supervision and oversight functions. It is worth mentioning that political correctness and tribalism has paralyzed the SSLA and prevented its diligent functioning. Some members openly block the SSLA's specialized committees from making their fellow tribesmen and women accountable for their actions and inaction in the executive branch of government. These entrenched ethnic politics led to the formation of ethnic causes in the assembly. A section at the centre of political and economic power, driven by Dinka ethnic nationalism, separated itself as the Jieng Council of Elders (JCE) and acted as a powerbroker around President Salva Kiir Mayardit. This loud expression of sociopolitical duplicity brought the concept of "the rulers and the ruled" that had dominated the Sudanese polity to the nascent South Sudan context. The Dinka had now assumed the role of *kayan al shamal* in relation to the other 63 nationalities of South Sudan.

The emergence of the JCE coincided with the political transformation of President Salva Kiir from a national to an ethnic leader, relegating his authority as chairman of the SPLM, as well as president of the republic, to the whims of the JCE. President Salva Kiir eschewed the SPLM and South Sudanese institutions in order to rule by presidential decrees, relying on the apparatus of the National Security and Intelligence Services (NSIS), which were modelled on the NCP's National Intelligence and Security Services (NISS). This sidelined and indeed emasculated the political, executive, and legislative instruments established by the Transitional Constitution of South Sudan (2011). The rise of the JCE in the corridors of power was virtually an ethnic capture of the state, with the expressed intention to construct a Dinka national state in South Sudan.[21] As mentioned elsewhere in this book, the formation of the JCE was the highest expression of Dinka ethnic nationalism, bringing in its wings the creation of a kleptocratic totalitarian regime that represents the social, economic, and political interests of the parasitic capitalist class that now controls the nascent state.[22]

This parasitic capitalist class built a close alliance with regional (East Africa) and international comprador capitalism for the extraction and plunder of South Sudan's natural resources. It is in this connection that we might better understand why President Kiir dragged South Sudan into the regional multilateral economic group, the East

---

[21] Some Jieng leaders, without shame or guilt, have drawn parallels between Jieng political and economic dominance in South Sudan and the dominance of the Kikuyu elite in Kenya's economic and political life.
[22] *The Sentry Report*, 2015.

African Community (EAC), and security organizations, including the International Conference of the Great Lakes Region (ICGLR). South Sudan's application and admission into the EAC and ICGLR was to protect the economic interests of the parasitic capitalist class and the political survival of the regime. The political survival of the regime was the main driver of the search for membership in these regional bodies. Indeed, South Sudan applied to join the Arab League in order to benefit from its military resources and as part of its growing relationship with Egypt, where the Arab League is headquartered. This is self-defeating: the southern Sudanese spent decades struggling to secede from the Sudan, not only because the *kayan al shamal* defined the Sudan within the parameters of Islam and Arab culture but also because they considered Sudanese nationality a step towards full integration of the African south into Arab nationhood.

The Republic of South Sudan joined the ICGLR at the time of its greatest social, economic, and political crisis. The regime assented to the ICGLR's Protocol on Non-Aggression and Mutual Defence Pact, Art 2 (106) as part of its survival strategy. It is an instrument to enable the regime to receive political, security, and military support from the region and the US administration, purportedly to bring peace and security to South Sudan. In fact, the regime's most important expectation of this regional support is for the ICGLR to declare all opposition groups opposed to Salva Kiir and his regime to be "negative forces." The protocol also allows President Museveni to keep soldiers of the Ugandan People's Defence Force (UPDF) in Equatoria in the guise of fighting global terrorism, while in reality they are there to plunder the teak, mahogany, and cedrela plantations in Yei, Maridi, and Yambio, and to poach elephants and rhinos.

The present stage of socioeconomic development in South Sudan does not allow it to engage in trade and commerce with the countries of the East African Community on fair and equal terms. It has no manufacturing capacity and its agriculture is at subsistence level at best. This makes South Sudan an economic colony of the EAC countries, particularly Kenya and Uganda, who are dumping their agricultural produce in the South Sudan market. Therefore, the regime kept a tight lid on information until it sneaked South Sudan into the EAC. The first shock in this hushed process was the disqualification of members to the East African Parliament appointed by President Kiir in 2017. A concerned South Sudanese lawyer blew the whistle, leading to the SSLA's procedural election of the nine representatives to the EAC

Legislative Assembly (EACLA). The admission of the Republic of South Sudan into the EAC before it could fulfil the conditions, and before it was ready to compete on equal terms with member countries, was definitely an act of political bad faith on the part of some regional leaders. It only served to expedite the laundering of stolen money by the parasitic capitalist class, moved in cash for deposit in the banks of East African countries.

By joining the EAC at this very early stage of South Sudan's social, economic, and political development, the elite in South Sudan only made the young country the dumping ground for cheap East African agricultural and manufactured products. Indeed, Uganda and Kenya have since 2005 been supplying the food markets in Juba and other major towns in South Sudan, precisely because the government of Southern Sudan did not make an effort to provide transport routes to surplus food-producing areas in Maridi, Yambio, and Yei. The roads to these areas were in perpetual disrepair, making it cheaper to import food commodities, including vegetables and even fish, from Uganda and Kenya. This suggests that the political elite cared little about developing the national productive forces, preferring to render the people of South Sudan, essentially an agrarian and agro-pastoral people, dependent for their survival on farmers in Uganda and Kenya.

The apparent asymmetry between the Republic of South Sudan and other countries in the region in terms of trade and commerce shows clearly in the flight of foreign currency, particularly the US dollar from South Sudan to the EAC countries of Uganda and Kenya. South Sudan pays in convertible currency rather than in the South Sudanese pound for commodities produced and sold in the currencies of East African countries simply because it exports nothing in exchange. This means that the US $4 billion to US $5 billion a year that South Sudan receives from the sale of its oil is visible only through its impact in the economies of Uganda, Kenya, and Ethiopia. This exposes the ignorant, corrupt, and unpatriotic nature of the South Sudan political elite. It has become obvious that selfish concerns and the protection of wealth stashed in banks and real estate in Kenya and Uganda were the main drivers of the application to join the EAC.

The socioeconomic transformation of an impoverished, multi-ethnic society like South Sudan requires more than just natural resources. It requires leaders conversant with not only the theory of social transformation but also capable of marrying that theory to their practice in the context of socioeconomic and political engineering of the country. This brings to mind what Mwalimu Julius Nyerere once said:

> Those of us who got education, we got it at the expense of our people. Each one of us is like a young man in a hungry village to whom the people give their last resources to enable him go to bring more resources from a distant village. If he fails to bring them the food, he will have betrayed the people.[23]

By failing to deliver social and economic development and instead stashing away money in foreign lands the South Sudan political elite betrayed its people. Indeed, the political elite in South Sudan demonstrated its betrayal of its people in multiple ways, which invokes questions as to why in the first place this elite led the people into the protracted struggle for independence. South Sudan's independence was not an accident of history, but it will be an unforgiveable historical mistake if the South Sudanese state remains stillborn because of the failings of its sons and daughters. These failings link to what I earlier described as the sociopolitical duplicity that the dominant political elite has displayed in the social, economic, and political engineering of the nascent South Sudan state. They stem from the duplicitous politics used to extricate themselves from the condition of power asymmetry in the Sudan, faking Sudanese nationalism in front of northern Sudanese while harbouring strong secessionist sentiments in the presence of southern Sudanese.

This lack of courage and integrity to be their real selves plays out in such pretences as pursuing a South Sudanese national agenda while in practice promoting a parochial ethnic agenda of hegemony and domination, as in the case of the JCE. Moreover, within the Dinka ethnic ideology that the members of the JCE pursue, they stoop so low as to support clan feuds and conflicts. This includes the case of Aguok and Apuk sections of the Rek Dinka in Gogrial, Warrap state, and Luach and Paweny sections of the Padang Dinka in northern Jonglei state. However, analysing this elite attitude and behaviour reveals that the underlying motivation is neither love for ethnicity nor solidarity with the people but personal ambition for power and wealth. The morally searing massacre of ethnic Nuer in Juba between 16 and 19 December 2013, undertaken by a Dinka private army, could not awaken the conscience of a fellow Nuer general who was then the Army chief of staff, Gen.

---

[23] Quoted from *We Must Run While They Walk: A Portrait of Africa's Julius Nyerere* by William E. Smith (New York: Random House, 1976).

James Hoth Mai; he was just protecting his power and privilege to prove the point. Then all hell broke loose and so began South Sudan's journey from fragility to state failure and collapse.

Since nobody was there to pronounce the collapse, the dominant and governing elite pressed on, pulling from the stomach of the earth a few barrels of oil to keep the wheels of war turning. A senseless war which made South Sudan an entangled bruise of traumatized, brutalized, terrorized, impoverished, alienated, malnourished humanity — all under the gaze of desensitized members of the United Nations Mission in South Sudan (UNMISS), Joint Monitoring and Evaluation Commission (JMEC) and the Ceasefire and Transitional Security Arrangements Monitoring Mechanism (CTSAMM), among others. Thus, like old disinterested watchmen in a deserted opencast mine, these organizations are there only to issue reports blaming all parties for violating the IGAD-brokered cessation of hostilities agreement. No one seems to entertain any hopes of a turnaround. A presidential advisor on military affairs told his Gok people to forget about Juba because there was "no government in South Sudan." And all the while, the president continues to appoint and disappoint people, cynically engaging in futile attempts to reunify the feuding SPLM factions instead of returning peace to the country.

I am convinced beyond a reasonable doubt that the failure to construct a state in South Sudan started long before President Kiir ascended to the helm. His leadership only worsened the already distorted national liberation process in the context of sociopolitical duplicity, as discussed above. The greatest danger facing the people of South Sudan is the surge in ethnic nationalism of the two largest nationalities: namely, the Dinka and the Nuer. The formation of the JCE, representing the socioeconomic and political interests of the Dinka, and the apparent hegemonic tendency triggered a parallel response from the Nuer. In their case, it was the mythology based on Ngundeng's prophecy, peddled by Dr. Riek Machar and power-hungry Nuer intellectuals. The Dinka and Nuer are the respective largest and second-largest nationalities in South Sudan; both are acephalous historically, with no tradition of indigenous statehood. The competition between their elites, based on ethnic hubris, constitutes an obstacle to the emergence of a national bourgeoisie capable of uniting the country.

The reason is simple: the ruling elite is composed of people who are ignorant and politically bankrupt, with no clear understanding of the politics or economics of a modern state. Their embrace of an ethnic ideology is part of the vacuous concept of constructing the state in South Sudan based on Dinka culture and patrimonialism. This pushes them to pursue parochial, personal, ethnic, and localized interests at the expense of broader national goals. They project ethnicity over a national agenda and, in so doing, the national and ethnic agendas have become synonymous and interchangeable. This confuses many people, particularly foreigners and those South Sudanese hailing from communities with strong traditions of indigenous statehood. Many in the JCE combine official executive positions in government and leadership of their respective clans/communities, suggesting that they are in government to represent their communities. This explains the exponentially high proportion of ethnic Dinka in every cabinet formed in South Sudan since 2005.

President Kiir has never hidden his Dinka ethnic chauvinism. Since assuming leadership of South Sudan, he has been bent on the political and economic empowerment of the Dinka of Bahr el Ghazal, especially those hailing from Warrap and Aweil. The political empowerment included appointments of people from Warrap for the positions of governor of the Central Bank, chief justice, inspector-general of police, director-general of National Intelligence Bureau, director-general of immigration, and director and administrators in the Office of the President. On the economic front, he empowered them through the selective awarding of inflated government contracts for procurement and construction. It is no wonder that his close relatives and business associates top the list of financial frauds already inventoried.[24]

In 2009, in an effort to reconcile the feuding Padang Dinka clans of Lauch and Paweny in northern Jonglei State, President Kiir awarded these clans land belonging to the Shilluk, triggering a civil war in the Shilluk Kingdom.[25] In a desperate attempt to scuttle the IGAD-brokered Agreement on the Resolution of the Conflict in South Sudan (ARCISS), Kiir decreed Establishment Order 36/2015, dividing South Sudan into 28 states. This decree awarded the Dinka nationality 14 states. This piece of legislation purports to empower the people through devolution of power. In reality, it concentrates and centralizes power in the hands of

---

[24] *Sentry Reports* 2015, 2016 and 2017.
[25] This was a travesty of justice to buy political loyalty. Decades before, in 1980, a committee appointed by the president of the HEC resolved that claims to the land brought by John Gejang Awol and Michael Miakol, the paramount and executive chiefs of Atar, were unfounded. After visiting and surveying the boundaries of Kodok and Fanjak districts, the committee concluded: "At no point along the Kodok/Fanjak borders did it cross both the Nile and the Sobat rivers at the point of reference, suggesting that the claim by the chiefs of Atar has no basis."

the president in Juba. Although the objective was to purchase Dinka loyalty, this potent drug caught the imagination of the poor masses, inadvertently reinforcing and perpetuating Dinka ethnic hubris and fascination with power, never mind that the creation of the new states offers no opportunity for socioeconomic development. It only benefits the local political elite in terms of appointments to state governments.

The legislation to increase the number of states was ill-advised, triggering intercommunal conflict and heightened tensions over boundaries, particularly in Warrap. In Upper Nile, this legislation, forced through by President Kiir, saw Shilluk land — the whole stretch of territory on the east bank of the Nile River, from Tonga in the south to Melut in the north — given to the Padang Dinka. This decision did not come in response to a sudden call from the Padang Dinka population for a colonial-type eviction of the Shilluk people from their ancestral lands. It was in the context of the JCE elite's speculation in land for mechanized commercial agricultural and livestock rearing. In fact, there are unconfirmed stories that some members of the JCE have taken huge amounts of money from some Gulf States speculators for the lease of land in Upper Nile.[26]

In a recently published study (Amir Idris, 2018), I discussed the role played by the South Sudanese political elite in the failure of South Sudan to transit to statehood and nationhood. One such reason, confirming the elite's backwardness, was its fleecing of the country of its wealth. As I wrote:

> The country's elite has built a kleptocratic regime that controls all sectors of the economy and have squandered the historic chance for development of a functional state. These predatory economic networks play a central role in the current civil war, because much of the conflict is driven by elites attempting to re-negotiate their share of the politico-economic power balance through violence.[27]

This report sums it up. It is an indictment of the SPLM/A leaders and cadres. It was not their commitment to the liberation that pushed them into the ranks of the SPLM/A: they were hunting for fortunes. This behaviour on the part of the leaders clashes with their image as

---

[26] A similar situation occurred in 2007, when a certain American claimed Paulino Matip had sold him a large part of Unity State; another American citizen claimed he had paid the local chief in Wondurba in Central Equatoria State money for the lease of a large swath of territory that included many villages. These cases have not been resolved.

[27] "The Nexus of Corruption and Conflict in South Sudan," a report published by Sentry, July 2015, an initiative of the Enough Project with its supporting partners, the Centre for Advanced Defence Studies and Not On Our Watch.

volunteers in the war of national liberation. It only proves that the ruling class in South Sudan is an ignorant, backward, and unpatriotic lot.

On inheriting the government of the subnational entity, the SPLM leaders had no idea of how to utilize the billions of US dollars it received in oil revenues. There were feasibility studies of development projects for the defunct Southern Region, which could have been the starting point for the socioeconomic development of southern Sudan. These included Portland cement in Kapoeta, hydroelectric power generation at the Fula Rapids in Nimule, an agro-industrial complex in Mangalla, cane sugar factory in Melut, fruit canning in Wau, kenaf in Tonj, tea project in Upper Talanga, and the Nzara agro-industrial complex. These were ready projects, which only required funding. It would not have taken much effort for the ruling elite to start implementing these projects. The Republic of South Sudan is now planning to import electricity from Uganda and Ethiopia, when the billions of dollars the leaders have stashed in the Ugandan economy could have built the Fula hydroelectric plant.

The ignorance, greed, and lack of patriotism of this class attracted to South Sudan all kinds of international criminals, including experts of the Bretton Woods institutions. By early 2013, South Sudan started to show signs of bankruptcy. In the course of eight years, the ruling elite had committed fatal mistakes, among them: failing to provide socioeconomic development and launching a border war against the Sudan. These mistakes fed into the power struggle within the emergent factions. No sooner did they plunge South Sudan into a destructive civil war, interrupting the transition from fragility to statehood and nationhood. There is no great ideological difference between these warring factions — namely, the one in government led by President Kiir, and the other one in opposition, led by Dr. Riek Machar — to occasion civil war except inflated ego and greed for power.

Conditions of extreme power asymmetry between southern and northern Sudan produced attitudes and social behaviours that triggered civil wars. South Sudanese spent six decades combating the outward manifestations of these asymmetrical relations, obtaining in the country until they seceded from the rest of the country. Instead of emancipating themselves and their oppressors in the process of liberation, they internalized these relations based on power asymmetry. Frantz Fanon in *Black Skins, White Masks* and Paulo Freire in *The Pedagogy of the Oppressed* speak to the situation of the current South Sudanese political elite, whether in government or in the current war's opposition. Their attitude and behaviour arise from deep-seated internalized oppression, deprivation, and discrimination, which can be traced to the colonial occupation and pacification. The urge among the ruling elite to dominate others and to treat others like pawns, and to accumulate wealth by any means available, is a reflection of an inner need to compensate for everything that they may have missed, not necessarily in physical reality but as something embedded in the subconscious.

The current civil war, and the exponentially violent manner its protagonists are prosecuting it, has created unimaginable hatred among the people. Some think South Sudan will not be viable again as one country. Several factors contribute to this thinking. The most excruciating factor is the ethnic dimension and the way it escalated into a war of all against all, rendering it more complex and difficult to resolve, even after isolating its political aspects as defined in the current IGAD-mediated peace talks. This is because the army and the security forces are predominantly ethnic Dinka, which makes the war essentially Dinka versus all the other ethnicities. This is by virtue of Kiir's presidency of South Sudan and the political and military support he receives from Uganda's President Yoweri Museveni. This has sucked all and sundry into the eye of the cyclone of rage and bitterness, which if not tended to immediately will make it impossible to end the war.

The deteriorating humanitarian situation, the intransigence and lack of concern for the people demonstrated by President Kiir, the ignorance, political illiteracy, and inability of the members of the JCE, who seem to be on a no-return journey to establish a Dinka-dominated state in South Sudan, have become a potent drug that is likely to perpetuate the conflict after whatever peace agreement is eventually reached. The war has displaced, dislocated, and disrupted people's livelihoods. They are unable to till the land to produce their own food and now depend entirely on international humanitarian assistance. Only a shift in the political thinking of the elite can make a difference. As the elites in government and in the opposition are absorbed in the struggle for power it means that any disputes, especially in elections after any transition period, will definitely rekindle the violence. Because of this, the priority of IGAD's special envoy to South Sudan should be to effect a paradigm shift that enables these elites to think outside the political box and discuss not power or its sharing but a path for social and economic development. This would transform the fundamental contradictions driving the conflict; namely, poverty, ignorance, and illiteracy.

The political and military weakness of the opposition, especially the SPLM/A-IO, is another factor that is perpetuating the condition of no-war no-peace. The formation and proliferation of different armed and political opposition groups would not have occurred had the SPLM/A-IO had a correct political reading of the situation. This would have enabled its leaders to chart clear political objectives and strategies for fighting Kiir and the JCE. The failure of Machar to transform the civil war into a revolution — a national democratic revolution, for that matter — has scattered and weakened the opposition outside and inside the country. The incarceration of Machar in South Africa further weakened the opposition. It also renders untenable the political opposition's political survival in a region decidedly in favour of the status quo in South Sudan under the leadership of President Salva Kiir Mayardit.

This has pushed some opposition groups, particularly the SPLM leaders now known as the "former political detainees", to propose some form of UN or African Union (AU) stewardship of South Sudan. Surrendering sovereignty, which this proposal implies, is characteristic of the group's political and ideological poverty. Forgetting that this is consistent with the now-recognised nonsense of "African solutions to African problems," the AU does not even have the capacity in terms of resources, while the UN stewardship might turn into a permanent situation, akin to its mission in the Congo, which has now spanned five decades. The idea of a stewardship should not be entertained: it would create a situation that could lead to South Sudan's dismemberment.

The solution to war and conflict lies with the political elite. The social and economic crisis that led to the pauperization of all, including the perpetrators of corruption and looting of the country's resources, coupled with the lack of democratic space and the dictatorial antics of President Kiir, has forced many to reconsider their political stance. The so-called "national dialogue" has failed to generate the required or anticipated results and has placed the onus of blame for the war on the government. It is creating a climate that will make reconciliation and other traditional methods of conflict resolution more attractive than the liberal peace that IGAD and the international community is pursuing. It might be necessary to consider recourse to the tradition method of conflict resolution successfully tried in the Wunlit Dinka-Nuer Peace Treaty (1999) to resolve the conflict in South Sudan.[28] This may be a

---

[28] The split in the SPLM/A following the Nasir Declaration (1991) transformed into an ethnicized conflict with immense and egregious human rights violations and abuses throughout the liberated areas to the advantage of the common enemy. A Church-sponsored traditional

better alternative to the IGAD's ARCISS, which speaks only to power sharing and superficial reforms to the system.

Short of sparking a national democratic revolution to construct a national democratic state in South Sudan, the political elite should be innovative and generate ideas and a political programme to pull South Sudan out of this self-inflicted agony. As discussed below, a national democratic revolution — involving all sections of South Sudan, in their various social, economic, and political formations — has the potential to address not only the issues of social and economic development but also those contradictions inherent in the country's national/ethnic multiplicity. The collective resolution of these contradictions is the only way that South Sudan can move from the present state of near collapse to peace, stability, and viable statehood. This is not only a condition for building a nation out of the existing ethnic, religious, cultural, and linguistic multiplicities in South Sudan; it is also a condition for freedom, justice, and fraternity. This would ennable "unity in diversity" and the construction of a national culture.

In conclusion, it is about time that the South Sudanese political elite, a section of the petty bourgeoisie, committed class suicide in order to resurrect in the guise of revolutionary peasants and intellectuals, to paraphrase Amílcar Cabral. This will enable these politicians to extricate themselves from ethnic parochialism, the sociopolitical duplicity, and duplicitous duality, which have plunged the nascent South Sudan and its people into the abyss.

---

peace conference in Wunlit, Bahr el Ghazal, involving the Dinka and Nuer sections involved in conflict, led to the Wunlit Peace Covenant and establishment of a people-to-people peace process, which ensued throughout Southern Sudan. The peace and reconciliation became a catalyst for the reunification of the warring SPLM/A factions, as well as the IGAD peace negotiations which resulted in the 2005 Comprehensive Peace Agreement (CPA) between the government of Sudan and the SPLM/A.

CHAPTER TWO

The Revolution That Never Was

> A revolution can be recognized not by what it calls itself but by the nature of its leadership; whether that leadership was conceived and delivered in the womb and warmth of society or manufactured in a laboratory test tube.
>
> — Debray[29]

The Republic of South Sudan, the highly hyped youngest country in the world, is in a dire state of affairs. This state of affairs confirms the misgivings many detractors, Sudanese or otherwise, had expressed about the ability of Southern Sudanese to govern themselves. The ability of a people to govern themselves is a function of many factors, some of which they themselves could construct socially and politically. At no time in our contemporary history, until the granting of independence in 2011, had southern Sudanese exercised sovereign power. Predictions that South Sudanese would not be able to govern themselves stemmed from social and political reality, historically occasioned by marginalization, oppression, exploitation, and discrimination. This narrative ignores southern Sudan's colonial realities and the political repression southerners suffered under the oppressive domination of their northern compatriots. This produced in them subjectivities and psychological complexes of inferiority, violence, and self-hate, which today seem to inform and drive their political attitudes and behaviours.

The present brand of South Sudanese political leaders emerged in the context of the struggle for national liberation against an oppressive

---

[29] Quoted from Régis Debray, *A Critique of Arms* (Penguin, 1978).

pan-Arab dictatorship. Most of these leaders were products and indeed commanders of the war of liberation. Most had had no prior experience in politics and government. They were moulded by the SPLM/A and, therefore, the ineptitude and avariciousness, vanity and lack of patriotism they have demonstrated in managing the young Republic of South Sudan must be linked to their genesis as a class in the liberation process itself. There is no comparison between the liberation-era leaders and those political leaders and technocrats who managed the ten years of self-rule experiment in the Southern Region (1972–1983) in terms of political space and financial and economic resources at their disposal. Those leaders who managed the Southern Region operated in a difficult political and economic environment, and yet they achieved some degree of success, albeit under a totalitarian political system that eclipsed their role in the systemic failure. The explanation for the failure of these leaders to place the young state on correct foundations of state formation and nation building, which underpin the current civil war and dire social and humanitarian disruption, must therefore be found in the political ideology of the SPLM/A, or its absence, during the war of national liberation.

It is necessary at this point to mention something about the evolution of organized political work in southern Sudan. Historically, at least after 1947, there has been no tradition of organized political work expressing the aspirations of the people. The resistance to colonialism and colonial occupation was physical and violent, rather than cerebral and political, in character. Political activities in southern Sudan evolved and sprouted under the political and economic tutelage of northern Sudan's theocratic and traditional political establishment. The only authentic southern Sudanese political party to emerge in the wake of the elections of the Constituent Assembly in 1954 was the Liberal Party, which called for federation with northern Sudan. The founding political leaders were characteristically right-wing conservatives or liberals who viewed politics through the lens of colonial officialdom.

The Juba Conference in 1947 sealed the fate of southern Sudan as an integral part of the Sudan, suggesting that the southern Sudan political elite would now play its role in the national body politics as equals with its northern counterpart. However, the substandard education of the elite's members, the lack of political culture, and financial weakness rendered unstable the political process towards independence, eventually triggering the mutiny of the Southern Corps of the Sudan Defence Force on 18 August 1955. The eruption of violence in southern

Sudan and the repercussions that followed set the ground for what became known as "the problem of southern Sudan." Southern Sudanese called for federation and self-determination, and made all kinds of political demands for greater constitutional protections.

This situation changed only in May 1969, when left-wing officers in Sudan Armed Forces (SAF) overthrew the liberal multiparty government. The May regime's initial recognition of the socioeconomic and cultural disparity between southern and northern Sudan, expressed in the 9 June Declaration, created the political and ideological conditions for the emergence onto the political stage of the hitherto neglected and marginalized southern Sudanese left-wing politicians and political activists. The idea of regional autonomy as a solution to the problem of southern Sudan began to spread. The strategy was that under a progressive leadership the people of southern Sudan would exercise regional self-rule to implement a social and economic development programme and bridge the socioeconomic and cultural disparity between the two parts of the country. This political development was short-lived; an ideological shift to the right occurred within the Sudanese revolutionary camp and the regime returned to conservative neo-liberal policies.

The July 1971 reactionary counter-coup prompted Gen. Gaafar Nimeri to jettison the national democratic revolution programme that had supported regional self-rule. This enabled Nimeri to negotiate peace with the Southern Sudan Liberation Movement (SSLM), the political leadership of Anya-nya Land Freedom Army, under the auspices of the World Council of Churches and witnessed by Ethiopian Emperor Haile Selassie. These negotiations led to the signing of the Addis Ababa Agreement on 3 March 1972, providing regional autonomy for the southern provinces of Bahr el Ghazal, Equatoria, and Upper Nile. The Addis Ababa Agreement was incorporated into the Constitution of the Republic of the Sudan as a distorted version of the regional autonomy provided by the 9 June 1969 Declaration.

The Addis Ababa Agreement ended the war in southern Sudan but this did not resolve the social, economic, and political crisis of the regime. The regime's incorporation into the imperialist orbit of influence to implement economic policies dictated by the World Bank and the International Monetary Fund fuelled the crisis. The regime transformed into a one-man totalitarian dictatorship to suppress social and political unrest occasioned by its ill-considered economic policies. The cycles of socioeconomic and political crisis eventually led to the regime's demise in a popular uprising in April 1985. These crises did not spare the Southern Region, where the political elite there set up a quasi-liberal democratic parliamentary subsystem that served as a peripheral subset of the totalitarian regime. The lack of socioeconomic development in the Southern Region triggered political unrest in its constituent provinces where armed groups started to operate against the government.[30] The clash between the totalitarian system in the centre and a quasi-liberal democratic dispensation in the Southern Region led Nimeri to abrogate the Addis Ababa Agreement and dismantle the Southern Region (June 1983) and impose an Islamic penal code (September 1983) on the country.

The abrogation of the Addis Ababa Agreement and the dismantling of the Southern Region were renewed strategic steps towards the Islamization of the Sudan. It is worth mentioning that the leftist coup in May 1969 aborted the promulgation of the Islamic Constitution. Abrogation of the agreement that granted self-rule would be the price Nimeri had to pay for inclusion of the National Islamic Front (NIF) in the system.[31] The imposition of the Islamic Sharia laws, especially the application of the so-called "instant justice", was intended to suppress opposition to the regime, amid growing popular alienation as the regime drifted more into the imperialist orbit.

American economic investments leading to discovery by the American company Chevron of oil in Western Upper Nile, later renamed Unity Province, rendered the Sudan an important US foreign policy interest. The Southern Region's elite viewed the oil discovery with enthusiasm as it was expected to contribute to development of the region. But President Nimeri's decision in 1980 to locate the oil refinery in Kosti rather than Bentiu, to suit Chevron's economic interests and those of the parasitic capitalist class in north Sudan, triggered political unrest in the Southern Region. The People's Regional Assembly (PRA) passed a motion against the decision, to the chagrin of Nimeri. Armed vigilante groups who would later become the Anya-nya II started to form in the area in opposition to the oil exploration. As the political situation deteriorated, Nimeri embarked on a strategy of administrative

---

[30] Some elements of the Anya-nya forces absorbed into the Sudan Armed Forces (SAF) resisted their transfer to northern Sudan and mutinied, including in Aweil (1975), Akobo (1976), and Juba (1977). They went on to establish what they called the Anya-nya II to fight for total liberation of Southern Sudan.

[31] The right-wing northern political parties (Umma Party, National Democratic Party, and the Islamic Charter Front) agreed with Nimeri in February 1977 (Port Sudan Agreement) to join the May regime on the condition that Nimeri abrogated the Addis Ababa Agreement with the South and dismantled the Southern Region.

decentralization of the Sudan as a means of breaking the political power of the Southern Region's government. Nimeri exploited the PRA's impeachment of Gen. Joseph Lagu in 1979 and the return of Abel Alier to the presidency of the High Executive Council (HEC). Nimeri relieved Abel Alier as vice president of the republic and appointed Gen. Joseph Lagu in his place. This cultivated the seeds of political divisions within the Southern Region along ethnic and provincial fault lines. It also accelerated Nimeri's administrative decentralization plans. Many politicians beyond Abel Alier's circle picked it up to divide the Southern Region for their own political reasons.

But the Southern Region, for some time, remained outside the turmoil that affected Nimeri's regime in Khartoum and northern Sudan. This was partly because of the separatist nature of Southern Sudan. Nevertheless, the power struggle among the Southern Sudan political elite was part of the general crisis of the regime, and indeed informed the call for re-division of the Southern Region and the subsequent mobilization for war against the regime. Opinion will definitely differ on whether or not the events leading up to the mutiny of SAF Battalion 104 in Bor on 16 May 1983 were in any way linked to the power struggle in Juba. There was no direct political linkage between the military action and the power struggle that led to the March 1983 arrest of two members of the Council for Unity of Southern Sudan (CUSS), PRA Speaker Matthew Obur Ayang and HEC Vice President Dhol Acuil Aleu.

Other politicians took to the bush after Nimeri abrogated the Addis Ababa Agreement and introduced the republican decree to dismantle the Southern Region on 1 June 1983. Among them were Joseph Oduho, Samuel Gai Tut, Akuot Atem, William Abdalla Chuol, Benjamin Bol Akok, and Martin Majier. There was frustration among the former SSLM leaders with the Addis Ababa Agreement's implementation and Nimeri's interference in the democratic process in the Southern Region. In fact, the gunrunning in Upper Nile and Bahr el Ghazal that accompanied the PRA's elections in early 1982 was proof that the politicians had decided to return Southern Sudan to war. It is worth mentioning that elements of Anya-nya II were already operating and engaging the armed forces in eastern Upper Nile and northern Bahr el Ghazal.

The narrative, therefore, that the mutiny in Bor was planned as part of the formation of the SPLM/A, as it is claimed in the SPLM Manifesto, requires a credibility check for the following reasons. First, the SPLM Manifesto was published nearly three months after the events in Bor and Ayod. Therefore, the mutinies in Bor and Ayod could not have been the precursor of SPLM/A formation. In most situations of this nature, a manifesto announcing the launch of an insurgency hits the media outlets well in advance of the event. In this case, the SPLM Manifesto post-dated its formation. Second, the events in Bor were linked to administrative indiscipline and the embezzlement of salaries by the commanding officer, Maj. Kerubino Kuanyin, and were therefore criminal in nature. However, this crime was for personal reasons not linked to any political struggle. Third, Kerubino was a former Anya-nya officer but was deeply involved in fighting the Anya-nya II insurgency in Eastern Upper Nile.

The events in Bor that led to the mutiny could have been the work of military intelligence linked to the country's political leadership through the commander of SAF's Southern Command, Gen. Sadeeq el Banna, who doubled as Kerubino's friend with cordial relations that transcended duty and professionalism. In light of this fact, it is imperative to investigate the mutiny in Bor in its own context, as an event linked to military discipline and the Army top brass in Khartoum, rather than being part of the power struggle in the Southern Region. In this respect, I offer two ways of looking at this period.

The first scenario has to do with Nimeri's strategy to instigate and foment political unrest in Southern Region in order to accelerate the abrogation of the Addis Ababa Agreement and dismante the Southern Region. The eruption of violence allowed Nimeri to circumvent the political process to amend the Constitution to expunge the Addis Ababa Agreement and dismantle the Southern Region. The war in southern Sudan would eventually lead to his downfall and transform the Sudanese polity.

The second scenario has to do with the presence in Bor of Col. Dr. John Garang, a senior officer in the SAF. The government knew the volatile situation in Bor and, as usual in such a situation, the army top brass would not allow a senior officer to holiday in a volatile place like Bor. However, in approving Garang's request travel to Bor, Nimeri must have been counting on Garang's specialization as a counter-insurgency officer to quell the unrest among the Bor mutineers. Garang could have behaved like the British officials whom the southern mutineers trusted and surrendered to during the Torit mutiny in August 1955, preventing the radicalization of the insurgency and its linking up with anti-imperialist forces in the Horn of Africa.[32]

---

[32] This was the concern of the American administration and the Central Intelligence Agency (CIA), which monitored superpower rivalries in the region and the Middle East.

The SPLM/A Manifesto speaks of a national liberation movement "to wage a protracted armed struggle,"[33] with the objective to "transform the Southern Movement from a reactionary movement led by reactionaries, concerned only with the South, jobs and self-interests to a progressive movement led by revolutionaries and dedicated to socialist transformation of the whole country."[34] Viewed from an ideological perspective and the objective reality then in the Sudan, this statement seems to be shrouded in speculation and dreaming, making it the subject of critical investigation in order to separate myth from reality.

The SPLM Manifesto noted that the remnants of Battalion 104 (Bor) and Battalion 105 (Ayod) formed the SPLM/A. If that was the case, then this fits into the analysis that the SPLM/A formation had much to do with Dr. John Garang's earlier revolutionary ideas about African revolution, informed by his perception of an oppressive Arab nationalism in the Sudan. This is expressed succinctly in his letters to Dominic Akec Mohamed (February 1972) and to Gen. Joseph Lagu and the SSLM negotiation committee at the Addis Ababa peace talks (January 1972).[35]

The mutiny in Bor and the presence of Col. John Garang was connected to the SPLM/A formation but only in a narrow context. This would mean that John Garang had since 1972 harboured the idea of waging a protracted war rather than negotiate with the moribund regime of Gen. Nimeri because, as he said, "The condition for permanent revolution have not as yet been sufficiently created within our own movement." This explains his contempt for the Anya-nya leadership, which comes up in the manifesto, disparaging them as reactionary, jobbist, and self-interested.

It is difficult to tie together the idea of constructing a socialist New Sudan, as the SPLM/A leadership desired, and southern Sudanese sensibilities. After the July 1971 counter-revolutionary coup, the south was intensely anti-communist and secessionist. The SPLM Manifesto was the height of hypocrisy and deceptive populism, its contents characteristic of the views of some leftist intellectuals who had returned from the West with an only superficial theoretical knowledge of Marxism. They failed to factor into their analysis the objective reality that people lived.

---

[33] SPLM Manifesto, Chap. 8, Art. 23(a), in PaanLuel Wël (ed.), *The Genius of Dr. John Garang* (2013).
[34] Ibid, Chap. 7, Art. 22.
[35] January 1972, quoted in *The Genius of Dr. John Garang*, vol. 2 (2013): pp. 20 and 23.

No one can decree socialism into existence, either politically or divinely, as in Genesis when God said, "Let there be and there was light." Socialism is a sociopolitical construct in the context of advanced development of the social and material productive forces. This means that it was a Cold War gimmick to make the building of a socialist New Sudan its prime objective, at a time when the socioeconomic development of Sudan was characterized by the low level of development of its productive forces. The Sudan remains at the stage that the Marxists usually categorize as the stage of national democratic revolution. It is a stage when the progressive forces accelerate the development of productive forces to address fundamental contradictions in state and society. The role of the SPLM/A therefore would be to liberate the masses from poverty, ignorance, illiteracy, and superstition, and consolidate national independence and fraternity among the masses.

The Sudanese political and ideological spectrum included the Sudan Communist Party, a Marxist-Leninist workers' party, on the far left, and, on the far right, the Islamic fundamentalists. There were also left- and right-wing and conservative liberal political formations. It will become clearer as we procede whether or not the SPLM/A was in reality part of the Sudanese national democratic revolutionary forces in the Sudan. From a Marxist perspective, the socialist ideology that the leaders of the infant movement projected did not spring from an internal social reality or genuine conviction of socialist ideals. It was an opportunistic move in anticipation of external political, diplomatic, and military support. This means that the SPLM/A leadership feigned socialist idiosyncrasies only as a deceptive strategy to link itself to Ethiopia and the socialist fraternity in order to solicit political and military support. I will come back to this point after completing the answer to the doubts expressed by others regarding the ability of southern Sudanese to govern themselves.

I would say that the ability of a people to govern themselves depends critically on the leaders they have produced or continue reproduce. However, leaders do not just spring up from nowhere to lead: they are the product of people's life experiences and they reflect people's historical aspirations. In this respect, I would say that the chaotic social and political mélange South Sudan is going through is not intrinsic to southern Sudan and its people. It is extrinsic, being the product of the obfuscations the SPLM/A introduced into the liberation process. Attempts to bypass or rush through a stage in the socioeconomic development of society could have unintended negative consequences. There was a high rate of suicide among Hungarians in the 1970s and

1980s, linked to the sharp gradient of the socioeconomic transformation from peasantry to industrial proletariat, which began with radical agrarian reforms following the triumph over counter-revolution in 1956.

The people of southern Sudan in their different social formations have historically governed themselves in the manner that suited them. The ethnic communities, no matter how rudimentary or primitively organized, had indigenous governance systems that created harmonious relations with their neighbours until the European colonial intrusion and occupation in the nineteenth century disrupted their social order. Since then they have never had peace and harmony among themselves. Therefore, the current situation, which impels others to doubt the ability of South Sudanese is a product of SPLM/A as it introduced traits, attitudes, and behaviours that were not only completely alien to society in Southern Sudan but also to liberation processes the world over. The outcome in post-independence South Sudan is comparable to other situations in the recent and contemporary world. At a certain level it compares to the Republic of Nigeria of the 1960s and 1970s when Nigerian leaders, propelled by greed and ambition, plunged the oil-richest country in Africa to what today is a caricature of itself before independence. Nigeria's resources ended up in the hands of a few fabulously rich individuals who created social and political disorder to prevent Nigeria from becoming a politically and economically powerful African country (Achebe, 1983).

In terms of regional and international conspiracy and rivalry to sabotage its progress, socioeconomic development and the prosperity of its people, South Sudan may compare to Belgian Congo, which successively became the Republic of Congo, Zaire, and finally the Democratic Republic of Congo with neither a republic, democracy, nor prosperity for its people, despite its enormous natural resources. However, in terms of the personality of its leadership, I can vouch that South Sudan compares with no other country after the tragic death of Dr. John Garang de Mabior. His successor, President Salva Kiir Mayardit, the accidental president of South Sudan, is a man of a rare character similar to that of the Cambodian leader Pol Pot. A leader, and a good leader for that matter, is critical to the country and its people's social and economic wellbeing. Discussing the totality of the sociopolitical environment that surrounds South Sudan and the presidency of Kiir brings to mind a scene in *Detained: A Writer's Prison Diary* (1981) by the Kenyan author Ngũgĩ wa Thiong'o. After meeting a colleague who had just been arrested and sent to prison, he quipped,

"Our freedom from detention in Kamiti Maximum Prison depended on the death of Kenyatta."

Many South Sudanese, including those who supported President Kiir based on ethnic solidarity, now believe he has turned into such an albatross that only his death will bring respite to the people of South Sudan. It appears unbelievably apocalyptic that the fate of a people could be contingent on death of its leader, particularly a former senior member of the liberation movement that led the struggle for the country's independence. This indeed can only be a true expression of despair and dismay in view of the busted expectations and the humanitarian catastrophe. The demise of Kiir, *suo moto* or otherwise, will not, however, arrest South Sudan's inevitable slide into the abyss. A military coup will make the situation even worst, which could degenerate into a Somali-type scene. It will only be with the concerted efforts of all those disenchanted with this kleptocratic, totalitarian regime that South Sudan will be saved.

The current South Sudan reality is characterized by a social, economic, and political meltdown. The unbridled greed for wealth and hatred among the leaders, to the point of sacrificing their own people for political expediency, cannot be the legacy of a socialist revolution, even under a right-wing leadership. We can find an explanation for how this situation has come about in the way that the SPLM/A leadership duped the people of the Sudan and the region about its left-wing credentials while pursuing a counter-revolution. It is a fact that Cold War exigencies, the superpower ideological rivalry in the Horn of Africa and the Middle East, and the ideological credentials of the Ethiopian Derg did not make it possible to thoroughly scrutinize the Marxist or left-wing ideological credentials of the SPLM/A leadership. However, political parties are sovereign and therefore no party would abrogate the right or mandate to scrutinize the other.

The Ethiopian Derg would have had the right of oversight over what the SPLM/A leadership did with the material support it received from it and other socialist countries and parties on the basis of solidarity. However, matters did not operate or function in that way. The SPLM/A operated in a manner that suited its political objectives. Only the people of the Sudan could hold it and its leadership to account or, as usual, things were left for history to either condemn or absolve. The SPLM/A leadership was, therefore, caught up in the web of regional and international intrigue, deception, and double-talking, as well as ideological shifts occasioned by the Cold War.

The SPLM Manifesto (1983) correctly enunciates that the socioeconomic and cultural backwardness in Southern Sudan epitomized the general situation in the peripheral Sudan. It went on to define the real and potential enemies of the SPLM/A, and to conclude in Chapter 11 that:

> The SPLA/SPLM is convinced of the correctness of its socialist orientation. The SPLA/SPLM programme is based on objective realities of the Sudan and provides a correct solution to the nationality and religious questions within the context of a united Socialist Sudan, thereby preventing the country from an otherwise inevitable disintegration.

The Communist Party of the Sudan (CPS), the leading workers' party and the revolutionary section of the Sudanese people, published its General Report in 1967, which was adopted by the fourth party convention.[36] This report spelled out in clear ideological terms the outstanding features of the regional and international situation at the time. It analysed the Sudanese political situation and the mass movement, and the prospects for the formation of the National Democratic Front as the means to heighten the mass movement, given that the Sudan was still at the stage of national democratic revolution.

The SPLM/A Manifesto appeared, to the political community within the Sudan, to be a revision of the theoretical understanding of the Sudanese situation as per the general report of the fourth convention of the Communist Party. In fact, the SPLM/A in its manifesto fails to acknowledge the presence of the CPS or any other left-wing or revolutionary forces in the country. Its discussion of the social, economic, and political reality of the Sudan in general and Southern Sudan in particular lacked an indepth analysis, suggesting that the ideas carried in the manifesto had been imported from a reality other than that of Sudan's.

There have been instances in history when revolutionary intellectuals, perhaps impatient with the slow but consistent political struggle the working class was undertaking, or forced by the objective political conditions of the country, took to armed struggle against the oppressive national bourgeoisie to effect social change. This was particularly true after the triumph of the Chinese Communist Party in 1949 and the establishment of the People Republic of China. The Cuban Revolution, led by the July 26th Movement, was one such example in

---

[36] *Marxism and the Problems of Sudanese Revolution* (Khartoum: Dar el Wasilla Publishers, 1967), in Arabic.

which revolutionary intellectuals defeated the oppressive regime while the authentic Communist Party remained, leading to class struggle in the cities and towns. Similarly, national liberation and anti-colonial movements in the former Spanish and Portuguese colonies in Africa followed the same revolutionary armed struggle. In retrospect, the SPLM/A emulated these movements in what would have appeared to be a social revolution in the Sudan carried out by rural peasantry and pastoralists rather than an industrial proletariat. Unfortunately, what the SPLM/A leadership failed to understand was that peasants and pastoralists, as a social class, do not aspire to build socialism. In most cases, peasants struggle for agrarian reforms, mainly to acquire land rights from their feudal lords. There is nowhere in Southern Sudan where feudal relations exist. Therefore, the reason why the SPLM/A undertook to mobilize the peasants and cattle herders to fight a protracted armed struggle comes within a context other than the building of a united socialist Sudan. We shall find out in the following pages.

The purpose of this discourse is to establish the revolutionary credentials of the SPLM/A. This stems from reading its manifesto, later publications and the speeches of its chairperson to the troops at different times and places. The SPLM/A was not a political party or organization that chose revolutionary warfare as its means of struggle against the oppressive minority regime in Khartoum. It kicked off as a military force, the politics of which had to be tacked on after the fact. The most important and critical factors in any revolutionary war and, which indeed accompany mobilization for war, are the political and ideological consciousness of the leaders, cadres, combatants, and the masses. A revolution is identified by its political ideology and organizational structure, which in turn defines its internal relations, as well as relations with the masses. It is also identified by the character of its leadership, whether or not the core leadership is a single man or woman, and whether or not the leadership was conceived somewhere in a laboratory test tube or conceived and developed in the womb and warmth of society.

The leadership of the SPLM/A hailed from a stratum of reactionary military officers from the SAF. The fact that it sprouted and espoused a national (Sudan) revolutionary agenda but ended up a regional (Southern Sudan) entity with a leadership in the person of Salva Kiir Mayardit who pursued a parochial ethnic agenda smacks of opportunism. This manifested itself immediately upon its formation in terms of a power struggle, which rocked the infant movement, and the refusal to undertake ideological training and political education and organization of the combatants. The greatest weapon in revolutionary war is not the types of guns the combatants carry but the level of their ideological consciousness and political awareness. The absence of this political education cast doubts on the SPLM/A as a genuine national liberation movement.

The Republic of South Sudan is a story that we must candidly tell, if only as a gesture of recognition and respect for the role the people of Southern Sudan, the Nuba, and the Funj played in the war of national liberation. I am sure that each time we scratch the surface of this inexhaustible story of our people's agony and suffering — caused by mindless, power-hungry leaders — we fathom the truth of what and where it all went wrong. We also tell this story to make people aware so that they emancipate themselves, and to stimulate them to action so they can transform the oppressive reality submerging them. It is inevitable that ethnic demagogy will one day cease to stir and steer people's lives. It will not be long before the people recognize that the unqualified support they offered their leaders because of ethnicity or provincialism is the source of their poverty, ignorance, and illiteracy.

Politicians, scholars, and students of South Sudan from a variety of ideological perspectives have authored and published books, research papers, and newspaper articles about the struggle of the people of South Sudan. Some South Sudanese wrote memoirs chronicling their respective roles in the long struggle. The most recent publication of note was by Hilde F. Johnson, who speaks to the tragedy that befell the people of South Sudan immediately after independence.[37] She was right in a multiple of ways, regarding her account of the events leading to December 2013's violent eruption. However, in the same vein, I could say that like many diplomats and international civil servants who worked in South Sudan, Dr. Hilde confused her responsibility and mandate as the special representative of the UN secretary-general, developing personal relations with the main actors in the government of the Republic of South Sudan. Experience must have now taught Dr. Hilde that relations of friendship, inspired by solidarity with a political cause, can be only shallow; they seldom transcend individuals, time, and space. Dr. John Garang de Mabior, as a leader, was different from Salva Kiir Mayardit and the louts who took over the SPLM leadership and the government of South Sudan following his tragic departure in 2005.

---

[37] *South Sudan: The Untold Story from Independence to the Civil War* (London: L.B Tauris, 2016).

Like their predecessor Sudanese compatriots, South Sudanese political leaders have perfected the arts of pretence to charm with a seemingly benign personal demeanour, hiding their official attitude and behaviour from the foreign diplomats and international bureaucrats they engage with. In this way, many foreign diplomats have fallen victim to the confusion of developing personal relations of friendship while carrying out their official functions. As a result they fail to report objectively back to their home countries about the situation in South Sudan. This may explain how the eruption of violence in Juba on 15 December 2013 took unawares the governments with diplomatic accreditation to South Sudan, particularly the USA, Britain, and Norway, as well as close neighbours like Ethiopia and Kenya. I have to omit the Republic of Uganda because it was part of the regime's planning team. In this way, through personal charm and feigning civility when engaging with his peers and their diplomatic envoys, President Kiir has dodged critical scrutiny of his decisions and actions in the country.

In a ceremony on 26 August 2015 to countersign the Agreement on the Resolution of the Conflict in South Sudan (ARCISS), the president presented himself as the victim of an imaginary regional and international aggression against his regime. Kiir categorically rejected the compromise peace agreement and considered it part of a scheme for regime change. Nevertheless, none of the IGAD heads of state and government officials present at the ceremony questioned why the president was appending 26 reservations to the agreement, even though he had attended the IGAD summit in Addis Ababa on 16–17 August, which imposed the compromise agreement. The reservations eventually translated into flagrant violations of the peace agreement. The way that people treat him suggests that relations with President Kiir transcend normal diplomatic etiquette, especially for those leaders who have businesses flourishing in South Sudan, or those who return to their countries with fat "khaki" envelopes in their briefcases.[38] This complacency or tacit support on the part of the regional and international interlocutors emboldens Kiir to act outside constitutional precincts, enabling him to emasculate the Legislature, the judiciary, and the civil service, as well as the ruling SPLM.

South Sudan, with its 64 component nationalities, is the result of history and demography. It is a unique mix of medieval social formations

---

[38] The term "khaki" is used to refer to the bribing of diplomats. The South Sudan government has used the country's last amounts of money to bribe regional leaders, buying political and military support.

juxtaposed to modernity in a complex pattern, underscoring the nature of its current predicament as a polity. The mix contains sociocultural ingredients with enormous capacities to block or undercut mutual advancement of the whole, and this underpins the failure of state formation and evolution of a nation in South Sudan. It is indeed an understatement, if not a misnomer, to compare South Sudan to a six-year-old toddler, suggesting that the world should forgive its leaders for their delinquency, for their uncouth and infantile public behaviour.

In this maze of absurdities, we may also come to face the oxymoronic ingenuity exhibited by some of South Sudan's leaders. An ingenuity that defies conventional wisdom, which makes a PhD holder in economics surround himself not with intellectuals of similar calibre but with functionally illiterate Sudanese Army brutes who have turned the national liberation movement into its very opposite and domesticated oppression. It is this ingenuity that created a leadership hitherto unknown in Sudanese leftist circles, one that proclaimed a socialist revolution in the dying days of the Soviet Union-led world socialist system. One may forgive those Sudanese on the political left who believed that the SPLM/A was an imperialist hoax or Cold War gimmick: they stand vindicated. The SPLM/A was anything but a revolution.

This is a discourse about the SPLM/A and its impact on the social and political environment in the Sudan, but more specifically in Southern Sudan, from where it sprang up. The objective of this discourse is two-fold: to deconstruct the myth that the SPLM/A was a national liberation force spearheading a socialist revolution. In this, I intend to make people more aware, particularly the Dinka ethnic chauvinists organized in the Jieng Council of Elders (JCE) as the power brokers around the presidency of Salva Kiir Mayardit. They believe the liberation myth and consequently accept their privilege in the SPLM/A. The myth and the Dinka ethnic ideology of hegemony and domination underpin the current social, economic, and political crises in South Sudan. This discourse therefore hopes to investigate the origin of "socialist New Sudan"' and the ideological shift to the right the SPLM/A leadership made after the first Gulf war.

The SPLM/A was essentially rural-based in terms of membership (largely peasants) and the low level of sociopolitical awareness of those members. The idea of building a "socialist" New Sudan from a backward rural environment exposes an obvious disconnect between myth and reality. The SPLM/A leadership spoke to different narratives while practicing their very opposite. They ignored the dialectics of a war of national liberation and consequently came out with something resembling the system against which they had struggled. In the concluding chapter of *The Politics of Liberation in South Sudan: An Insider's View* (Nyaba, 2000:198), I asked a rhetorical question, "What is the SPLM and where is it?" If I were to ask the same question today the answer would be that the SPLM/A was the greatest deception. The SPLM leadership treated the Sudanese people, in both the north and south, to this great deception. The SPLM today is not even a caricature of what it was in 1983. This is what I mean by transmorphization, in the manner of Goebbels transforming lies into truth through repetition.

The people of South Sudan will for generations tell and retell the story of the SPLM/A as part of their history. They will speak of the political and military leaders who emerged and how they rose to fame during the war of national liberation. A popular anecdote in the People's Republic of Hungary during the Cold War goes that a Russian asked how the Turks had managed to rule the rebellious Hungarians for nearly 500 years. In response, the Turk coldly said, "In all these years, we did nothing to remind the Hungarians of our presence." In the same measure, with their never-ending power struggles and greed for wealth, the SPLM/A leaders will keep fresh in the minds of the South Sudanese people the memory of their iniquities, corruption, and ruthlessness. It is awful if this is how the people will remember the SPLM/A leaders. This statement lays credence to what I said earlier, that questions hang over the SPLM/A as a national liberation movement. The proof of which should be visible in the current reality in South Sudan, reflective of its internal organization in the form of institutions and instruments of its power and leadership, in the manner it conducted the war, in the relations it built within the ranks, and between it and the masses.

Was the SPLM/A a Reincarnation of SANU?

The authentic written or oral material with which to judge the SPLM as the engineer of the current social, economic, and political reality of South Sudan is its manifesto. A critical political and ideological evaluation of the SPLM Manifesto reveals a falsified narrative of SPLM/A origins as a national liberation movement. This is not just because of the putschist nature of its leadership but because it lacked ideological clarity. This confirms the fear many in the political leftist harboured: that the SPLM/A was a right-wing Trojan horse in the socialist stockade.

The social origins and ideological training of its leadership betray its right-wing and neo-liberal inclinations. The emergence of a liberation movement led by right-wing leaders could not be anything more than a counter-revolution. In the context of Southern Sudan, counter-revolution is expressed through ethnic ideology to supplant the historical Arab-dominated northern Sudanese political hegemony and domination. No matter how they have tried to fudge it, the ethnic context nevertheless comes out explicitly in the manifesto in the form of "an early determination of the SPLM/A leadership to prevent the hijacking of the Movement." In looking at this quote, it becomes obvious that the SPLM/A suffered from a certain form of determinism expressed not in class struggle terms but in populist sloganeering.

This determinism comes out clearly in the script, in the social and political processes leading to the emergence of Dr. John Garang as the leader of the nascent movement. Without the Derg's military intervention to resolve the power contest, Garang would not have become the leader. This support for Garang was not based on ideological grounds but on his military and academic credentials. That putschist decision and action of the Ethiopian army general who came to mediate the power wrangle in the nascent movement in support of Garang — "the early determination of SPLM/A leadership" — marked the beginning of military capture and the distortion of the SPLM/A development as a genuine national liberation movement. The emphasis was on power and whoever wielded it rather than on the revolution and the political programme underpinning it. This closed the door to political dialogue with the Anya-nya II forces, which were mainly Nuer, ostensibly to set the ground for military confrontation of the two movements, ignoring the possible social and political repercussions for the nascent movement.

The withdrawal of the Anya-nya II into the Sudan and its alliance with the oppressive regime inadvertently led to the numerical dominance of the Dinka in the nascent movement. The ethnicization of the political and ideological differences between the SPLM/A and the Anya-nya II played out negatively and turned into mutual exclusion. The attitude of the SPLM/A leadership, which the rank and file echoed, calling any Nuer *nyagat* (traitor) not only exacerbated Dinka-Nuer ethnic tensions, it also entrenched the sense of military superiority within the Dinka and their resolve to protect that advantaged position. The early determination of the leadership clause literally meant protecting the Dinka leadership of the nascent movement to prevent other ethnic or ideological groups hijacking it. This will become clear as we discuss the ostracisation of the revolutionary democrats and the surge of Dinka ethnic nationalism in the SPLM/A.

It is important to offer some background knowledge of the political struggle in Southern Sudan, to enable a clearer understanding of some of the attitudes and behaviour of some leaders. The SPLM/A leader, Dr. John Garang de Mabior, came from the same political school of thought as his mentor William Deng Nhial, which glorified Dinka ethnic nationalism and its ideology of hegemony and domination of the other ethnic minorities. According to this school, without a Dinka leadership, Southern Sudan would never become free from the North Sudan. True to his belief, William Deng in 1965 abandoned in East Africa his colleagues Aggrey Jaden, Joseph Oduho, and others to come back to the country. They had collectively founded the Sudan African National Union (SANU) in 1961. After the collapse of the Round Table Conference on the problem of Southern Sudan in March 1965 Deng Nhial remained in the country to establish and lead a variant of the SANU (Inside) to play politics in Khartoum. The Arab-dominated northern political establishment assassinated Deng Nhial in 1968. His politics, in collaboration with Sadiq el Mahdi and Hassan el Turabi in the "Congress of New Forces", rubbed on the wrong side the traditional and theocratic feudal political establishment, prompting his assassination in Rumbek in May 1968.

In the SPLM/A, Garang tied a knot with Salva Kiir Mayardit in this Dinka ethnic ideology. In fact, the two represented the terminals in this Jieng power circuit until a low-capacity wire, which ran from Oxford through Khartoum to Yei, short-circuited their relations in 2004, in what became known as the "Yei crisis". This event rocked the SPLM/A to its core. The personification rather than institutionalization of the SPLM/A leadership's power and public authority meant that differences between Garang and Kiir could lead to the destruction of the movement. It was rumoured that Garang wanted to promote Nhial Deng Nhial to the second position in the SPLM/A leadership hierarchy. He wanted to do this as a gesture of respect for the late William Deng Nhial, his mentor. The second reason was to ensure that in any event power would never shift away from the Dinka fraternity, particularly after the return to the SPLM/A fold of Dr. Riek Machar and Dr. Lam Akol Ajawin, whom Dr. John Garang did not trust but believed were more adroit than Salva Kiir or James Wani Igga. Having long been a loyal and effective number two, Kiir would not hear any talk of Nhial Deng's promotion. Indeed, Kiir had become the SPLM/A vicar general of Bahr el Ghazal and therefore would not tolerate Nhial Deng, his junior in the military hierarchy, replacing him as deputy to Garang. Surrounded by SPLA officers and men from Warrap and Aweil, Kiir dug his feet down in Yei to challenge the leadership of Dr. John Garang. It took the intervention of SPLM/A friends to defuse the crisis and restore the harmony. This was a serious risk, one which Kiir should not have taken. It was the eve of the signing of the Comprehensive Peace Agreement, which Garang and Ali Osman Taha had spent time negotiating in Naivasha, Kenya. Nevertheless, Kiir survived to inherit the helm and to implement the project of social, economic, and political empowerment of the Dinka.

In the more than two decades of its life, the SPLM/A did nothing to disprove the perception of many leftists in and outside it that the SPLM/A was a right-wing Trojan horse in the revolutionary camp. Of course, revolutionaries recognize each other by their ideology, organization, and the emphasis placed on the political education and organization of the masses to raise social awareness and political consciousness. The Ethiopian Derg had hesitated to support the Anya-nya II even on a reciprocation basis against the Sudan government. It was a separatist organization, which made it difficult for the Ethiopian government to support its reactionary leadership lest it would be shooting itself in the foot politically and diplomatically. However, the Derg immediately elected to support Garang, based on the contact made in Khartoum.[39] It is worth mentioning that an Ethiopian Air Force helicopter picked up Col. John Garang at Adura inside the Sudan.

The Derg leadership must have decided to support and determine the leadership of the new movement. The Sudanese revolutionaries who congregated in Itang in western Ethiopia to launch the new movement that would now spearhead the revolutionary war of national liberation were only to endorse that decision. This declared Col. Dr. John Garang de Mabior the chairperson and commander in chief of the SPLM/A. It was to the chagrin of the politicians who had wanted the political movement (SPLM) and its leadership separated from the military (SPLA). This explains the little time allotted to the process and the skirmishes provoked by the Ethiopian soldiers to remove from the venue the bulk of Anya-nya II who supported the leadership of Samuel Gai Tut, a Nuer from Lou. This Ethiopian intervention not only cultivated the seeds of discord and war between the infant SPLM/A and the Anya-nya II, which was now forced to ally with the government of Sudan, but also distorted the political and ideological evolution of the SPLM/A and strengthened its militaristic character. It also set the stage for the

---

[39] A cell of progressive Dinka intellectuals in Khartoum contacted the Ethiopian Embassy in Khartoum and informed it of the fighting in Bor. They also reported that a progressive officer by the name of John Garang was on his way to Gambela and would require assistance from the comrades in the Derg.

personification rather than institutionalization of the SPLM/A's power and public authority, something that continues to haunt the people of South Sudan to this day.

Once the contest for leadership had been resolved with the Anya-nya II, one expected that the SPLM/A leadership would settle down to undertake the necessary political and organizational imperatives of the nascent liberation movement. The immediate task would have been to complete the organization and structure, and establish the political authority of the movement (SPLM) over and above the military (SPLA). This would have defined the roles and responsibilities of the different organs and individuals exercising those powers. The next task would be to define the social, economic, and political objectives of the war. The political objectives would determine the strategies and tactics required for achieving the objectives. These would be the steps a revolutionary leader would undertake to establish people's power as he embarked on an armed struggle to transform the oppressive reality in his country.

There was something suspicious about the SPLM/A leadership line-up. Apart from the fact that it comprised former officers of the SAF, it was predominantly Dinka in composition. Garang was the chairman and commander in chief; Maj. Kerubino Kuanyin came second as deputy chairman and deputy commander in chief; Maj. William Nyuon Bany became the SPLA's chief of general staff; Captain Salva Kiir Mayardit became director of military intelligence (MI), while Maj. Arok Thon Arok was made a member of the Political Military High Command (PMHC) without portfolio. As director of MI, Kiir became the commander of the SPLA training centres in Bonga and Bilpam, where they cultivated and instilled militarism and total obedience in the recruits.

Something peculiar lingers about the relationship that bound Garang to Kiir, something more than their common ethnicity. Another knot tied the two men together in their professional training which facilitated the transformation of the SPLM/A from a national liberation movement into a patrimonial political patronage network and, finally, into an ethnocentric, totalitarian dictatorship. Kiir trained as an intelligence officer in the Sudanese Army, rising to the rank of captain by the time the SPLM/A was formed. Garang, a university graduate in economics, joined the military as a captain, rising to the rank of colonel.[40] As an army officer, he specialized in counter-insurgency — US strategic war

---

[40] Garang joined the Anya-nya in 1970 after graduating from the University of Dar es Salaam. He was then absorbed into the Sudan Armed Forces as a captain following the Addis Ababa Agreement in 1972.

against liberation movements in Africa, Latin America, and Asia during the Cold War. This begs the innocent question of whether or not a good counter-insurgency officer could lead a successful insurgency.

In retrospect, Garang had all that he required, in terms of human resources and military logistics, to rise to power in Juba or even Khartoum. This, however, will come later in the discourse. I raise it here in the context of the suitability of a counter-insurgency officer leading an insurgency, leave alone a revolutionary insurgency. The strategies Garang employed to conduct the war between 1983 and 1987 resembled more the waging of a counter-insurgency, which depleted his own human and material resources, than an insurgency against an enemy. As a result, the SPLM/A lost thousands of combatants, including strong officers who could have competed for leadership positions in the nascent movement, in tactical and less important battles, especially in Jekau, Malual, Yabous, and other loctions. Could it possibly have been that his professional training as a counter-insurgency officer interfered with the conduct of the war? The SPLA victories were usually pyrrhic and contrary to the laws of guerrilla warfare: destroy the enemy and preserve your men.

It is important to note that Dr. John Garang de Mabior and Salva Kiir Mayardit forged a working partnership. This relationship witnessed, over the years, the elbowing out of SPLM/A leadership and the subsequent demise of permanent members of the PMHC; namely, Kerubino Kuanyin Bol, William Nyuon Bany, and Arok Thon Arok. This partnership also witnessed the unexplained demise of many political leaders, including Benjamin Bol Akok, Martin Majier Gai, Joseph Oduho, and Joseph Malath, and competent military officers like Martin Makur Aleyow and Martin Kajivoro, and many others. Many of these officers did not fall in battle but were executed without public notice and in dubious circumstances.

In their outward appearance and public pronouncements, these former SAF officers, now leaders of the national liberation movement, presented themselves as revolutionaries, sharing fidelity to the revolutionary cause. But deep down, beneath the wheeling and dealing, it was a partnership of subversion of the revolution. It was a partnership between imperialist agents and the burgeoning parasitic capitalist class that the Sudan's Nimeri military regime fronted. It was a very complicated enterprise: Nimeri allowed Garang to lead an insurgency in South Sudan in order to complete his Islamic project in the Sudan. It was like killing two birds with a single stone. The strategic objective was to stop the radicalization of the insurgency in Southern Sudan by preventing it from joining the popular uprising against Nimeri in the Sudan and with the revolutionary and anti-imperialist forces in the Horn of Africa and the Middle East. In subverting the SPLM/A, Nimeri and his imperialist friends were able to exploit the relations that evolved between SPLM/A and its Ethiopian benefactors.[41]

The 1970s and 1980s witnessed profound social and political changes in the Greater Horn of Africa. The US had lost its military base in Ethiopia after the coup that overthrew Emperor Haile Selassie in 1974. The Derg had moved closer to the Soviet Union and Cuba following the defeat of Siad Barre in the Ogaden. Across the Gulf of Aden, the Yemeni People's Democratic Republic was in the Soviet zone of influence. In the Sudan, Gen. Gaafar Nimeri had just reversed the leftist coup, executed the top leadership of the Communist Party of the Sudan (CPS) and was inching towards warmer relations with the US administration. This created the climate that enabled the World Council of Churches (WCC) to broker the Addis Ababa Peace Agreement between Nimeri and Gen. Joseph Lagu Yanga, leader of the Southern Sudan Liberation Movement (SSLM), under the auspices of Emperor Haile Selassie.

In the early 1980s, the Horn of Africa, encompassing Sudan, Ethiopia, and Somalia, was in the eye of intense superpower ideological and strategic geopolitical rivalry. The region was experiencing social and political upheavals. Eritreans were fighting to secede from Ethiopia. In the Sudan, Nimeri, now a friend of the Reagan Administration, was facing serious political and economic problems, which triggered strikes and demonstrations against the regime in the north. In the Southern Region, a different kind of socioeconomic and political unrest smouldered but was not directly related to events in the north. There were serious political challenges linked to the discovery of oil in western Upper Nile and Nimeri's decision to demarcate the borders, which placed the oil fields within northern Sudanese territory. A rebellion was imminent.

The importance of Sudan's strategic position as a link between Africa and the Middle East and its long borders with Ethiopia was not lost on US administration. Chevron had a US $1 billion-plus investment in the oil fields in southern Sudan. A rebellion or a revolution in southern Sudan that threatened to close down or nationalize Chevron's operations

---

[41] The SPLM/A, while completely dependent on the Ethiopian government, which was fighting wars in Eritrea and Tigray, started a conventional war in Southern Sudan. This indeed was subverting the Ethiopian regime.

would constitute a US national security threat, and therefore the CIA would try to prevent such an event. This may provide the answer to the speculation that there may have been a strategy linked to Cold War geopolitics to subvert revolution in South Sudan. It is not impossible to subvert a revolution. Indeed, history has shown that many revolutions failed to achieve their objectives. This was because of either internal weaknesses or because of external intervention.

Notwithstanding its restive and political fragility, the Southern Region was the least likely place in the region for the launch of a socialist revolution, as called for in the SPLM Manifesto. The objective conditions and subjective factors were not ripe for any kind of revolution, leave alone a socialist revolution, which would need an industrial proletariat to lead it. The improbability of socialist revolution in Southern Sudan stems from the absence of an advanced working-class movement. Conservatives and right-wing politicians had dominated southern Sudan since independence in 1956. By their nature and their failure to grasp the fundamental contradictions inherent in the socioeconomic and cultural backwardness of the region they could not stimulate revolutionary action in the masses.

The geostrategic position of the Sudan renders any revolutionary movement in the area susceptible to subversion, even in the most subtle manner. In the context of the Cold War's geopolitics and superpower rivalry in the Horn of Africa, the Americans would not tolerate a revolutionary movement with the potential to link up with the Derg in Ethiopia or other revolutionary forces in the Middle East to rise up in South Sudan. Such a political development would be a big problem for imperialism. It was therefore imperative to nip it in the bud, necessitating the professional expertise of Garang and Kiir to undertake sustained though subtle counter-revolutionary actions within the SPLM/A. The objective was to prevent its development and evolution into a genuine national liberation movement, one in which a political and ideological consciousness was developed among its combatants and the masses.

I have discussed the external factors linked to superpower rivalry in the Horn of Africa. These factors by themselves would not succeed in subverting the SPLM/A as a liberation movement without corresponding internal factors. The internal factors linked to southern Sudan's objective reality were the personality of Garang and his personal ambition for power. Without that personal character it would not have been possible to build the SPLM/A into a huge army encompassing the marginalized Sudanese people, who trusted him and joined in their tens of thousands to fight for freedom, justice, and fraternity. The nexus between the SPLM/A as a liberation movement and a personal power project is subtle and sometimes difficult to notice. Garang tragically died before he could exercise the power he had worked so long to achieve.

Promotion of Militarism: A Culture of Fear and Self-Preservation

One of the dictums of Mao Zedong was that "power comes out of the barrel of the gun," suggesting that anyone desiring power must build an army that is loyal only to him. Whether it was for social revolution, overthrowing an oppressive despot, or to serve a personal agenda for power, the army was a fashionable tool, glossed in national liberation idiosyncrasies in the Horn and Great Lakes regions of Africa, particularly towards the close of the Cold War. Before the turn of the last century, regimes in Sudan, Ethiopia, Somalia, Uganda, Rwanda, Zaire, Central African Republic, and Chad had been replaced. Whether or not these liberation/resistance movements/fronts influenced the social, economic, and political situation in their respective domains is another matter outside the scope of this investigation.

The SPLM/A emerged in the context of the destruction of the "old Sudan" and the construction of the "New Sudan." But this would mean compromising to share power with the National Congress Party (NCP). It failed to achieve its political objectives and instead settled for Southern Sudan, to the chagrin of the Nuba, the Funj, and other marginalized northerners in eastern and northern Sudan. The objective of this section is to discuss how the SPLM/A transformed from a revolutionary army (militant) to a reactionary (militarist) outfit to serve the personal power agenda of its leader. Dr. John Garang de Mabior was one of the few African intellectuals fascinated by the use of military methods in the process of national liberation. Thus, after graduating from Dar es Salaam University in 1969, he joined the Anya-nya. Gen. Nimeri assumed power that year in a leftist military coup that placed the Sudan on the path of national democratic revolution, albeit for a very short period. It could not have been a coincidence that a revolutionary pan-Africanist opted to join the reactionary Anya-nya instead of returning to participate in building a democratic movement in Southern Sudan following the May revolution. The question that people ask is whether or not Garang used his counter-insurgency knowledge to camouflage his intention to join the mutineers in Bor.

The ease with which the SPLA formed, in terms of the availability of human and material resources, could have been a source of difficulty for someone interested in person power. This pushed to the fore "the early determination of leadership", necessitating stringent security measures that straightjacketed the SPLM/A's development into a closed and secretive, intrigue-infested army. The SPLM/A adopted the same security and intelligence code as that of the Sudanese Army. Thus, from the beginning the SPLA was modelled on the reactionary Sudanese Army, in terms of training, military doctrine, morale orientation, and relations between officers and men. It slanted towards militarism, militancy rendering more important the hierarchical (power) than horizontal (comradeship), to shape and condition the relationships between the members of the SPLM/A and enforced by a network of military intelligence (MI) officers and informers whose task was to instil fear and spread rumours and falsehood.

This situation in the SPLM/A generated a culture of suspicion and fear. People were obsessed with self-preservation and gossip. There was a general apathy and a lack of confidence or solidarity among the troops and officers. Comrades were suspicious of each other and maintained allegiance to only one person: the chairman and commander in chief. It was a climate of leader worship, of flattery and court jostling; where people accepted anything a leader said no matter how uncouth and in bad taste it was; and where everybody wanted to endear himself to the leader. It was an artificial atmosphere where comrades discussed private as well as public issues in whispers; where gossip was spread, especially concerning the attitudes and behaviour of SPLA officers, men in the general headquarters, and among the bodyguards of the PMHC members. It was an environment of intense fear, self-preservation, and competition for higher ranks. This meant spying on fellow soldiers, gossiping, double-crossing, and making false witness. This attitude and behaviour permeated the rank and file throughout the liberation movement. Militarism, therefore, was a potent drug to make people submit. It was the antithesis of liberation.

In a personal power project one seldom factors other people into the leadership scheme. As a rule, a leader will take great care to see that only the mediocre and nonentities rise to positions of power and authority. Many great leaders have behaved in this manner, their manipulations and shunning of merit noticed immediately when they vacate the stage. Thus, Jacques Mallet du Pan's statement that "the revolution devours its children" literally suggests that the leader destroys the best brains around him or those suspected of harbouring an appetite to lead. There were many unexplained deaths, disappearances, and prolonged detentions of SPLM/A leaders and cadres between 1984 and 1996. In an environment characterized by fear and self-preservation, it is difficult to find out exactly what happened to those who died or disappeared.

In building personal power in a national liberation movement like the SPLM/A it was important to suppress people's political awareness and ideological consciousness and create an uncritical mass. It is worth mentioning that patrimonialism and political patronage overwhelmed any revolutionary ethos in the SPLM/A and made it easy for the leader to manipulate the combatants by appealing to ethnic sensibilities. However, this was not enough. It was necessary to promote militarism for two reasons: to enforce the cult of personality around the leader and to combat Dinka egalitarianism, which does not countenance autocracy and a cult of personality. It is worth mentioning that the majority of the combatants were ethnic Dinka hailing from northern Bahr el Ghazal.

Therefore, the suppression of an ideological and political awareness and the promotion of militarism in the national liberation movement supported the leader's cult of personality, which served multiple purposes linked to Garang's power ambitions. First, the idea was to invoke absolute and personal loyalty to Dinka leadership in the person of Garang, whom they considered an incarnation of William Deng Nhial and his successor in Dinka leadership.[42] This image links up with Garang's emergence in the leadership of the war of liberation, which was Deng Nhial's supposed role in the Anya-nya movement. Therefore, in the training camps, the Dinka recruits would spend long hours composing and singing morale songs in praise of Garang and Deng Nhial rather than in praise of the revolution.

Second, some Dinka leaders from Bahr el Ghazal like Kerubino Kuanyin (Gogrial), Benjamin Bol Akok, and Kawach Makuei (Aweil) had emerged in the context of the political mobilization for the war of national liberation. They questioned and challenged Garang's leadership because he hailed from a minority Dinka section (Bor) in Upper Nile and was not from Bahr el Ghazal. It was therefore necessary to thwart their leadership ambitions by inculcating Dinka ethnic ideology, which overlooks the minor sectional or clan variations within the Dinka nation. In the light of this logic, the Dinka combatants should feign

---

[42] The late William Deng Nhial was the unquestioned leader of Dinka from Bahr el Ghazal and the party he led, SANU, controlled all the Dinka districts in Bahr el Ghazal except for some parts of Rumbek and Gogrial.

indifference to, and prevent acts of solidarity in the case of any power struggle that simmered between Garang and his deputy, Kerubino Kuanyin Bol, or any other Dinka leader. Not only that, but they should also stand with Garang in any power contest with a leader from another ethnicity, as was in the case with Samuel Gai Tut. This paid off when Garang ordered the assassination of Benjamin Bol Akok and the arrest of Cdr. Arok Arok, who commanded the loyalty of most SPLA officers and men hailing from Bor.

Third, this was to elevate Garang almost to the level of a deity in Dinka social psychology, and to instil a feeling of loyalty and fidelity to Garang above any other individual, whatever his social background, in the Dinka realm. Indeed, this stratagem of projecting Dinka ethnic ideology through his own personality worked very well. Garang managed to get away with the execution of some brilliant Dinka political and military leaders on flimsy charges that they wanted to hijack the movement. They had no opportunity to put their case because the Dinka ethnic ideology had paralyzed or trumped their individual rights to question the leader all the Dinka held in such high esteem, almost like a messiah.

A Dinka who has managed to capture power was more important than any other individual who had not. This muted the reaction of members of Malual Dinka to the cold-blooded murder of their charismatic leader Benjamin Bol Akok in 1984; or of the Twic Dinka for the arrest and detention of Kerubino Kuanyin in 1987 and Arok Thon Arok in 1988, both of whom were members of the High Command. The incarceration of Cdr. Arok Thon was more dramatic because none of the SPLM/A rank and file hailing from Bor came to his rescue. He was able to escape from Garang's jungle prison thanks to the glitch that was the Nasir Declaration in 1991. The Dinka ethnic ideology therefore propelled Garang to the status of state president, enjoying red carpet treatment in regional capitals, while still only a guerrilla leader in the bushes of South Sudan.

Political and Ideological Subversion of the Revolution

It was not an absolute necessity that the peasants who made up the SPLM/A would be Marxists or capable of internalizing Marxist philosophy. However, it was impossible for them to engage, without a minimum of ideological orientation and training, in a revolution that aimed to transform their lives. The call was for a "united socialist Sudan", an expression of left-wing ideology presupposing knowledge of revolutionary theory. Without some grounding, this call had the reality of something found in a fairy tale. I have already established that southern Sudan was in such a low state of social and economic development that the culture of organized leftist political work was lacking. The leadership of this nascent movement hailed from this environment — the most socioeconomically underdeveloped and culturally backward part of the Sudan, where conditions for a socialist revolution did not exist.

In situations of extreme ignorance and poverty, the simplest means of duping poor people into following a course of this nature is to dangle in their face the prospect of a heavenly life where milk and honey flow. Both Islam and Christianity guarantee a better life after death if a person converts and follows their teachings. Nobody has ever come back to tell us if this is the truth. At least socialism promises a better life before death, and many people have witnessed how socialism improved the lives of millions of Chinese. This is the picture "socialism", as a socioeconomic system, spurs in the minds of the downtrodden and prompts them to action. A socialist movement that promised freedom, justice and prosperity (led by a south Sudanese, for that matter) attracted thousands of followers, particularly from the peripheral Sudan in the far north, east, west, and in central Sudan. They saw the SPLM/A as a redeemer and joined in the tens of thousands across ethnic and regional fault lines in the country.

The SPLM Manifesto could easily pass for a piece of ultra-leftist literature. It was precise and surprisingly preclusive of coalition politics characteristic of liberation or nationalist movements. It unkindly disparaged and castigated the Anya-nya leadership, which smacked of an expression of personal disdain. Thus, an examination of its content reveals its ideological emptiness. It was a document tastelessly over-spiced with socialist jargon and slogans, some of which did not suit conditions in Sudan or South Sudan. A few, or perhaps one intellectual, versed in leftist literature and phraseology must have authored the SPLM Manifesto with the sole intention of gaining political and military assistance. It lacked the ideological touch that usually comes with leftist literature. The manifesto did not lay down a programme for addressing the fundamental contradictions that underscored the struggle it claimed to be spearheading. The concept and vision of the "New Sudan" hung somewhere between political fantasy and bluff.

A socialist revolution presupposed two important premises: the class nature of the struggle and a high level of political consciousness among the combatants and the people. The section of society that is capable of waging class struggle are the working classes and a section of petit bourgeoisie, by virtue of their possession of the necessary ideological and political tools for struggle. This political consciousness enables a correct perception of reality through theory (reflection) and practice (action). There cannot be a socialist revolution without a revolutionary theory, goes the Marxist adage, and every liberation movement must have its ideology, encapsulating its theoretic analysis of the context and a practical programme for achieving that objective. In the words of Amílcar Cabral, the liberation struggle is of necessity an expression of internal contradictions in economic, social, cultural, and historical reality, including in the Sudan or southern Sudan, for that matter. This meant that the national liberation movement should lend itself to the concrete knowledge of this fundamental reality in the articulation of its objectives and political programme for transforming that reality.

The first thing the SPLM/A leadership did was to denigrate education and knowledge. This came out in one of Garang's speeches addressing SPLA recruits, most of whom were illiterate cattle herders in the Bonga Training Centre:

> Tell them [former officials and students] to throw away their certificates and degrees. They have no use here. Those of you peasants and cattle camp dwellers will be the directors and managers. They will just be your secretaries whose work is to write what you want.

What kind of socialist revolution or revolutionary government is run by illiterate and ignorant people?[43] This was the beginning of populism, which quickly translated to the proscription of an organized and systematic political training and education of the combatants. It is not permissible to engage in a political struggle, leave alone revolutionary armed struggle, without a minimum of political education and knowledge that informs and mediates the combatants' social and political relations with themselves and with the masses among whom they interact in the context of the war of liberation.

Given the low level of social awareness and shallow knowledge of organized political work among the peasants and the pastoralists in southern Sudan, the idea of proscribing political education was intended to prevent the evolution of a revolutionary consciousness among the SPLM/A leaders, cadres, and combatants, as well as among

---

[43] This contrasted with Cabral who believed the pencil was better than the gun in the process of national liberation in Guinea Bissua, and with Thomas Sankara, who contended that a soldier without political education was a potential criminal.

the masses. Therefore, what appeared as the SPLM/A's failure to trigger the evolution of mass revolutionary consciousness was in reality deliberately engineered to subvert the revolution. The objective was to produce in the people of South Sudan an uncritical and docile mass. This reality — the absence of revolutionary consciousness — correlates with the emphasis placed on militarism and military routine in the SPLM/A, which shaped and conditioned relations between the leaders, cadres, combatants, and the masses.

Inculcation of revolutionary consciousness and political awareness in a war of national liberation is more important than the rifles the combatants carry. As Thomas Sankara once said, "A soldier without political or ideological training is a potential criminal." It is a literal truth and indeed resonates with a certain reality that revolution creates awareness, which prompts the combatants in a rebel army to behave distinctively different from the elements of the oppressive regime's army. Short of revolutionary consciousness there would be no difference between these uniformed and gun-toting individuals. It was a radical departure from revolutionary ethos to hear Garang tell the passing out of a batch of SPLA combatants in Bonga Training Centre: "Through this AK-47, you will get all you want — food, women." It indeed turned out to be a licence for the SPLA soldier to loot, rape, and kill the very people for whom they had taken up the gun.

The SPLA training camps were manned by reactionary instructors who had been trained by the SAF. They instilled and reproduced in the recruits a culture of militarism, of instantaneous obedience to orders and instructions. This created a dichotomy in the attitude and behaviour of the combatants in their contact with people in their villages. While the SPLA officers and men chanted the slogans of freedom, justice, and equality, democratic governance and prosperity for all, they engaged in acts that went counter to these values. This generated confusion in the minds of the people. No wonder some people in the Aliab area of Lakes State protested when the SPLA combatants addressed them as "comrade." This was on the grounds that a "comrade" was somebody who behaved badly, beating innocent people and stealing other people's livestock. The suppression of political education and ideological training meant that combatants were depoliticized and insensitive to the concerns of the people. The people are intelligent and quickly grasped the difference between words and deeds.

There is something poignantly sinister about depoliticizing combatants in a national liberation movement. This has to do with the power relationship in the liberation movement between the officer corps and the soldiers, and between the movement and the civilian population. Political awareness and an ideological consciousness connote knowledge of a struggle's social and political context. The people acquire these attributes through learning and unlearning, through reflection and action, to paraphrase Paulo Freire (1974), in the process of conscientisation. The leaders and the people learn and act together to transform the oppressive reality that has submerged their consciousness. This ideological consciousness moulds the revolutionary intellectual and peasant in thought and character, to enable internalization of concepts and core values, and to stimulate a change of attitude that enables the correct perception of reality. It is the revolution's raison d'être to trigger a change of attitudes and a correct perception of the oppressive reality in order to trigger the drivers of transformative action.

The Ethiopian and Cuban governments provided the SPLM/A with opportunities and facilities for the political and ideological education of its leaders, cadres, and activists. This was provided through the 2nd Yekatit Political School in Addis Ababa, and a school on the Isle de Juventus in Cuba. It was indeed an opportunity, particularly in Cuba where many liberation movements in Africa, Latin America, and the Middle East sent their cadres. This was an opportunity to learn together, to compare and corroborate experiences of revolutionary practice. The SPLM deliberately sent to those facilities individuals who hardly could benefit, in terms of literacy or the will to learn progressive ideas, from the courses offered. They came back from the training courses in Cuba and Addis Ababa as counter-revolutionaries.

There is a direct connection between the proscription of political and ideological work in the SPLM/A — the perversion of awareness and consciousness, the emphasis on militarism — and the cult of personality around Garang. The Derg's support to the nascent SPLM/A was premised on ideological solidarity, which explains the Derg's reluctance to support the Anya-nya II, which originated after the Akobo mutiny in 1975. This solidarity stance, in addition to the military logistical support, presupposed supporting the evolution of ideological clarity and political organization in the SPLM/A. The Ethiopian ideologues would help to identify and select prospective SPLM/A candidates for political and ideological training as political commissars, who would then undertake political and moral orientation within the army. Unfortunately, this was not the case. The SPLM/A leadership made a special selection of officers who were unable to absorb or internalize aspects of Marxist philosophy and political economy, or practice those teachings. They hardly understood the underlying concepts, and therefore could not interpret or carry their correct meanings to the combatants or the masses.

The socialist façade that the SPLM/A presented was created by the imagination of many progressive-minded and leftist people, including some members of the Communist Party of the Sudan. These comrades would have formed the core of socialist cadres of the SPLM/A, to double up as the most informed and ready-made political commissars. It is always prudent to deploy cadres with a good command of revolutionary politics, who understand the contradictions that underscore a war of national liberation, to undertake political work, particularly at a very low level, as in the army and among the civilian population. This political and ideological work would also mediate the relations between the army and the masses. It would help define the class character of the war, and define who the enemies or friends were. It would also spread the envisioned nature of state and society that the SPLM/A sought to construct during and after the war of liberation.

This was not the case. The SPLM/A leadership reduced the political work to the mere chanting of slogans by the combatants and the masses. This explains why the SPLM/A leadership deliberately identified particular individuals fit for this kind of political work, which eventually produced tricksters and criminals in the guise of political commissars and revolutionaries. Thus, in their march to defeat the enemy, the SPLA contingents invariably left in their trail cases of rape, murder, and the brutalization and dehumanization of civilians, especially women and girls (Nyaba, 2000: 51). The very people for whom they purportedly carried their guns became their victims. It was obvious that ridding the SPLM/A combatants and cadres of any preoccupation with politics was to produce and enhance the culture of sycophancy and indifference, to encourage a preoccupation with hierarchies and ranks, and ensure an instinctive and instantaneous obedience to orders. This culture created robots armed with AK-47s who had been trained only to kill people, including friends.

Not only that, this culture also disparaged the intellectual and any kind of erudition. An instructor in our Sonki (bayonet) Battalion told me, "Your doctorate is useless here. Roll it into tobacco and smoke it." It was a display of authority, reducing me in size and aping what Garang had said earlier in one of his lectures to the recruits. This form of insult really set me off. Without caring about the consequences, I defiantly told him, "The doctorate is not a paper: it is knowledge located here in my head." I spent a week doing extra drills as my punishment for defying the instructor. I knew some university graduates who emerged functionally illiterate after six months in the SPLA's training centre in Bonga. It was later known as the Institute of War and Revolutionary Studies, though there was nothing revolutionary in the institute's curriculum to warrant the name.

It was not difficult to conclude that the brutalization and dehumanization of the SPLA cadres and combatants were intended to produce a docile militarised force. Inevitably, they replicated the way they had been treated when they encountered the civilian population. This indeed occurred where the SPLA deployed outside their bases and behaved like an army of occupation, treating the people as if they had been conquered. The kind of abuses they committed would never have been contemplated in their own homes, like raping girls, lactating mothers, and elderly women. The SPLA and the Didinga people fondly remember the commander of Bee Battalion, Cdr. Martin Manyiel Ayuel, for his military professionalism. Cdr. Martin asked the commander in chief to order the battalion back to Bahr el Ghazal in order to avoid an imminent conflict with the Didinga people, who had wiped out an SPLA platoon of 51 men after they went on a raping and brutalization spree in Didinga villages.

The war of national liberation is a process leading to the emancipation of society from all kinds of social, economic, political, and psychological problems. This would be the response to the rhetorical question a Sudan Socialist Union (SSU) apologist asked after the SPLA hit the headlines in 1984: "Liberation from who?" Many SPLA combatants believed, however, that liberation was carrying an AK-47 rifle, shooting at enemy soldiers, and taking over their positions. Thus, by the end of the war there was a sense of entitlement for positions in government, ranks in the organized forces and, above all, privilege and wealth. Then came the chest-thumping "We liberated the country" to intimidate potential competitors, especially those who might have remained working as public servants under the oppressive northern regime, the product of the Al Ingaz Revolution.

This attitude and sense of entitlement did not come out of nowhere. It is the product of the evolution of the SPLM/A and the way it conducted the war of national liberation outside its political and ideological context. It is the direct consequence of shunning ideological training and political enlightenment of the leaders, cadres, and combatants in the SPLM/A, which substituted rent-seeking for the selfless sacrifice and volunteerism that initially drove recruits into the rank and file of the SPLM/A. I established earlier that ideology is one of the most critical elements in a war of national liberation. The other elements include, inter alia, political enlightenment, organization, and institutionalisation.

It is dangerous to call people to arms without giving them a political education. It is even more dangerous to postpone to later stages the political work of national liberation because of immediate military confrontation with the enemy. It amounts to severing the dialectical relations between the two functions of the national liberation. The military is effective and necessary only within the context of a political objective. The SPLM/A started organizing and building its military SPLA before the political SPLM component; in fact, the SPLM did not exist except in the vagaries and confusion when the two were united in a dialectical relation. The SPLA preponderated over the SPLM in all practical matters of the movement. The initial standoff between the politicians and the military officers, warded off by the Ethiopian intervention, must have pushed the SPLM/A leadership to shun political work in general and organization in particular. Everything occurs for a reason and the preponderance of the military in the nascent movement was indeed to concentrate and centralise the power and authority of the movement.

It is worth mentioning that after the resolution of the leadership wrangles, the SPLM/A leadership, comprising the politicians and the military officers, could not agree on the organizational structure, which would vest authority in the political rather than the military leadership. The inordinate influence the Derg's envoy exerted on these leaders clearly decided the contest in favour of military leadership of the movement in the person of Dr. John Garang de Mabior. His credentials as a PhD holder and a colonel in the army tilted the scales and he emerged as chairman of the SPLM Provisional Central Committee, as well as commander-in-chief of the SPLA. In practice, the distinction between the chairperson of the movement and commander-in-chief of the army would be evident had the two components differentiated into their professional spheres. This did not happen and, therefore, the political and military functions of the nascent movement merged into one thing. The overemphasis on the military in the liberation movement imperceptibly led to the complete marginalization and ostracisation of politicians.

The negative attitude towards politicians and a desire to rid the movement of all political enlightenment was evident in the SPLA training centres. The recruits would spend hours, even late into the night, chanting empty slogans or singing morale songs praising the chairman and the leadership of the movement. Attempts to offer a political explanation for certain episodes in or outside the Sudan were vehemently rebuffed by the instructors, who usually responded, "This is not parliament." I was later to understand why, after I was ordered at about one o'clock in the morning to meet with the chairman. It stunned me that they had construed the political classes I offered recruits in the Sonki Battalion as negative agitation against the movement.

"My intelligence officers informed," said the chairman.

"They must have lied to you," I responded.

"Leave that," he said, cautioning me to change the topic. And then he started lecturing me about how the Ethiopian revolutionaries had waited 12 years before they launched the Ethiopian Workers' Party. "We should do the same. We do not have to hurry."

I replied, "Our situation is definitely different from the Ethiopian situation. The revolutionary officers seized power in a coup, and because of Ethiopia's objective reality, it could take the officers that much time to achieve that task. They were busy implementing other important tasks, like freeing land from feudal ownership, literacy campaigns to disseminate revolutionary knowledge, and many others. For us, we start with the people spearheading a revolutionary armed struggle to capture Khartoum. This means that the people should know and understand all the steps we take for them to support the revolution."

Garang was not amused. "Attention!" he shouted. "Go out. I will call you again."

He did not call me again.

This short interview, conducted in the middle of the night, placed me in an intellectual swirl that prevented sleep until sunrise. I called to the fore of my thoughts the SPLM Manifesto and began to question most of its chapters, particularly the clauses about the protracted revolutionary armed struggle. I found it incomprehensible to conduct a revolutionary armed struggle without a measure of political education among the peasants, who made up the bulk of the SPLA's recruits. My ideological and political background and the brief contact with Garang brought me to the conclusion that either he had little knowledge of the people's war or he was exploiting the conditions created by the people's war for personal power ambition, as I discussed earlier.

This explains his contempt for the political leaders who joined the ranks of the liberation movement in the early days of the war. It was really a difficult time to be a politician and, more particularly, the right-wing politicians were not familiar with such situations. They virtually were at the mercy of those ruthless military officers who found delight in humiliating former ministers in the Southern Region's government. Many of these politicians ended up in SPLA jails and detention camps. The degrading treatment meted out to the politicians and intellectuals in general marked the end and complete neglect of organized political work in the liberation movement. Military training became obligatory for all persons joining the liberation movement, regardless of their age and physical fitness.

Everything has a purpose. It does not matter whether you realize it immediately or some other time in the future. The purpose of organization in any system — more specifically, in a political movement — is to bring all its parts together to make the system function effectively. In a political party or national liberation movement the different parts together constitute the whole, and the whole cannot operate effectively without the component parts. In this respect it would be difficult to undertake political work without organization that connects the different parts in a political and ideological unity. Therefore, organization translates to unity, harmony, and discipline in the rank and file, based on conviction in and commitment to the cause. This, a priori, is contingent on political awareness and consciousness on the part of the combatants and the people.

Theoretically, the SPLM/A, in this configuration, subsumed in a dialetical relationship the dual functions of the political and military dimensions of the national liberation. However, in practice the two did not disengage into their respective professional domains. The SPLM/A leadership adamantly refused to separate the movement (M) from the army (A), such that the "M" would lead while the "A" subscribed to its authority, as practiced in modern states where the armed forces are subordinate to political and civil authority. The chairman of the SPLM/A political structure would still be the C-in-C of the military without any qualms, though these positions are held by the same person. But the SPLM/A leadership laid so much emphasis on the "A" being dominant over the "M" that organized political work disappeared from the liberation movement.

The strategic political objective of the party or the liberation movement is to capture the state in order to transform society in accordance with its ideology. In the political struggle to capture state power, the party or the liberation movement must subscribe to a certain degree of organizational structure, which should be simple and permit easy circulation within it of ideas and party communications. This enables bona fide members to participate in the decisions of the party. The fundamental instruments in political work are the constitution, internal regulations, and a political programme encompassing the social, economic, and political spheres of the party or movement's work. The party or movement's constitution defines its world outlook or its ideology, guiding principles, strategic political objectives, the party organs, and relations between them. The internal regulations, as the name implies, define the membership, rights, and obligation, and their relationships, in addition to the functions of the different organs of the party. This implies a clear definition of roles and responsibilities.

Military settings differ from political organization. In the SPLM/A, where the military and political functions fuse into one, it would require a high degree of political and ideological dexterity to function effectively without sacrificing either of two disciplines. The army regiments into constituent units like squads, platoons, companies, battalions, brigades, and divisions, and operates on commands and orders delivered hierarchically from the top to the bottom. There is instantaneous obedience to orders and commands. It is not permissible to dissent or display indiscipline in the army; it could easily lead to prosecution, which could include death by firing squad, imprisonment, or dismissal.

A political setting such as the party requires only fidelity to principles, the constitution, and commitment to the party's programme. Comrades maintain both horizontal and hierarchical relations in carrying out their party function. Comrades discuss and debate issues and, in revolutionary parties, they subscribe to the principles of democratic centralism and criticism and self-criticism. Political and ideological difference is managed through democratic political and ideological struggle. This struggle helps to clarify and sharpen the points of difference, rendering it easy to resolve them.

Adherence to both military and political traditions at the same time in the SPLM/A constituted a serious discrepancy and disconnect between theory and practice. This is because military issues require orders to execute while political matters require debate and possible disagreement. This was the difficult situation many conscious and progressive cadres and combatants found themselves in when dealing with senior reactionary commanders. In most cases, the military order held the field. The SPLM/A leadership went for easy solutions and quick results to resolve the contradictions inherent in this organizational configuration. It imposed strict military order and discipline, which betrayed the falsehood that in the SPLM/A one was both a soldier and a politician. They tried to justify this falsehood with a rejoinder that the decision the individual took to enlist in the liberation movement was a political decision. The soldier/politician individual in the SPLM/A was the personification of a robot soldier, having no conscience and, therefore, was not a revolutionary engaged in a war of national liberation.

As I mentioned earlier, everything has a purpose. Speaking of the purpose, motive, or reason for the military-political set-up in the SPLM/A, it cannot be anything less than an intention to monopolize and personify the SPLM/A's power and public authority. In a political movement the power and authority rests with the political leadership, which in itself is an institution. The best practice the world over is that power and authority institutionalizes in the form of institutions and instruments. The SPLM/A leadership refused to construct institutions and instruments of power and authority apart from the dysfunctional Political Military High Command (PMHC), which was just form without content. It had no rules for the conduct of its business. Indeed, the PMHC never met until its natural death in 1994. The reason is simple: Garang did not want to share decision making with anyone in the movement, including the PMHC members. Creating institutions would mean that some people would be there to make decisions on some aspect of the liberation movement, and Garang would not contemplate any delegation of authority.

The consequence of shunning political organization and the building of democratic institutions in the SPLM/A played out negatively in many episodes. For lack of space, I will discuss only three important disruptions that rocked the SPLM/A to its core. The first major political and military shock in the SPLM/A followed the Nasir Declaration on 28 August 1991, led by three commanders, who were alternate members of the PMHC. This move, christened as a "sweeping revolution", revealed the lack of democracy in the liberation movement, although the Nasir commanders raised the objective of self-determination for the people of southern Sudan. Four years earlier, in 1987, Cdr. Kerubino Kuanyin Bol, the deputy chairman and deputy C-in-C, supported by some progressive SPLA officers, raised the issue of democracy in the SPLM/A. Garang, with the assistance of Ethiopian security, suppressed this move to reform the SPLM/A and had Kerubino and 26 other officers arrested and detained.

It is worth noting that the SPLM/A had grown large in terms of the quality and quantity of people who had joined. A time was bound to come when the political functions would preponderate over the military functions and, therefore, it was necessary, indeed imperative, to build democratic structures as a means of training the leaders, cadres, and combatants for democratic governance. The call for reforms and structuring of the SPLM/A was in order. The problem was that Garang had closed all avenues to democratic discourse in the movement, relying on a repressive security and intelligence apparatus to suppress and nip in the bud any agitation for reforms. This suffocating political atmosphere produced the Nasir Declaration. It happened at a time when the SPLM/A was at its weakest. The Derg has just been overthrown and Garang could no longer receive support from Ethiopia to quell the rebellion.

However, the Nasir Declaration had its difficulties and weaknesses, linked to the general lack of organization and political awareness in the liberation movement. This showed clearly in the poor preparation, in terms of political work, and the military execution of the move. The SPLA Military Intelligence had wind of the plans and arrested officers sent to Equatoria to agitate for the move. It also showed how impossible it is, without solid organization, to take over a liberation movement spread throughout the territory of southern Sudan. Making a simple announcement in a remote location like Nasir, without first capturing Garang, was an ill-advised beginning. Classic military coups to take power occur by first neutralizing the elements and instruments of that power, together with taking over the communications and public broadcasting systems like radio and television. This was not the case with the commanders in Nasir, and this explains why their move was eventually defeated.

The Nasir move failed to snatch power. There was no way the move was going to succeed. Its thrust was against what had become the hallmark of the liberation movement: the shunning of political organization and suppression of awareness. The commanders in Nasir employed the same undemocratic methods, ostensibly to construct democracy in the liberation movement. It was putschist rather than a political move; as a result, they ordered the summary execution of the mainly Dinka dissenters in Nasir. The Nasir Declaration forced a split in the SPLM/A and this triggered internecine fighting between these SPLA factions with enormous destruction of life and property. The Dinka people of Jonglei took the brunt of this destruction, including the abduction of children and women and theft of livestock. It is noteworthy that some groups in Jonglei still hold a grudge against the Nasir leaders for the destruction. In fact, that episode remains a reference point that still defines the relations of some Bor leaders to the Nasir leaders. Suffice to say, the Nasir move was a revelation for many people in southern Sudan. That these events took a quick turn to ethnic animosity speaks volumes about the SPLM/A.

There were many lessons that should have been learned from the Nasir move, in terms of what the liberation movement should have done to improve inter-ethnic relations in southern Sudan. It was surprising that the SPLM/A leadership (Torit faction) in its national convention in 1994 did not draw lessons from this episode, in terms of re-organization and structuring of the faction, taking into consideration the mistakes that led to the Nasir Declaration. Many issues at the national, regional, and international levels required critical analysis and evaluation. This would redefine the movement's development trajectory following the defeat of the Derg and ascension to power by the Ethiopian People's Revolutionary Democratic Front (EPRDF). The SPLA's sudden and unplanned withdrawal back into the Sudan and the worsening internal situation led to the detention or rebellion, respectively, of three permanent and four alternate members of the SPLM/A Political Military High Command (PMHC).[44] These were not adequately discussed and, therefore, the convention could not give any clear direction.

Social and political contradictions do not dissolve or disappear by themselves; they must be resolved by addressing the conflictual elements inherent in the contradiction. Fudging, ignoring, or refusing to address these conflictual elements, in the hope that they will dissolve or disappear, is to ensure their violent recurrence. They generate kinetic energy of themselves and erupt with a force that could destroy the organization. In retrospect, most of the social and political upheavals that afflicted the SPLM/A were avoidable had the liberation movement constructed institutions and instruments for addressing them. The SPLM/A's first national convention, held in 1994, did not problematize the Nasir Declaration and the split that followed in order to not expose or identify the system's internal weaknesses. This would have helped to rectify these weaknesses and strengthen internal unity and discipline in the movement. It was therefore a missed opportunity to assess and

---

[44] These were Cdr. Kerubino Kuanyin Bol, Cdr. Arok Thon Arok, Cdr. William Nyuon Bany, Cdr. John Kulang Puot, Dr. Riek Machar Teny, Dr. Lam Akol Ajawin, and Cdr. Gordon Koang Chol.

evaluate the movement's political and military performance since its inception in 1983. This was the first time the SPLM/A leaders, cadres, and officers had met each other since leaving the training centres. It was an exciting moment, coming three years into the SPLM/A split.

The SPLM/A's first national convention was indeed a school from which to learn through criticism and self-criticism. Unfortunately, the culture of overconfidence makes it impossible for people to learn or unlearn. The convention was just a rush to "forget the past", "open a new page", and to "forge ahead", all in the SPLA mode of "business as usual." The proceedings of the convention, entitled "Watershed Resolutions", carried nothing spectacular in terms of ideas or plans. It was obvious that the organizers did not come from a culture of organized political work; they did not possess the technical knowhow to conduct a convention of that magnitude, involving thousands of participants from all parts of the Sudan. The consequences of ignoring the need for organization were apparent from the technical, ideological, and political aspects of the SPLM/A's first-ever convention.

The second disruption to rock the SPLM/A ship after the Nasir Declaration was the Yei crisis, which affected its top leadership. The personal differences between Garang and his deputy, Cdr. Salva Kiir Mayardit, were eclipsed by underlying structural and organizational weaknesses, reflected in the personification rather than institutionalization of SPLM/A power and public authority. This remained the main driver of the SPLM/A's internal contradictions and the underlying cause of the failure of both of the SPLM/A reconciliation agreements with Anya-nya II (1988). The agreements, which respectively brought back into the SPLM/A Machar (2002) and Lam Akol (2003), triggered the Yei crisis in 2004. It is not feasible to resolve a contradiction within the same plane as the elements driving it. The return of Machar, Lam, Ochang, and others without structural changes that defined their roles and responsibilities in the new SPLM/A setup was bound to trigger another disruption.

The conference in Rumbek convened in December 2004 to specifically address the Yei crisis did not do much to address the underlying structural weaknesses of the movement. Like all SPLM/A meetings and conferences before it, the meeting in Rumbek appeared to ignore the real issue. It turned out to be a blame game against an amorphous "leadership" without pinpointing where the problem was situated. It ended with the sentiment of "Let us open a new page", allowing Garang and Kiir to reconcile. Conferences cannot resolve internal movement contradictions; only relevant institutions can do that. After the conference closed no one made any reference to resolution of the Yei crisis. The half-hearted attempts to restructure the SPLM/A's power and authority fell by the roadside as soon as the CPA was signed with the NCP. Belatedly, having failed to prepare the movement for the running of a state, Garang dispatched SPLM/A leaders, cadres and activists en masse for training in South Africa.

What could have been remembered as one of the resolutions of Rumbek conference was the appointment of Cdr. Salva Kiir Mayardit to re-organize the army (SPLA); Machar to organize and structure the Civil Authority for the New Sudan (CANS); and Cdr. James Wani Igga to organize the liberation movement into a political party (SPLM). These were daunting tasks coming 21 years late. The trip to South Africa must have relieved the three leaders of the discomfort of implementing the orders. It would have been, however, an opportunity to effect some reforms before the SPLM embarked on managing the subnational entity — the Government of Southern Sudan. This failure to address the power configuration, distribution, relations, roles, and responsibility triggered a third disruption. This political conflict was between President Kiir and his deputy, Machar, which played out finally in the form of a violent eruption on 15 December 2013, and led to the onset of a new civil war.

These disruptions underscore the importance of organization in a political military movement like the SPLM/A. The most autocratic and totalitarian regimes the world over are highly organized and run efficient systems that keep them in power. It was rather shocking that the SPLM/A was so averse to the evolution of a formal governance system. The SPLM/A was now worse than the Nimeri regime, which it used to despise and categorize as a "one-man, no-system rule"; at least under Nimeri there was a bureaucracy to run the state. The SPLM/A, in its 21 years of existence, could pass for a huge informality, which eventually became impossible to formalize, especially after the death of Garang. He alone could manage it.

This brings us back to factors underlying Garang's refusal to organize and institutionalize the SPLM/A, and whether or not this was linked to his personal ambition for power or has to do with the wider dimension of superpower rivalry in the Horn of Africa. The refusal to organize and institutionalize the SPLM/A was the other side of efforts to stifle democracy and growth of awareness within the liberation movement. Being two sides of the same thing, the SPLM/A could have been a dialectal expression of theory and practice of the national liberation movement. On the one side would be the political dimension and its functions, which manifest as political awareness and consciousness. In this dimension the comrades would democratically discuss, debate, and decide on the issues of liberation. On the other dimension would be the military, which operates on orders and commands. To stifle one dimension of the liberation struggle was the very antithesis of liberation, especially the one that entails suppressing people's social awareness and political consciousness. Therefore, in the situation that obtained in the SPLM/A, it was clear that this dialectal relation was not the objective for conjoining the military and politics. The preponderance of militarism was to instil instantaneous obedience, and to preoccupy the combatants *only* with military routine, hierarchies, and etiquette, and at the same time to channel awareness in a manner that does not question the leader. This betrayed the falsehood that in the SPLM/A the individual was both a soldier as well as a politician.

Stifling democracy in practice serves the dictator in building his dynasty in the same way that it serves imperialists interested in the extraction and plunder of a country's natural resources. Garang could achieve his desire for absolute and personal power by building an army rather than a political movement. Several factors contributed to the evolution of personal rule in the SPLM/A. The large numbers of illiterate peasants, isolated within their own languages, did not demand address for their social-psychological needs. This was considered unnecessary for such an army. The inordinate reduction in the numbers of other ethnic communities in the SPLM/A due to desertions, splits that followed the Nasir Declaration and the Khartoum Agreement, which attracted many Nuer to the government of Sudan, increased the dominance of the Dinka, particularly those from Bahr el Ghazal, in the movement.[45]

By 1995, no one referred to the manifesto, and SPLM/A cadres and activists had jettisoned the use of socialist idiosyncrasies in their oral and written communications. The words "your excellency" supplanted "comrade." The clutch had slipped and the revolutionary gears disengaged. The liberation movement beat a retreat to where the SSLM and the Anya-nya had left off in 1972, in a manner that said, "If you cannot beat them, join them." The concept and vision of the New Sudan

---

[45] Most of the Equatorians, unfamiliar with the kind of the conventional warfare and battles the SPLA fought in areas far away from their homes, deserted and went back to their homes. The internecine fighting that followed the Nasir Declaration also forced the Nuba and the Funj to abandon the SPLA and return to their home territories.

disappeared into thin air. The SPLM/A could not complete the journey of national liberation; the revolutionary armed struggle to destroy the minority clique had stalled. It was no longer easy to speak of and about the "New Sudan". The retreat to liberal peace had begun in earnest.

The SPLM/A had failed to revolutionize the war of national liberation. The SPLM Manifesto spoke to populist sensibilities but failed to radicalize and energize the movement beyond those sentiments that push people to take up arms. In fact, local feuds and the urge to acquire firearms drew many of the peasants who joined the SPLM/A at the beginning of the war (Nyaba, 2000: 24). This failure to radicalize was not only because of the lack of ideological training, political enlightenment, organization, and institutionalization, but because the SPLM/A lacked a political programme. The absence of a revolutionary programme made it difficult if not impossible to convert the military victories the SPLA scored into social or economic incentives for the masses.

The drawbacks connected to the SPLM/A's lack of a political programme played out in the social, cultural, economic, and political life in the villages and towns that came under the administration of the SPLM/A. In classic guerrilla warfare, when an insurgency controls part of the country these liberated areas become the "rear base." The social, economic, and political importance of these so-called liberated villages and towns cannot be overemphasized. Politically, the "rear base" should have constituted the SPLM/A's bourgeoning counterstate. This counterstate grows in geography and demography at the expense of the areas left under the oppressive regime as the war progresses, and the growing strength of the revolution forces the enemy to retreat and make acomplete withdrawal.

This "rear base" would have been where the SPLM/A started to implement its vision and concept of the "New Sudan", characterized by freedom, justice, fraternity, and prosperity, which the combatants sang about daily in their morale songs. This is where the SPLM/A would organize and institutionalize the executive, legislative, and judicial organs of the people's power. Institutionalization would have necessitated the differentiation of the liberation movement into its professional domains, with the SPLM becoming the people's party and the SPLA the people's army, with the political authority resting in the SPLM. This would enable the SPLM to organize the administration, economy, and social services of the nascent state. This would mark the zenith of political mobilization throughout the country where everybody except those in areas still controlled by the oppressive regime participate in one way or the other in the war. The SPLM would stimulate the development of people's productive forces in all sectors of agriculture, the new country's economic mainstay. It would build an economy in which the people were engaged in productive activities like food production, trade and commerce, and cottage industries, while the SPLM administration would provide security; social services including health, education, and veterinary; and build roads to connect the different parts of the country. In this respect, the revolution would generate and enhance in the people a sense of self-reliance, and at the same time free the national productive forces from foreign control or domination.

But the SPLM/A's failure to construct a programme for prosecuting the war of national liberation, apart from the military engagement with the enemy, was one of the factors that pushed it towards a heavy reliance on external material and moral support. The SPLM/A could not meet the resultant exigencies and deficiencies the people experienced as a result of cutting communication with the garrisoned towns. This prompted a large-scale migration of the population, particularly in Upper Nile and Jonglei, to refugee camps in western Ethiopia. It marked the beginning of South Sudan's heavy dependence on international humanitarian assistance, both inside and outside the country. As discussed in other sections, it proved the vacuity of the revolutionary slogans that the SPLM/A raised, particularly the idea of a protracted revolutionary armed struggle. A protracted war can only obtain and succeed under conditions where people's resilience and innovation enable them to rely on themselves rather than on external resources. This explains the reason why we raised the development of people's productive forces to encourage self-reliance. This in turn enhances people's determination, their resolve to be free, and their readiness to make sacrifices.

What did the SPLM/A do as large parts of southern Sudan, Nuba Mountains, and Southern Blue came under its military control? The Nuba were very lucky; they had a political leader in the person of Cdr. Yousif Kuwa Mekki, who managed to establish an administration run by local social and religious leaders. The situation in the Nuba Mountains demanded exactly that kind of leadership to construct a foundation for resilience and self-reliance. In the Southern Blue Nile and southern Sudan, conditions in the liberated villages and towns were dire. It was reminiscent of a colonial military occupation in the real meaning of the word. The SPLA treated the civilian population like conquered people and, indeed, many preferred to foot it to the refugee camps. The SPLM/A experimented with an administrative system unknown in the Sudan. Instead of the traditional provinces and districts, the SPLM/A introduced the "Independent Administrative Areas" to which a senior SPLA commander was deployed in charge as the civil-military administrator. He had executive, legislative, and judicial power over the people.

The experiment of the Independent Administrative Areas, together with the independent area command structure, was a disaster, leaving sad memories with the civilian population. The civil military administrator doubled as the independent area commander of the SPLA based in the area. He was invariably a young SPLA officer who had risen in the military hierarchy but had no prior civil service experience. Most of them were intermediate or secondary school dropouts when the war began. Most of these commanders were Garang's former bodyguards, who had to learn how to command by trial and error far away from SPLA headquarters. This endeared them to the chairman and commander in chief because they were able to amass fabulous wealth through corruption and direct extortion.

By 1990, the swath of territory lying east of the River Nile south of the Sobat River, down to the Sudan borders with Kenya and Uganda, and the whole of western Equatoria had come under the control of the SPLM/A. It was a population of three to four million in a territory larger than Kenya. Because of the lack of political and administrative institutions, and with no economic activities, the liberated areas were like one big refugee camp with survival dependent on the beneficence of the international community. The SPLM/A's failure to carry out political organization and refusal to create political and administrative institutions in the areas under its military control boomeranged in the form of internal political conflict.[46] An analysis of these internal dynamics — particularly the Nasir declaration (1991), the Yei crisis (2004), and the civil war (2013) — demonstrates that the common denominator is autocracy and personification of power and public authority in the liberation movement. This was in contravention not only to democratic principles and practice but also the egalitarian traditions of a predominantly peasant society.

---

[46] Since the SPLM/A's inception in 1983, splits within the ranks occurred in 1985 (Oduho and Majier), 1987 (Kerubino), 1988 (Arok Thon), 1991 (Riek, Lam and Gordon), 1992 (William Nyuon), 2004 (Salva Kiir), 2009 (Lam Akol), and, 2013, the current civil war (Machar et al.).

Ethnicity and the Upsurge of Ethnic Nationalism

The politics of administrative decentralization triggered conflicts among the communities as they struggled to determine the boundaries of their area councils. With the help of Nimeri's intelligence agents, the communities began to arm. It is important to note that the intention of many of the youth who initially joined the SPLA was to collect firearms, then return home to settle local conflicts. Thus, the youth from Abyei and northern Bahr el Ghazal had their conflict with the Baggara Arabs (*Marahaleen*) while the Bor youth had perennial conflict with the Murle over cattle rustling and child abduction. In northern Jonglei, the Padang Dinka had their land problems with the Shilluk of Panyikango. The formation of the SPLM/A redirected these smouldering conflicts into the war of national liberation.

It was important that the people understood that the contradictions between them because of boundaries were a secondary contradiction triggered by the primary contradiction between them and the oppressive regime. When the SPLM/A shunned political education and enlightenment it inadvertently raised a false consciousness and entrenched in the people reactionary attitudes to other ethnicities that they considered their enemies. Marxists would categorise this action as "separating the people from their means of struggle." It was important to direct the people's anger against the oppressive regime towards liberation as a transformative action, but that required an ideological and political orientation.

The censuring of ideological training and political work among the essentially rural people who comprised the majority of the SPLA combatants left a psychological void that was filled with parochial ethnic attitudes engendered by their new situation. The rise of parochial ethnic ideologies can be blamed on the ideological and political vacuum created by the SPLM/A's neglect. The power struggle that rocked the nascent movement at the beginning of the movement's formation ran almost along ethnic lines, pitting Garang (Dinka) against Samuel Gai Tut (Nuer).

The intervention of Ethiopia and resolution in favour of Garang, although based on a completely different reason not linked to his Dinka ethnicity, played into the Dinka-Nuer historical rivalry, which prompted the Anya-nya II (mainly Nuer) to desert and ally with Nimeri's regime against the liberation movement. It was no wonder that Dinka ethnic nationalism and its ideology of hegemony and domination surged to the point of monopolizing all aspects of the SPLM/A, taking on another narrow dimension of being the only counterforce in southern Sudan to the Arab-dominated northern political elite in the Sudan.

The numerical dominance of the Dinka in the nascent movement fuelled the Dinka ethnic nationalism, becoming at times the SPLM/A's existential defining phenomenon as a national liberation movement, notwithstanding the presence of other Sudanese ethnicities. This attitude of treating the SPLM/A as a Dinka movement, underwritten by the fact that four out of five members of the movement's leadership were ethnic Dinka, underscored other ethnicities' sensitivity to the Dinka sense of superiority and ethnic hubris that tended to alienate others. This led to the emergence of counter-ethnic ideologies that stalked the movement throughout southern Sudan, Nuba Mountains, and Southern Blue Nile. This played out in the form of mass desertions of troops back to their home turfs, leading to paralysis of the SPLA's operational plans.

The surge of Dinka ethnic nationalism is attributed to their numerical strength in the nascent movement, the use of Dinka language, and the fact that the movement's leadership was predominantly Dinka. This could not have been a coincidence in a movement of more than 70 ethnicities, hailing from South Sudan, the Nuba Mountains, and Southern Blue Nile. It is therefore necessary and of paramount importance to problematize the surge of ethnic nationalism. Although it began imperceptibly in the early stages of the war of national liberation, nevertheless, together with state power and the primitive accumulation of wealth, it has now evolved into an explosive alloy.

Sixty-four nationalities and national groups at different demographic weights and at varying levels of socioeconomic and cultural development inhabit South Sudan. The European colonial occupation in the 19th century, beginning in 1821, interrupted and froze at that primeval stage the region's natural socioeconomic and political development. This interruption remains the only reference point for the physical, psychological, and political existence of South Sudan as an entity. Hitherto, these nationalities coexisted in relations that characterize a pre-capitalist mode of production. The Azande, Shilluk (Chollo), and Anyuak (Anywaa) had constructed centralized quasi-states with standing armies in their territories. The Dinka and Nuer, the largest and second-largest single groups respectively had no tradition of indigenous centralized authority. They remain to date effectively leaderless and in the process of continuous segmentation.

The most profound feature of the Turco-Egyptian state in the Sudan (The Turkiyah) was its ruthless extraction of slaves and other resources to fund its administration. The Turks, Egyptians, and Arabized Nubians slavers roamed the forests and swamps of southern Sudan for slaves. The absence of modern weapons and the lack of solidarity with each other constituted the individual and collective weakness of these nationalities, enabling the Turco-Egyptian and Arabized northern Sudanese collaborators to brutalize, defeat, enslave, and colonize them. Nevertheless, they resisted in a variety of ways and means. It is worth mentioning that slavery depleted the population of many communities because their habitation and lack of solidarity rendered them vulnerable.

This asymmetrical resistance and demonstration of valour the different national groups offered to colonial enslavement and the slave trade created subconscious and psychological images, perceptions, attitudes, and behaviours towards each other. The social, economic, and politically constructed relations between these national groups, and even between the different sections and clans of the same nationality, were refracted through the asymmetrical resistance to slavery and slave trade. These psychological attitudes and self-perceptions also informed their behaviour and treatment of their neighbours. They named each other in a manner connoting their behaviour during times of existential threat.

The sections of Dinka nation in Bahr el Ghazal, namely the Malual and Rek, call themselves Muony Jieng, unlike all other Dinka groups in Lakes, Jonglei, and Upper Nile, who identify themselves as Jieng. Essentially, there is no great difference linguistically in the meanings of *muonyjieng* and *jieng*. They mean the same thing and every Dinka would understand them. However, between the Rek in Tonj-Gogrial and Malual in northern Bahr el Ghazal, *muonyjieng* takes on another meaning of machismo, almost along the lines of "*Deutscheland über alles*." This derived from their purported exceptional role in the resistance to slavery and slave trade in the 19th century and therefore connotes numerical strength and valour.[47] This self-perception, deposited in their subconscious, encourages them to overlook or despise those

---

[47] In Dinka traditional warfare one assures of victory by amassing large numbers of combatants, which then becomes the basis for claiming power or superiority over other sections or tribes with whom they share the same quality of armament (spears and sticks). This may explain why the Dinka (Bahr el Ghazal) claim leadership of South Sudan because of their numerical superiority.

neighbours like the Bongo and Fertit, who are referred to collectively as *door*.[48]

The war of national liberation brought together the people of southern Sudan from varied social and ethnic backgrounds. Some came into the liberation movement with a feeling of superiority due the experience we have just discussed. The absence or censuring of political awareness, considered divisive, entrenched that sense of superiority in some of the combatants hailing from the Dinka ethnicity. The numerical superiority of the Malual and Rek Dinka in the SPLA training centres spurred those distant memories, as reflected in the morale songs they composed in the training centres. In this context, the Dinka ethnic ideology emerged in the SPLM/A as an expression of superiority. The political elite exploited these collective social and political sensibilities to justify Dinka privilege to power and wealth in an independent South Sudan.

This Dinka sense of superiority makes leadership of South Sudan a Dinka birthright. This drives their quest for power and leadership of all social organization and associations. They are ready to fight among themselves or with other ethnicity communities on the question of power and leadership. That a Dinka must always lead impelled William Deng Nhial to abandon his SANU colleagues in East Africa in 1965 to return to play politics in the Sudan. The formation of SANU (Inside), as it was then known, was predicated on the political mobilization of ethnic Dinka in support of a Dinka leadership to pursue an agenda that appealed to Dinka power sensibilities: if the Arabs or Arabized Nubians ruled the Sudan, the Dinka must rule in southern Sudan. This stretches to such extremes that a weak Dinka leader is better and preferable to the best leader of any other ethnicity. This reactionary attitude disrupted the unity and solidarity among the southern Sudanese political elite and divided their efforts to win social and political rights from a succession of Arab-dominated northern regimes. The cultivation of ethnic politics based on the populist ideology of demography, valour in war, and self-righteousness began to take roots in southern Sudan's body politics in 1965. In this configuration of things, SANU appeared to represent the social, economic, and political interests of the Dinka (Bahr el Ghazal) while Southern Front, which played elitist right-wing politics,

---

[48] *Door* derives from the Arabic word for "move." The word was used by slavers to order the slaves to move or start moving. Since the Dinka villages were located along the slave trail, they witnessed the slaves, mostly from the Bongo, being ordered in Arabic and therefore gave them the name to differentiate them from the Dinka.

represented the interests of all other southern Sudanese, including the Dinka in Upper Nile.

This Dinka ethnic ideology is a phenomenon linked to, and ingrained in, the psyche of the Malual and Rek Dinka of Aweil, Tonj, and Gogrial, the bedrock of SANU during the liberal parliamentary democracy (1965-1969) and in the defunct Southern Region (1972-1983). The assassination of William Deng Nhial in 1968 deprived SANU and the Dinka people of Bahr el Ghazal of a charismatic populist leader. The May leftist revolution (1969) exacerbated SANU's decline as a predominantly Dinka political outfit. The Dinka leadership and power shifted to Bor, Upper Nile, in the person of Molana Abel Alier Kwai. A renowned lawyer, Abel Alier negotiated the Addis Ababa Agreement, won Nimeri's confidence, and was appointed by him as interim president of the High Executive Council (HEC), serving from 1972 to 1978. Opposition to Abel Alier came largely from fellow Dinka from Bahr el Ghazal, especially during the "wind of change" (1978), which catapulted Gen. Joseph Lagu Yanga to the helm of the HEC.

Lagu was an outsider to southern Sudanese politicking. Of course, he rose to this leadership position from the military, having been the leader of the Anya-nya and the Southern Sudan Liberation Movement (SSLM). Coming from a military background, Lagu was not familiar with the political brinkmanship in the Southern Sudan. Not only did he scuttle the coalition that brought him to power, he also quickly lost that power through an impeachment vote in the People's Legislative Assembly (PLA). This allowed Abel Alier to recapture the political stage on the wings of a Dinka unity programme orchestrated by Andrew Wieu, a veteran SANU diehard hailing from Padang Dinka in Upper Nile. Although the political jockeying in the Southern Region occurred within the perameters of the Sudan Socialist Union (SSU), nevertheless they ran along SANU-SF fault lines, and by extension along ethnic and provincial cleavages. No matter what coalition they built, the SANU bulwarks failed to shift power to Bahr el Ghazal. A Southern Region-based coalition brought Engineer Joseph James Tambura (Azande) to the presidency of the HEC in 1982, with Dhol Acuil Aleu (Dinka) as deputy, and Matthew Obur Ayang (Shilluk) as speaker of People's Regional Assembly.

The digression above was necessary to underline the dictatorship of numbers in politics in southern Sudan and in the liberation movement. In the SPLM/A, the numerical weight of the Dinka helped impose the use of Dinka language as a de facto medium of communication in movement. This enhanced and entrenched the Dinka ethnic ideological symbols of superiority. The withdrawal of the SPLM/A into southern Sudan after the defeat of the Ethiopian Derg witnessed the circulation in the liberated areas of such messages as "*Awich ku aŋich ku*" (We know what we want). The sudden appearance of such utterances suggesting, as mentioned above, that the Dinka comrade knew what his comrades from other nationalities did not know was a precursor of what was to come in South Sudan once it became independent. This was perhaps to signal the complete ideological shift from revolution and the vision of "New Sudan" to Southern Sudan and its secession.

The idea of projecting Dinka ethnic ideology over South Sudanese patriotism and fraternity comes in the context of protecting personal power. However, the Dinka political elite developed the idea into a comprehensive programme of constructing a Dinka state in South Sudan. This came following the tragic death of Garang and Kiir's ascension to the helm of the SPLM and the government of Southern Sudan, along the lines of the Arab-dominated northern political elite, the *kayan al shamal* that dominated the Sudanese state. President Kiir defined its features as the political and economic empowerment of the Dinka people. It is worth recalling why the Rumbek conference did not address the Yei crisis but glossed over its manifestations. This was perhaps done to prevent the development of a permanent rift among the Dinka rank and file in and outside the SPLM/A. The false grievance of marginalization some political and military elite hailing from Bahr el Ghazal initially raised to drive the Yei crisis was struck off the agenda of the conference as it was distractive and would not serve the wider Dinka power agenda.

In retrospect, the construction of the Dinka state in South Sudan must have been the SPLM/A's raison d'être. This conclusion stems from the discussion about the SPLM/A's refusal to organize and democratise: doing so would open opportunities for people from non-Dinka ethnicities. A democratic environment would not have permitted the germination and growth of the Dinka ethnic ideology. This may explain why an "early determination" of the Dinka leadership was necessary, as spelled out in the SPLM Manifesto of 1983. The obnoxious chest thumping, which some Dinka intellectuals and political leaders do in local, regional, and international fora, that the Dinka singlehandedly fought the war and brought the independence of South Sudan, notwithstanding its falsehood, is meant to lay credence to the Dinka state thesis. In the absence of an open and transparent discourse to expose its vacuity, the Dinka political elite embarked on modelling South Sudan state on Dinka tradition and customs. It only required a few committed zealots surrounding President Kiir to push the crazy idea of ethnic exclusivity in the SPLM/A, now the ruling party in South Sudan.

The six-month period that followed the death of Garang witnessed a strange phenomenon of unprovoked hostility, intrigue, and witch-hunts involving first- and second-row leaders in the SPLM. It was a power grab, part of the culture of competitiveness, hierarchy, and rank that took over the SPLM/A's leaders, cadres, and activists. Rising up within the system was the major concern of any SPLA combatant. An intense political pressure built up inside the SPLM. Its parameters revolved around the question of power, with hints of the Yei crisis defining who, and from where, should wield power. It became so dangerous that some members threw in the towel and left the scene. The political game of entrenching Kiir's personal power continued unabated into the botched SPLM 2nd National Convention in 2008. The tragic death in a plane crash of two principal movers, whom I am reluctant to mention here, did not deter the project and its strategic objective to define the ethnic and hence power configuration by elbowing out of the SPLM hierarchy some prominent non-Dinka SPLM leaders.

The SPLM's 2nd National Convention was a fiasco, notwithstanding the enormous financial and political resources placed in the scheme to elbow out of the SPLM hierarchy some leaders, mainly Dr. Riek Machar as the SPLM's first vice chairman and Pagan Amum Okiech as the SPLM's secretary-general. This failure to use the SPLM convention to get rid of Kiir's political enemies in the SPLM and GoSS infuriated him and the Dinka political elite, prompting a new strategy. President Kiir could no longer hide his disgust and disdain for these two leaders, but there was no way other than democratic means for him to get rid of them. He had to bide his time until the right opportunity presented itself. In the meantime he put into operation his Plan B, which was to render the SPLM party completely dysfunctional. With the collaboration of the Dinka political elite, Kiir resorted to presidential decrees to govern South Sudan. Thanks to the Transitional Constitution of South Sudan (2011), some of his legal cohorts worked to make him an absolute ruler. It was in this context that the Dinka political and business elite established the Jieng Council of Elders (JCE) as a power broker around Kiir's presidency of South Sudan. It replaced the SPLM in its political function as the ruling party.

The Dinka ethnic ideology of hegemony and domination, built on the total control of the country's economic and political resources, was bound to trigger a counter-ethnic ideology. The exigencies of the war of national liberation have increasingly broadened people's social awareness, although within the parameters of their own ethno-cultural formation in reaction to the dominant ethnic ideology. Proponents of ethnic nationalism should be extremely careful lest they unleash ethnic animosities that lead to war of all against all. The Nuer pride themselves for resisting British pacification during the colonial era. This precipitated the war in Lou Nuer in the 1920s. Their perception of the Dinka as cowardly and greedy drives their rejection of Dinka leadership of South Sudan. This has translated into a revival, and even elevation into a religion, of Ngundeng's prophecies preserved in songs. Some of these prophecies claimed that the Nuer people would govern South Sudan after the end of war with the Arabs. It is unfortunate that some Nuer intellectuals and political leaders believe this narrative. They have internalized the myth and spread it in response to, or as a counter to, Dinka ethnic nationalism.

So much about the genesis and evolution of Dinka ethnic nationalism is linked to the war of national liberation. It is essentially reactionary in nature, divisive, and conflictual. It rests on the politics of exclusion, social discrimination, and economic marginalization. It can obtain and be sustained only when politics are organised and power exercised based on ethnicity. In this connection, demographic weight becomes the only criterion for wielding power. But the prevailing social and economic conditions in South Sudan cannot permit the building of a Dinka state based on the parameters listed above. The state as superstructure evolves in a society where the dominant mode of production has crystallized and consolidated.

Accordingly, a Dinka overlord must first emerge as a uniting factor in the Dinka society of over 200 clans and subclans, around which a Dinka state can germinate and grow. As alluded to above, Dinka and Nuer societies are in a state of perpetual segmentation. The process makes every Dinka section completely independent of other sections, rather than interdependent. The apparent oneness of the Dinka was the outcome of the expansion of the colonial state in the Sudan. The colonial policy of indirect rule, which necessitated the building of indigenous institutions of governance alongside colonial state administrative structures, accelerated this sense of oneness.

A reality that the Dinka political elite never want to mention in their representation of the Dinka ethnic nationalism/ideology is that the emergence of the JCE as the presumed superstructure of the Dinka nation has heightened the process of segmentation and even fragmentation among the Dinka sections and clans, leading to inter- and intrasectional feuds consequent to competition and struggle for power among their respective political and military elite. In fact, although the JCE comprises some senior people in the state apparatus, this has not prevented the bitter conflict among their respective sections and clans. Therefore, the struggle among these leaders for ascendency has fed into the inter- and intrasectional feuds, particularly in Warrap (Gogrial). The never-ending perennial conflict in Gogrial between the Aguok and Apuk has at its roots their respective community chairpersons. The competition between former chief justice Ambrose Riiny Thiik and Justice Chan Riech Madut, the current chief justice of the Republic of South Sudan and chairman of the Aguok Community, has fuelled the conflict between the two communities. It is worth mentioning that the two justices are both close friends of President Kiir. Regardless, they have not put this relation to the service of peace between their communities. Both sides have committed atrocities and human rights violations, killing women and children, and throwing toddlers into burning huts.

In Lakes State, the Agar clans have been fighting among themselves for a very long time. The governor of Lakes State was unable to quell these conflicts, notwithstanding the huge SPLA and police force under his command. The reason is simple: the governor became part of the conflict because of his overt support to his clan, providing weapons and ammunition. The situation in Lakes State due to the clan conflicts involving Agar-Gok, Agar-Ciec, Ciec-Aliab, and Ciec-Atuot led to the declaration of a state of emergency. In Jonglei, where the Dinka sections had previously been peaceful, the disease of sectional and clan rivalry for power has also begun to affect the state. A similar situation obtained in Malek, south of Bor, where a section was threatened with eviction from its ancestral lands. These are examples to prove the emptiness of the claim of Dinka nationalism peddled by the political elite.

The Padang Dinka is a section of the Dinka, its people scattered over a large territory in Upper Nile (Abialang, Agier, Nyiel, Dongjol, and Ngok), Jonglei (Luach, Rut, and Paweny), Unity (Pan Aru and Alor), northern Bahr el Ghazal (Abyei), and part of Tonj (Lauch Jiang). Only the Dinka language unites them. Their recent historical records point to internal feuds between themselves rather than between them and the neighbouring Shilluk, Nuer, and Maaban. This mutual hostility and continuous segmentation supports the thesis that it is improbable that a Dinka state can emerge in South Sudan, even if the political elite, the JCE, desires it.

The Dinka ideology expressed in the context of hegemony and domination of other nationalities is nothing more than the Dinka political and business elite trying to control power and wealth in the young Republic of South Sudan. This Dinka nationalism and its ideology arose during and indeed in the context of the war of national liberation in southern Sudan. However, the multi-ethnic character of the liberation movement did not allow it to spread because of the risk of splitting the movement. As a tool for personal power, Garang had to militarize and promote militarism, along with the leader's cult of personality, in order to produce a docile and uncritical mass in the liberation movement. In essence, Dinka nationalism was an elite's ploy to blindfold and hoodwink the Dinka, to divert their attention from the failure of the political elite to provide socioeconomic development.

Dinka ethnic nationalism is essentially an elite power project. Like the liberation movement that spurred it to life, it is built on the false and deceptive idea of a predetermined personal leadership of Dr. John Garang de Mabior, rather than a political programme for addressing the fundamental contradictions that underpinned the war of national liberation. It is also built on patrimonialism and the political patronage of a close network of individuals who understood and internalized this concept. In the absence of Garang the concept started to wobble due to competing power centres within the Dinka realm. President Kiir promoted Dinka ethnic nationalism but, unlike Garang's version, it was in the context of the political and economic empowerment of the Rek Dinka cartels in Warrap and Aweil. His disdain for the Agar (Lakes) and Bor (Jonglei) betrayed the hollowness of the ideology.

President Kiir elevated the Dinka ethnic ideology to a policy of social, economic, and political empowerment of elements of Dinka elite. Nevertheless, it remained vacuous and cannot be sustained, particularly as the financial and economic resources he gave to the cartels have been spent. In this connection, he destroyed the South Sudanese fraternity and social capital that united the people throughout their struggle for freedom, justice, and prosperity without building something substantial in lieu. In fact, South Sudanese fraternity and solidarity died on 16 December 2013, when hordes of Mathiang Anyoor and Dotku Beny massacred thousands of their compatriots hailing from the Nuer nationality in Juba, and the subsequent revenge killings by Nuer of Dinka, Shilluk, and other nationalities in Bor, Bentiu, Malakal, Nasir, Akobo, and other parts of South Sudan. This was the consequence of the ethnicization of national politics and the personification of public power and authority.

The upsurge of Dinka ethnic nationalism came against a backdrop of the power shift to the Aweil-Warrap politico-military-business elite — the new parasitic capitalist class that emerged following the death of Dr. John Garang. It grew out of the Yei crisis. The attempt to snatch power from Garang, which was the Yei crisis, centred on the assumption that the majority of the SPLA combatants hailed from Bahr el Ghazal and, therefore, leadership of the movement and of South Sudan must come from there. The lack of institutions in the SPLM/A, which placed all power in the hands of Kiir, entrenched the idea that SPLM/A power belongs to the Bahr el Ghazal political elite. Their control of the state enabled the burgeoning parasitic capitalist class to build relations across the region as a means of consolidating its power both internally and externally.

The alliance between the burgeoning parasitic class and the regional and multinational comprador capitalism built on the extraction and plunder of South Sudan's vast natural resource potential. This transformed the regime into an ethnocentric and kleptocratic totalitarian dictatorship in order to facilitate the extraction and plunder. This heightened the internal contradiction leading to the civil war. Notwithstanding the massive destruction of life and property caused by the civil war, it was good that the Dinka ethnic ideology sparked off as early as it did in order to trigger the civil war. The civil war provides conditions for transforming the situation of poverty, ignorance, and illiteracy in South Sudan. Everybody in South Sudan, including those in government, are now dependent on food aid supplied by the international community. The security forces prey on the civilians to cover their costs. The country is on the verge of social, economic, and political collapse. Every South Sudanese, including those in the diaspora, have come to understand what an ethnic ideology can do to a multi-ethnic country like South Sudan.

Whether linked to a deliberate subversion of the revolution, or to prevent the evolution of social awareness and political consciousness in the SPLM/A combatants and the masses, the shunning of political and ideological work in the national liberation movement gave rise and entrenched ethnic nationalism in every ethnic group. Dinka ethnic nationalism became dominant because of their numbers and their links to the power at the top of the liberation movement. Whatever has happened in South Sudan, including the civil war, links directly to the lack of ideological and political consciousness of the leaders, cadres, and political activists.

The Ideological Shift to the Right and the Search for Peace

The final two decades of the last century wrought fundamental changes in the world. It marked the end of the Cold War between the West, led by United States of America, and the Socialist Camp, led by the Soviet Union. The collapse of the Soviet Union, leading to the retreat of the world socialist system, had a precipitous impact on the bipolar world system. It triggered the collapse of many satellite states that depended for their existence on its solidarity and beneficence. It was a phenomenal change that forced many liberation movements into the imperialist orbit through ideological retraction. This wind of change did not spare the Horn of Africa. In Ethiopia, the Derg collapsed, leaving the Ethiopian People's Revolutionary Democratic Front (EPRDF) to march into Addis Ababa, and the Eritrean People's Liberation Front (EPLF) to take power in Asmara. These profound developments have transformed for all eternity the political configuration of the Horn of Africa that rested on and was sustained by post-World War II realities. It was just a matter of time before the Eritreans conducted a referendum to formalize and legalize their independence from Ethiopia. The Somali state disintegrated into component clan fiefdoms, with a devastating impact on the security architecture of the Horn of Africa. In other parts of Africa, South Africa's apartheid regime collapsed and the ANC under Nelson Mandela assumed power in democratic elections.

This spectacular development on the regional and world stage caught the SPLM/A completely unprepared. Preparedness and readiness to respond to change is always a problem for a system that depends on a single individual for it to function. The writing on the wall started to appear as early as the end of 1990: it was only a matter of time before the Derg would collapse. The Ethiopian Army was so demoralized that soldiers had started deserting the frontline without even shooting their rifles. The flight of Mengistu Haile Mariam from Addis Ababa on 20 May 1991 accelerated the collapse of the regime, catching unawares the SPLA contingent that was deployed to defend Asosa against the joint forces of the Oromo Liberation Front (OLF) and the Gambela People's

Liberation Movement (GPLM). The SPLM/A leaders had not anticipated the sudden loss of their indispensable friend.

The defeat of the Derg would not have had such a dramatic impact on the struggle of the Sudanese people had the SPLM/A organized and subscribed to the theory and practice of revolutionary armed struggle. From its inception in 1983 and until its sudden and unorganized withdrawal into southern Sudan, the SPLA had fought the war from its bases in western Ethiopia. This in itself speaks volumes about the SPLM/A leadership and its ideology of liberation. This is because by 1991 the SPLM/A was in complete control of the whole of western Equatoria, parts of central and all of Eastern Equatoria, parts of Upper Nile region south of the Sobat River, and large parts of Bahr el Ghazal. Indeed, the SPLA controlled rural South Sudan. The logic of maintaining those bases in western Ethiopia and not in southern Sudan spurs questions, the answers to which may cast light on the nature and the political objective of the war the SPLM/A prosecuted.

We place "rear base" between quotes because its importance to a liberation movement is like water to the fish, in both the literal as well as the euphemistical sense. In its political and military sense, "rear base" connotes all the territory behind the guerrilla frontline adjacent to the territory controlled by the enemy. In the southern Sudan context, it must include the area that the SPLM/A had liberated from the enemy. In strategic and tactical language, the enemy forces abandoned the area due to the strength of the revolutionary forces. This is where the liberation movement sets up its proto-government and begins to construct the state and society it envisaged in the concept and vision of the New Sudan. In this territory, a new socioeconomic and political order would begin to cultivate, germinate, and take root. The rear base is the school where the movement trains its leaders, cadres, and activists in everything, including the art of government. It is where a new culture of fraternity and solidarity evolves, uniting the army and the people as well as the people in their different sociocultural formations, all in preparation for the the emerging state and society christened the New Sudan, as opposed to the Sudan under the oppressive regime based in Khartoum.

It is imperative and of paramount significance to problematize why the SPLM/A continued to position its rear bases in a foreign land when it was in control of parts of Southern Sudan, far away from government-controlled, garrisoned towns. This would assist in understanding the SPLM/A paradigm shift from revolution to liberalism and the search for liberal peace with the Sudan government. It is, however, simple to explain. The response of large numbers of enthusiastic southern Sudanese to receiving arms, coinciding with huge supplies of adequate armament, forced an early conventionalisation of war (Nyaba, 1997). These essentially were external resources; the decision to conventionalize the war was subjective, not corresponding to the fact that the movement's message had not reached everywhere in Southern Sudan. At this early stage of the war, the first skirmishes with the government army only affected and influenced the people in Jonglei and, to some extent, Upper Nile Province.

The arrival of large numbers of recruits necessitated establishment of transit camps before they proceeded to the SPLA training camps. An arrangement with the Derg made it possible, through the agency of the UNHCR, to feed these numbers recorded as refugees with the Ethiopian Refugee Administration (ERA). This meant that the SPLM/A, to ensure continuous supplies from the UNHCR stores, had to supply similar numbers of recruits (refugees) to fill the vacuum left by those going for training. The transit camps were the refugee camps at Asosa, Itang, Tharpam, Piny-udo, and Dimma in western Ethiopia, which indeed were SPLM/A logistical rear bases. Thus, in order to maintain a constant population level, as registered in these refugee camps, the SPLM/A encouraged communities, particularly in Jonglei, Upper Nile, Blue Nile, and parts of Equatoria, to migrate to western Ethiopia. It was a ploy to attract international humanitarian and relief assistance, some of which would be sent to feed the SPLA inside southern Sudan. This may explain the commitment to maintaining rear bases in western Ethiopian, rather than within southern Sudan.

The conventionalization of war in response to the huge numbers of combatants alone and not in response to the development of the war requires some discussion. As Mao Zedong said, war conforms to natural laws, and laws of war are developmental in that each stage in the war of liberation corresponds to certain specific laws of conducting it. According to the Vietnamese independence hero Gen. Võ Nguyên Giáp, "If you override the laws of nature, the laws of nature will override you." Therefore, conventionalization of guerrilla war, or a war of national liberation, in South Sudan should not have occurred at the beginning of the war. It should have occurred consequent to the development of the war from isolated ambushes and small-scale, platoon-level (tactical) to battalion- or division-level (strategic) engagement with the enemy. This strategic-level engagement presupposes that the SPLM/A was in control of military production and supply (guns, artillery, ammunition, uniforms, and food for the army) in addition to transport and communication system. The SPLM/A could never have sustained the early conventionalization of the war without its heavy reliance on the external injection of resources. This forced the absolute dependence on the Ethiopian government, further necessitating maintenance of its bases in western Ethiopia.

It may read like ignorance on the part of the SPLM/A leadership of the cardinal principles and laws of revolutionary armed struggle, or was it perhaps an exercise of counter-insurgency skill on full display? A person trained in counter-insurgency must first commit professional suicide in order to rise in the guise of a competent revolutionary guerrilla combatant, imbued with the principles and theory of revolutionary warfare, to lead an insurgency war, to paraphrase Amílcar Cabral. In retrospect, many of us witnessed some counter-revolutionary practices in the SPLM/A. It was as if it was subverting itself. It was understandable, indeed permissible, for the SPLM/A to accept political and military support offered, based on solidarity with the people's cause of liberation. It was, however, rather difficult to understand or stomach the idea that a guerrilla army depended on relief food, which was the reason for the maintenance and location of the "rear bases" in western Ethiopia. It defeated the essence of revolutionary warfare, which puts self-reliance and dependence on a movement's own resources at the top of its priorities.

This was an unintended negative consequence of the first act of Ethiopian beneficence and solidarity. However, it could have also been ignorance and the lack of political awareness that led many in the SPLM/A to believe that the Derg would meet all the exigencies of a war of national liberation in southern Sudan. Thus, they received the assistance as a matter of right. Perhaps, to many people in the SPLM/A, it did not occur to them that the revolution was entirely a Sudanese affair and that whatever the Ethiopian people and government gave was only on the basis of solidarity. Revolutionary armed struggle is a people's war that subscribes to certain codes of conduct, translating essentially into an organic unity of the people with the guerrilla army in the common pursuit of freedom, justice, and prosperity. In this context, each group has specific functions in the liberation process.

The guerrilla army would fight the enemy and create conditions for the civilian population to produce all the life necessities for themselves and for the guerrilla army operating in their midst. The idea of uprooting communities from their homes in order to become refugees in western Ethiopia was one of the political failings of the SPLM/A leadership. It deprived the revolution of the natural habitat where it could develop in the daily practice of the masses. It rendered the SPLM/A vulnerable to unnecessary external influences and, more specifically to the liberal peace-making processes, in addition to the culture of relief-dependency syndrome. This explains the nexus between the international humanitarian intervention and the liberal peace initiatives forced on the SPLM/A.

Cdr. Salva Kiir supervised the sudden and unorganized SPLM/A withdrawal back into southern Sudan. It was a major operation involving refugees, the combatants, and their families, undertaken in a hurry and, as a result, led to an enormous loss of life. Many SPLA combatants hailing from the Nuba Mountains and northern Bahr el Ghazal drowned in the Gilo River at Abwobo: they did not know how to swim. It was rumoured that a contingent of EPRDF, together with elements of SAF, were in hot pursuit of the SPLA. It caused panic and led to a stampede among both the refugees and the combatants.

Back in the liberated areas of South Sudan, the returnees and the combatants were shocked when they reached their towns and villages: Nasir, Akobo, Pochalla, Boma, and others were empty and deserted. In fact, nature had started to take over the permanent buildings. This was the epitomy of the SPLM/A's idea of liberation: fight pyrrhic battles to chase away the enemy in the direction of Khartoum while the people move into refugee camps. Thankfully, the SPLM/A had already negotiated for international humanitarian intervention through the Operation Lifeline Sudan (OLS).

The international humanitarian intervention to provide relief for war-torn southern Sudan started in 1989. It was the result of a tripartite agreement between the United Nations, the government of the Sudan, and the SPLM/A to establish OLS under the auspices of UNICEF as the lead UN agency. The UN/OLS turned out to be a multibillion-dollar business that continued for 15 years, attracting the World Food Programme (WFP); development partners, including the US Agency for International Development (USAID), and the Canadian International Development Agency (CIDA); and a large number of international humanitarian and relief agencies. The withdrawal into southern Sudan created conditions for the SPLM/A to relocate its political and diplomatic activities to Kenya where its relief wing, the Sudan Relief and Rehabilitation Association (SSRA), maintained an office. Nairobi was the hub of regional and international comprador capitalism, now at the crest of a new world order led by the USA. It was also the hub of international humanitarian intervention and relief activities inside war-torn southern Sudan, the Nuba Mountains, and Southern Blue Nile. The nexus between the SPLM/A's relocation of its political and diplomatic functions to Nairobi and the liberal peace-making process followed from the ready availability of donor support for the peace efforts. The liberal peace-making processes sought liberal and neo-liberal solutions to the fundamental contradictions underpinning the war in the Sudan.

It is worth refreshing our memory of the Nasir Declaration and the split that followed within the SPLM/A. The split within the SPLM/A occurred at the movement's weakest moment. The Nasir faction charted a shortcut with the NIF regime and became its main agent against the SPLM/A Torit faction. The attempt to reconcile the two factions failed but confirmed the permanence of the split and emergence of the two SPLM/A factions, which were soon engaged in fierce battles. The Nigerian peace initiative led by President Ibrahim Badamasi Babangida in Abuja (1992) brought together the two SPLM/A (Nasir and Torit) factions with the government of Sudan. The Nigerian government designed the Sudanese peace talks with the Biafran crisis in mind and, therefore, glossed over the fundamental reasons for the war in the Sudan. It therefore registered as a failure.

The IGAD peace process was the initiative of the government of the Sudan. It was more of a political and diplomatic move to regionally isolate and expose the SPLM/A as a warmonger. This was at a time when it was fighting joint assaults against the SAF and the Nasir faction forces, with its back to the borders of Kenya and Uganda. The government of Sudan was certain of military defeat of the SPLA and therefore only needed the cooperation of the region to isolate and neutralize the SPLM/A. However, the national liberation regimes in Eritrea, Ethiopia, and Uganda saw the situation differently, causing rifts with the Islamic fundamentalist regime. It took a long time (1994–2005) to negotiate the Comprehensive Peace Agreement (CPA).

I discuss the liberal peace-making process in the context not only of imperialist attempts to control and align the process to its security and economic interests in the Horn of Africa, but also in the context of its objective of subverting any radical resolution of the conflict. A liberal peace leaves the oppressive reality intact, creating conditions for a renewed eruption of conflict. I look at two processes in this connection: the CPA of 2005 and the Agreement on the Resolution of the Conflict in South Sudan (ARCISS) in 2015, both brokered by the regional Intergovernmental Authority on Development (IGAD). Suffice to say that the CPA may have addressed the issue of South Sudan secession but failed to resolve the fundamental problems that led to the war.

Despite the ideological and political differences between the NIF regime in Khartoum and US imperialism, the NIF was nevertheless representing the social, economic, and political interests of the parasitic capitalist class in the Sudan, in one way or the other in the service of international comprador capitalism.[49] Therefore, at a certain strategic level and consideration, the NIF was an ally of imperialism. There was an urgent need on the part of the US administration to bring together the NIF regime and the SPLM/A, through the liberal peace-making process, in order to stop the war and reach a settlement to restore peace and stability and facilitate the extraction of Sudan's natural resources, especially the oil deposits. I spoke earlier about the Chevron investments in the oil fields. This constituted a US strategic national interest in the Sudan, hence the strong link to a peace settlement that would enable Chevron to resume its oil exploration and development in the Sudan.

The recent history of the Sudan is awash with liberal peace agreements. Abel Alier (1990) categorized them as "too many agreements dishonoured", suggesting that these agreements essentially were and remain public relations exercises. Dictatorial regimes engage in these agreements to save time, as well as face, while plotting to outwit their opponents. When the opportunity arises, they will dishonour the agreements. In this way, Gen. Gaafar Nimeri dishonoured the Port Sudan Agreement (1977) with the National Front.[50] He also violated and abrogated the Addis Ababa Agreement in 1983, telling southern Sudanese politicians that it was "neither the Quran nor the Bible." President Omar el Beshir violated and refused to implement the Dar Fur Peace Agreement he signed with the Sudan Liberation Movement (SLM) in Abuja, Nigeria, forcing Menni Menawi Arkoi to return to arms. President Beshir also refused to implement the Abyei Protocol and the Popular Consultation provided in Southern Kordofan and Blue Nile protocols of the CPA, returning these areas to war in 2011.

---

[49] The NIF regime hosted Osama bin Laden in Khartoum. Sudan was implicated in the attack on the USA embassies in Nairobi and Dar es Salaam (1998), and by extension the World Trade Centre in New York in September 2001. Since then it has been on the US list of countries sponsoring of terrorism.

[50] The right-wing political coalition engineered by the Umma Party (UP), the Democratic Unionist Party (DUP), and the Islamic Charter Front (ICF) to fight against the leftist military coup, which brought Nimeri to power on 25 May 1969.

In the same vein, while signing the IGAD-brokered Agreement on the Resolution of the Conflict in the Republic of South Sudan (ARCISS), and in order to justify his reservations on the agreement, President Kiir said the "agreement was neither the Bible nor the Quran," confirming our fear that this most recent liberal peace agreement would most likely be dishonoured.

The main problem with liberal peace agreements lies in their failure to link the war to the fundamental problems of poverty, ignorance, and illiteracy of the masses. This is not a discovery but a fact established long ago (Garang, 1970). The SPLM Manifesto (1983) also confirmed that the so-called "problem of southern Sudan" was in fact a general problem of socioeconomic and cultural backwardness in the peripheral Sudan, characterized by abject poverty, ignorance, illiteracy, and superstition. This fundamental problem underscored the civil war and the socioeconomic and political crisis that afflicted the country. The liberal peace agreements, which invariably provide for some form of power and wealth sharing, cannot resolve this fundamental problem. The resolution lies in the radical transformation of the oppressive nature of the state in order to address these problems. It also leaves intact the oppressive system, which by its nature is incapable of transforming itself, creating conditions for the rekindling of war. The CPA left intact the oppressive regime that the NIF had built after its military coup toppled the democratically elected government of Sadiq el Mahdi in June 1989.

The NIF regime had deformed so much that reforming was not feasible or permissible. It had so polluted the sociopolitical environment in the country with its toxic Islamic fundamentalist ideology that it required a radical transformation, not a liberal peace agreement. However, since the NCP controlled 52 per cent of the government's seats, it vetoed the "democratic transformation" envisaged in the CPA and touted it as bait for confirming the unity of the Sudan. The National Democratic Alliance (NDA) could not achieve democratic transformation under the liberal peace arrangement; it required a different peace format predicated on the complete destruction of the NCP system. Since the majority of the component parties of the NDA did not subscribe to the armed struggle it was not possible to force democratic transformation of the oppressive system by the constitutional and legalistic means offered by the CPA. The CPA provided the SPLM/A with 28 per cent power in the Government of National Unity and 70 per cent power in the government of Southern Sudan. Like the NCP, the new SPLM/A leadership was not keen on democracy or a political struggle to realize democratic transformation of the Sudanese polity. From the word go President Kiir wanted only the control of the government of Southern Sudan in order to pursue the region's right to self-determination.

The CPA created institutions and instruments of governance in the subnational entity. It provided an equal share of oil revenues, which made the government of Southern Sudan's annual budget larger than some countries in the region. However, this alone could not address the fundamental contradiction in the Sudanese state and society. It required that once they had reached agreement to stop the war and end hostilities, the NCP, SPLM/A, NDA parties, and the other different Sudanese social and political formations should engage in a national dialogue to reach consensus on how to address the fundamental problems of the country. The Koka Dam (1985) and Ambu (1989) conferences of the Sudanese political forces laid down the basis of that national dialogue. Had it not been for the Umma Party's procrastination, which triggered the NIF coup, the war could have ended not through a liberal peace agreement but through a consensus that would have preserved the Sudan's territorial unity.

The conditions for preserving the territorial unity of the Sudan were eroding because of non-implementation and the dishonouring or abrogation of political agreements between the political elite. The SPLM/A rode on the crest of a popular uprising, bordering on a social revolution, and raised the slogans of restructuring the Sudanese polity. The downtrodden identified with the SPLM/A and joined its ranks in their tens of thousands. In fact, given the situation that obtained then, the SPLM/A would not have had to negotiate peace with the NIF government. It should have pursued the war to its logical conclusion, as happened in Cuba, Vietnam, and the Portuguese colonies of Mozambique, Angola, Guinea Bissau, and Cape Verde. However, after the political and ideological shift taken by Sudan's leaders, the SPLM/A was put in a narrow corner; its survival thereafter depended on the liberal peace process.

This shift would not have been necessary had the SPLM/A prosecuted its war of national liberation according to the laws of revolutionary armed struggle. Because of the careless neglect of these laws, the SPLM/A committed many strategic mistakes in the conduct of the war and in the management of areas that came under its military control. It is difficult to not consider Garang's declaration of a ceasefire, in May 1989, when the SPLA was winning the war in southern Sudan, anything other than a mistake. The SPLA's repeated victories on different fronts demoralized the SAF to the effect that some garrisons withdrew to Uganda when the SPLA announced the start of the ceasefire. This lull in the war gave the NIF an opportunity to launch its coup against the democratic government of Sadiq el Mahdi. The NIF then re-organized the army, infused it with Islamic jihadism and launched a counter-offensive, pushing the SPLA out of its liberated areas. If we were to discount an external subversion of the revolution, as discussed above, then it is possible that the SPLM/A leaders were not genuinely committed to the revolution, or had no conviction in the ability of the people to effect change, but exploited the war as a political ladder to personal power. In this case, the SPLM/A leaders decided to negotiate their positions in the Sudan's power configuration. That the CPA provided for Garang, or whoever was the SPLM chairman, to become the first vice president of the Republic of the Sudan did not come out of thin air. It suggested that the objective of the war of national liberation was to build sufficient political pressure on the NCP regime to share power.

This may explain the reluctance to undertake political education and organization of the combatants and the masses. The stifling of politics and democracy within the SPLM/A and in the society was intended to produce a docile and uncritical mass, one that would not question whatever came from the leadership. The dependence on militarism and military routine was in support of the leader's cult of personality and construction of a regime of personal power based on political patronage and patrimonialism. The SPLM/A had to negotiate peace not because it could not win the war but because its leadership structured the conduct of the war of national liberation in such a way that it would end as planned. The high-sounding socialist rhetoric at the initial stages was just a ploy to hoodwink the Derg and the socialist camps into providing military support. This rhetoric led to the draining of the Derg's meagre economic and financial resources, already committed to the waging of two wars in the north, as well as the total dependence of the SPLM/A in its war in the Sudan.

In fact, I would argue that it is wrong to speak of an ideological shift because the SPLM/A did not have an ideology. The vision was neither left wing nor right wing for the simple reason that the SPLM/A was shrouded in deceit and intrigue. The setup was indeed modelled on the SAF Military Intelligence and Nimeri's National Security Organization, the main objective of which was protection of the system by weeding out dissent. The projection of socialist rhetoric was to expose and trim off the genuine revolutionaries who joined the ranks of the liberation movement and to entrench the counter-revolutionaries. It was no wonder that the SPLM/A leadership embarked on making peace with the Islamic fundamentalist regime after the collapse of the Derg in 1991. The liberal peace-making process was the logical consequence of the strategic planning and execution of a scheme that politically, economically, and militarily exhausted the Derg, leading to its defeat. This strategic planning included subverting the revolution in the Sudan with the collaboration of the SPLM/A.

Corruption in the SPLM/A: The Evolution of the Parasitic Class

One of the consequences, intended or accidental, of ridding the SPLM/A of any kind of political and ideological work was the evolution of a dominant political military elite. This goes back to the quote from Thomas Sankara that a soldier without political consciousness is a potential criminal. This elite class preyed on the same people for whom they had taken up the gun.

In a casual conversation on the premises of the Law Society of the New Sudan in Rumbek, the SPLM chief political officer, who also was then the deputy governor of Bahr el Ghazal region, took everyone present in the crowd by surprise when, out of the blue, he said, "We will only declare our wealth." This interjection was quite astonishing given that the conversation had not touched on anything close to wealth or its declaration. It was a red herring. This was sometime in 2000, and the commander must have borrowed a leaf from the Ugandan National Resistance Movement's (NRM) leaders.[51] The jargon at the time, preached by the international community, particularly the non-governmental organizations (NGOs) and relief agencies, in southern Sudan in the execution of their mandate included "transparency" and "accountability." They conducted seminars, workshops, and meetings to "sensitize" their workers and the recipients of relief. Therefore, speaking of declaring one's assets was an idea that appealed to the sensibilities of the relief agencies. It was appropriate and timely in view of the attitude to property, public and private, that captivated persons in position of authority in southern Sudan.

However, the question that stands out boldly is: How can a volunteer in a war of national liberation accumulate wealth? Thus the surprise

---

[51] This was about the time that the NRM, in the face of mounting allegations of corruption, asked its leaders and former combatants to declare their personal assets and wealth.

that a deputy governor would speak of declaring his, or anyone else's "wealth." In fact, instead of declaring the wealth acquired, the individual should voluntarily declare *how* he accumulated that wealth without any known income. The SPLM/A did not formally remunerate its officials and operatives: they seized whatever they wanted. In this manner, the deputy governor was right that they should declare what they had seized from the populace and from the international relief agencies through extortion, corruption, and outright theft. I believe this is an appropriate introduction to a discussion of the subject of corruption in the SPLM/A during the war of national liberation and its exponential growth after its leaders, cadres, and combatants took over the reins of government in southern Sudan in 2005.

Liberation movements are invariably associated with altruism, emphasising selflessness, volunteerism, and sacrifices, including one's life. I believe this propelled many people into the rank and file of the SPLM/A to participate in the war of national liberation. However, without ideological training and political consciousness it is difficult to instil these values. Not everyone who joined the SPLM/A was a revolutionary; in fact, many were fugitives from Sudanese justice system and needed rehabilitation through intensive ideological and political training to turn them into revolutionaries. In the absence of this re-orientation, they continued their criminal activities as combatants in the SPLM/A. Without political education in the SPLM/A training there was no way that former criminals and fugitives of Sudan's justice system would abandon their antisocial habits. Indeed, it was shocking to find Nimeri's former security and intelligence agents wielding authority in the SPLM/A camps. It was like a bad joke — revolution, liberation, "New Sudan" — when considering the dubious personalities who were lecturing us about the SPLM/A. It was an insult to our revolutionary sensibilities. Those who tracked down and tortured Nimeri's opponents were once again at their job, but now working with the same revolutionaries. Someone quipped, "This 'New Sudan' is going to be older than the old Sudan." He was right. Membership in the SPLM/A was a licence to do all kinds of things, some of them previously unheard of in the Sudan.

The presence of corruption in the SPLM/A is not a new revelation. However, we speak of it as something for which the SPLM/A should have combatted as a matter of principle. Corruption is a social cancer that eats away the soul of society. It existed in the Sudan and, indeed, was among the reasons that the Nimeri's regime was overthrown. As a socioeconomic phenomenon, corruption becomes apparent only with people's increased awareness.[52] It is difficult, if not impossible, to list every corrupt act that occurred in South Sudan. Suffice to say that corruption was central to the movement's formation, considering that the theft of soldiers' salaries triggered the mutiny in Bor in May 1983 that led to the formation of the SPLM/A.

In the SPLM/A, everywhere under its administration corruption and abuse of power was the norm rather than the exception. As a practice, it started benignly in the form of diverting food rations and money that essentially belonged to those who were under one's supervision or command. It grew to involve the complex management of crossborder trade and commerce. It was a quest for financial resources to satisfy a certain lifestyle to be enjoyed not in South Sudan but in East Africa and further afield. In this, the South Sudanese elite could be very innovative. The "slave redemption exercise" in northern Bahr el Ghazal was one such enterprise, run by senior SPLM/A commanders and a church-linked international NGO that became a million-dollar business. Instead of operating to punish the perpetuators of the crime of slavery and slave trade in the 21st century they collected money to "redeem" the enslaved. It became so lucrative (and embarrassing) that the attempt to stop it triggered internal conflict.

What business then did the deputy governor conduct to derive the wealth he now wanted to declare? The people in the Law Society compound knew that the deputy governor was in the business of armed raids to acquire cattle from neighbouring cattle camps in western Upper Nile. When an onlooker asked him to declare how he had come into possession of more than 4,000 head of cattle, he angrily stormed out of the compound. This is the paradox of authority flouting respect for regulations and laws. The abuse of power is the foundation of corruption in all its manifestations now in South Sudan.

Before the eruption of war in 1983, society frowned on those accused of embezzling public money, and indeed artists composed songs to ridicule such anti-social behaviour. There were traditional practices, like cattle rustling among the agro-pastoralist communities, which the

---

[52] On assuming power in a military coup in May 1969, the rumour mill had it that the merchant class that was the Democratic Unionist Party (DUP) was corrupt, and that Ismail el-Azhari, then the president of the Supreme Council of the State, had built a second floor on his house from the proceeds of corrupt deals. Gaafar Nimeri was embarrassed and had to settle the 2,000 pounds debt Azhari had accumulated to improve his private house in Aburouf in Omdurman. I include this to underscore that respect for public property was a core value in the Sudan until the May regime perfected the abuse of office.

state criminalized because of the violence and conflict they caused. The breakdown of law and order and the proliferation of firearms among the communities saw a resurgence of these practices, making them part of the SPLA corruption as it involved combatants. These were the modest beginnings of corruption, which came to afflict the wider society. First, the word "liberation" came to be substituted for "theft" or "robbery" in the conversations of the SPLA combatants. Second, the word "comrade" was denigrated among civilians to connote a "thief" or a "robber", based on what they had observed in the behaviour and attitude of the SPLA combatants. The militarised culture was not revolutionary in either its content or scope.[53]

Corruption in the SPLM/A, the abuse of the words "liberation" and "comrade", marked the beginning of the primitive accumulation of wealth in the areas under rebel control. It happened in almost exactly the way that characterized the stage of primitive accumulation of capital in Europe. The difference in South Sudan was that the social stratification it created was based on an individual's control over the distribution of relief assistance rather than control of any means of production. This led to lifestyles that not only promoted the corruption of the recipients but the providers in this relief business. It also created conditions for the flow of this assistance ad infinitum, which resulted in the spread of the relief-dependency syndrome.

Being an SPLA commander in an area where several relief agencies operated was such a lucrative assignment that officers would fall over each other to take up the post. The command would enable them to access resources from relief agencies, either voluntarily or through extortion. The international humanitarian intervention was a multibillion-dollar business that moved in and out of South Sudan's war economy, lubricating the network of corrupt commercial activities some SPLA officers transacted with relief agencies. This involved the large-scale diversion of resources, distributing food aid in the markets of neighbouring countries and across the frontlines in government garrison towns. In a way, corruption was institutionalized and became fashionable, to the extent that a small group of SPLA officers realised enormous wealth in form of cattle, money, and other property in and outside South Sudan.

---

[53] "Why do you call me comrade? Do I steal other people's goats?" were the words of an angry Aliab man to an SPLA soldier who drew his attention by calling him "comrade." The implication was that use of the word "comrade" was only for those who steal other people's property.

The rush for wealth and its primitive accumulation among the SPLM/A leaders and cadres pushed them to mortgage the country's natural resources like timber, minerals, wildlife trophies (elephant tusks, leopard skins, rhino horns, etc.), and cultural artefacts found in western Equatoria to sustain a lifestyle of conspicuous consumption. It heralded the birth of a small class of combatants, politicians, and petty commercial workers whose attitudes and behaviour completely alienated them from the masses. This group of wealthy SPLA officers maintained their families in expensive rented or purchased residences in posh suburbs of East African cities. This group constituted the precursor of the parasitic capitalist class that now controls the economy of South Sudan.[54] It is possible to draw a line linking the international humanitarian intervention, corruption, and the emergence of this parasitic capitalist class. There is also a nexus between this parasitic capitalist class, their collaboration with the regional and international comprador capital in the extraction and plunder of natural resources, and the emergence of the ethnocentric, kleptocratic, and totalitarian dictatorship in South Sudan.

The SPLM's running of the Government of Southern Sudan (GoSS) could not have been any different from the manner that the SPLM/A operated in the liberated areas during the war of national liberation. It had no programme or clear policy direction at the government level. As during the war, the SPLM leadership did not attach criteria on conditions for the appointment of its cadres into government. Some of the leaders appointed ministers who had never worked before in responsible positions in government or private sector, notwithstanding the high ranks they had in the military. Some were civil society activists who went into government with a different work ethos. The president and his deputy were also new to the task. It was therefore "trial and error" and, in this connection, the notions of meritocracy, transparency, and accountability were completely alien or, if they were known, ignored.

Some of the SPLM/A leaders and commanders were quickly enmeshed in a social and economic environment that was already polluted by the NCP politics of survival through blackmail and corruption. Like hungry wolves, their appetites for wealth already whetted by corrupt practices in the bush, the SPLM/A leaders, cadres, and commanders, notwithstanding their government positions, established all kinds of businesses through

---

[54] Means to *earn a profit* in an extractive economy; i.e., to behave like a parasite by attaching to a nutrient-rich host and sucking the value out of it.

which they laundered stolen public money in collaboration with their foreign friends and associates. The rot began in earnest, engulfing all government departments. It is worth mentioning that Southern Sudan started from scratch. They had to ferry in everything, big or small, for northern Bahr el Ghazal, Unity, and Upper Nile from Khartoum; and from the East African countries of Uganda and Kenya for the Equatoria states, Jonglei, Lakes, and Warrap. This meant that for the first two years of the interim period the GoSS was involved in building the physical infrastructure and purchasing capital goods.

The businesses the leaders set up profited from overpriced government contracts that were dished out based on personal links to government ministers, parliamentarians, army generals, and SPLM cadres and activists. This was the beginning of "payback time", which was characterized by obscene and opaque deals. Some contractors did not implement their projects, even though they walked off with millions of dollars paid in cash by the Central Bank of South Sudan. It is indeed unbelievable that leaders of a national liberation movement could engage in such obscene levels of corruption. However, to help the reader visualise the affair, I will illustrate the case of Juba International Airport Terminal Project under the GoSS Ministry of Transport and Communication. The project began in 2006 with a budget of US $40 million. The contractor, an Eritrean national, disappeared with the money, never to show up again. This episode of contractors running away with money was repeated twice, and still no criminal case was launched by the Public Prosecutor. In most contractual agreements the successful bidder must provide evidence of his ability to undertake the contract and receive the payment in instalments corresponding to the amount of work done. The contractor receives the last instalment only after certification that the work done has met the terms specified in the contract. This was not the case in most of the GoSS contracts. It is possible that the officials managing these contracts could have been ignorant as they lacked experience. Nevertheless, in some of the cases the culprits must have just paid themselves in the guise of foreign contractors. The project remained until 2016 without being completed, before finally being awarded to a Chinese company through a loan paid by the Chinese government-owned Export-Import Bank of China.

The most spectacular case of corruption linked to senior officials in government at the national and state levels was what became known as the "Dura Saga." This fraud exposed the criminal nature of some South Sudanese leaders. As part of its food security policy, the GoSS

Minister of Finance and Economic Planning budgeted US $1.6 billion for the purchase of grain (dura and maize) to be delivered to vulnerable states in Bahr el Ghazal, Jonglei, and Eastern Equatoria. The Ministry of Finance paid out the money to the contractors after state governors gave false confirmations of receipt of consignments.[55] The lie was revealed by the death from hunger of thousands of people in Aweil, Warrap, and Lakes states. A forensic investigation by the World Bank revealed that the GoSS paid 57 contractors linked to the president, including some senior ministers, the speaker of the Legislative Assembly, and SPLA commanders, US $800 million for delivering no grains. The GoSS minister of finance and economic planning could not pursue the case because it involved the principal himself and his close associates, some of whom were very important personalities in Uganda and Kenya.

The other high-level case of corruption revolved around the issuance of letters of credit (LC). The quest for money renders corruptible everything within the realm of South Sudan's political, military, and business elites. This is how these elites reduced to a criminal enterprise a noble international business transaction tool. The LC saga was another way that politically connected individuals helped themselves to huge sums of money. Unlike in the Dura Saga, the LCs involved a criminal innovation, which changed the normal practice of commercial banks issuing LCs to a white paper business: approval for and issuance of the letters of credit moved from the commercial banks to the Ministry of Finance and Economic Planning (MoFEP). This meant that applicants did not require a business or commercial licence as a basis for issuance of an LC. Instead, those with political connections could get the approval for a certain amount of foreign currency (US$) at the official rate of the Central Bank of South Sudan. Many politically well-connected individuals got fabulously rich by fleecing the state coffers while at the same time inflating the parallel rate of the dollar.

An illustration of this LC transaction involves someone getting approval, which is nothing but a white paper, addressed to the governor of the Central Bank for US $1 million. This individual, who is not a businessperson and has no money at all but that is a well-connected South Sudanese, takes this approval to a Somali or Kenyan businessperson and sells it for its equivalent in the local currency, SSP 2.9 million. The Somali businessperson would than sell the imported

---

[55] The governors of Lakes, Warrap, and Northern Bahr el Ghazal (Daniel Awet Akot, Tor Deng Mawien, and Paul Malong Awan, respectively) lied when they claimed that they had received the dura shipments, allowing the contractors to receive payment.

goods at the black market rate of SSP 29 million or more, depending on the market rate that particular day. More often than not, the LC recipients or their business partners would not honour the deal to bring the goods; instead, they would recycle the dollar notes in the black market. In this way, the political elite and their associates informalized the economy. So much so that it became difficult to identify who was a bona fide businessman: everyone, including ministers and judges, was in the market.

Wonders do not cease in South Sudan, as everything is corruptible. Another financial fraud involving the top GoSS leadership occurred in February 2014. This was in the aftermath of the December 2013 eruption of violence. President Kiir named a Crisis Management Committee (CMC) and gave it a budget of SSP 800 million. Vice President James Wani Igga headed the committee, which included the minister of cabinet affairs, the speaker of the Council of States, and others. The CMC's terms of reference were to coordinate the government's emergency response to the exigencies of the war, particularly in Upper Nile, Jonglei, and Unity states. Instead of visiting the disaster areas in Jonglei, Upper Nile, and Unity states, the comittee toured Western and Central Equatoria states, which were peaceful. It turned out the whole affair was a ploy to syphon funds in order to line the pockets of some GoSS top executives and buy their political loyalty. President Kiir provided proof of this thieving when he intervened to stop the auditor general from conducting any audit of the missing money.

There appears to be no limit to the theft, and one could go on bringing out cases of corruption in South Sudan. This was despite the president making pronouncements about "zero tolerance for corruption" at every public occasion. Just under his nose in his office, a cartel comprising the chief administrator, a director, a security detail, and their business associates operated to fleece the government of millions of dollars. The group would send financial requests to the Ministry of Finance, directing the director of budgets to divert budgetary allocations from certain ministries to the Office of the President to fund certain projects not found in the enacted Financial Allocation Bill. The cartel exploited the president's weakness for signing letters in compromised conditions.[56] It took a very long time to expose and bring the cartel to book, despite the repeated reports of stolen money in the Office of the

---

[56] The governor of the Central Bank of South Sudan, the late Elijah Malok Aleng, warned President Kiir against using his signature to draw money from the bank.

President. This explains how the Office of the President, the Ministry of Finance, and Ministry of Defence and Veterans Affairs would overspend by between 100 and 400 per cent of their respective budgets. The victims of such illegal diversions were the service ministries — agriculture, higher education, and health — which never received their respective allocated budgets.

The Sudan People's Liberation Army (SPLA) was another dirty spot. The corruption here could be considered an extension of the wheeling and dealing that occurred in the army during the war of national liberation. The transition from war to peace did not occur in an orderly manner, especially with the tragic and sudden death of the chairman and C-in-C. Many things went berserk. The non-military assets of the SPLA were considered the property of the individuals who managed them. The main preoccupation was relations with the NCP and SAF. The general expectation, therefore, was that the SPLA would be reorganized, trained, professionalized, and armed so it became an effective and efficient combatant force capable of meeting any emergency. The Southern Sudan Legislative Assembly allotted the military 40 per cent of the GoSS's annual budget, which ran into billions of US dollars. The SPLA High Command did not reciprocate this patriotic gesture. On the contrary, the SPLA became a bastion of corruption, where the generals, particularly those deployed in procurement and logistics commands, enriched themselves.[57]

Some SPLA generals not close to the general headquarters, or who were in command of sectors, divisions, or larger SPLA contingents, preyed on their divisions and battalions whose exact numbers they would not divulge in the hope of pocketing the excess money. The situation became even more desperate with the absorption into the SPLA of the other armed groups (OAG), the former tribal militias the SAF had sponsored in its proxy war against the SPLA. Many SPLA contingents would go for months without receiving salaries simply because the commanding officer had pocketed the money to build himself a mansion in Juba or across the border in Uganda or Kenya. Many SPLA generals set up businesses with some foreigners for quick profits. One type of business was in the domain of higher education: bogus universities were established without meeting even the most basic requirements for accreditation in Juba and other towns in South

---

[57] Police in Melbourne, Australia, impounded a house for the former SPLA chief of general staff, Gen. James Hoth Mai, bought in 2014 for US $1.5 million after his name appeared in *Sentry Report 2015*. It was part of the money gained fraudulently.

Sudan. These universities registered for degree courses people who had never been to school. When the minister of higher education, science and technology ordered the closure of these bogus universities they threatened him with dire consequences.

President Kiir's "zero-tolerance for corruption" was just a bluff, to say the least. It was just to fill in some of his boring speeches and solicit applause from the audience. In reality, the president would not hesitate to intervene to stop the minister of justice from investigating a case or force him to withdraw a corruption case from the court. These were cases involving government contracts where the contractor was the president's business associate. In the prevailing situation in South Sudan, where particular sections of society are deliberately economically empowered, it would be a misnomer to categorize it as simply corruption. It was politically engineered kleptocracy to put at advantage the Dinka from the Warrap-Aweil axis. This is because the Ministry of Justice, the Anti-Corruption Commission, and the South Sudan Police Service silently and helplessly watched this scourge under their watch and could not stop it.

The government of South Sudan pursued liberal economic policies and free-market ideologies that, in the absence of strong institutions, engendered corruption and strengthened the burgeoning parasitic capitalist class and its hold on public and private economic sectors. It was part of the social and economic empowerment of persons and businesses linked to the president and influential ministers in his government. It thrived on the preferential giving out of inflated government contracts. This class, which also was part of the political patronage networks of the system, survived on the domestication of corruption and strong links to the regional and international comprador capitalism anchored in the extraction and plunder of South Sudan resources. Businesses and citizens of neighbouring East Africa and the Horn of Africa invaded South Sudan when it had not yet developed its systems for conducting business formally.

Ugandans, Kenyans, Somalis, Ethiopians, and Eritreans started to do business with South Sudanese in often dubious partnerships, both in the formal and informal sectors. By their vocations, South Sudanese are seldom petty traders. Most of the retail commercial business in South Sudan, down to the level of small villages, was the preserve of the *jellabah*, the Arab merchant class from northern Sudan. As a rural people, South Sudanese valued livestock and cultural assets rather than money. A Dinka or Nuer working in government or the private sector will save money to buy cows and goats; an Azande, Moru, or Bari will save money to build the tombs of a parent or grandparent. This explains why the only businesses owned by South Sudanese were those linked to corruption in government.

The Eritreans and Ethiopians were involved in hotels, transport, water tankers, construction, and banking.[58] They invested mostly in leasing land from the locals and built hotels, restaurants, and coffee houses. Some elite Eritreans and Ethiopian, particular those with military backgrounds who must have mixed and interacted with SPLA commanders, engaged in more lucrative government and army contracts. This was real payback service as these businesses were linked with the political system in their home countries. The Ethiopian Commercial Bank had branches in Juba and Malakal and the Ethiopians monopolized air transport from Juba to Addis Ababa and some domestic routes.

The Ugandans were in all kinds of informal businesses, including even medical services, operating unlicenced clinics in Juba and its suburbs, exploiting the lack of regulatory mechanisms and the ignorance of many people in South Sudan. The most popular Ugandan business was operating *boda boda* transport services in Juba and dumping second- and third-hand Japanese vehicles into the South Sudanese market. The food market in Juba was filled with cheap Ugandan agricultural and dairy produce as well as fish, displacing and putting out of work local farmers and anglers. The Somali businesses were mainly in transport, the supply of building and construction materials, and the supply and management of fuel depots. The Kenyan businesses were in engineering, information and communications technology, air transport, and banking. Three Kenyan banks — Kenya Commercial Bank Ltd., Equity Bank, and Eco Bank — operated branches in major towns in South Sudan. Kenyan Airways monopolized the Juba-Nairobi line, including frequent charters for President Kiir's foreign trips.

The invasion of the country by foreign businesses, big and small, betrays a salient fact that South Sudan had leaders who did not have a strategic plan for the country. Some of the businesses were initially given only short-term licences, albeit in anticipation of permanent solutions, endured because the permanent solutions never arrived. For instance, the

---

[58] This was a business triggered by the lack of piped water in most South Sudanese towns. It was carrying untreated water from the Nile River for sale in the residential areas, the cost of a barrel of water approximating that of a barrel of oil. This easy but lucrative business attracted an SPLA general who purchased secondhand tankers from Kampala and employed Ethiopian and Eritreans drivers to run the business.

use of water tankers in Juba was considered a temporary measure until the construction of the Juba water pipe system had been completed. This project was never undertaken because the SPLA generals who operated water tankers, selling untreated Nile water, sabotaged it. The same thing occurred with the Juba electricity project: importers of diesel-operated generators demonstrated against and killed the government plan on the grounds that the government project would kill their business.

The question arising from this mess would be how did the foreign nationals repatriate their money back to their home countries. Most informal businesses transferred their money at one of the more than 127 forex bureaus in the country. This informs the extent of capital flight from South Sudan. In fact, large amounts of money left the country in cash, making an account of the transfers difficult. Both nationals and foreigners competed to send money out of the country. The South Sudanese political, military, and business elite, particularly those returning from the diaspora in USA, Canada, and Australia, repatriated large amounts of money to purchase property. The economies of Uganda and Kenya benefited directly from the situation in South Sudan. Many South Sudanese refugees remained in Kenya and Uganda. There are about 200,000 South Sudanese outside the refugee camps who are studying at different levels of the educational ladder in both Kenya and Uganda.

The case of Uganda is particularly important in this discussion about corruption and the evolution of the parasitic capitalist class in South Sudan. It transcends social, economic, and political domains, which define the relations between the countries' leaders, President Yoweri Museveni and President Salva Kiir. It has become clear that the Uganda citizens in South Sudan were part of Museveni's plan to improve Uganda's economy. Apart from the remittances they sent home and the payment of taxes, Ugandan immigrants in South Sudan were part of the solution to the unemployment crisis in Uganda. This explains Museveni's deceptive, and unflinching, political and military support for President Kiir, going so far as to have the UPDF and Air Force actively participate in the civil war.

It really is deceptive on many counts as Museveni's support for Kiir connects with the extraction and plunder of South Sudan natural resources. Since 2006, President Museveni has maintained a contingent of UPDF in South Sudan, ostensibly to track down and engage in battle with the Lord's Resistance Army (LRA). In all these years of roaming the forests of Equatoria the UPDF has never had meaningful contact with the LRA. And yet, throughout this period, there have been constant reports of the LRA's wanton killing of civilians in Western Equatoria State. This prompted the governor, Bangasi Joseph Bakasoro, to form a local vigilante group — the Arrow Boys —to protect the Azande people.[59] It emerged that the UPDF, rather than combat the LRA, were engaged in harvesting timber, poaching elephants and rhinos for their trophies, and prospecting for gold and diamonds, which they transported back to Uganda.

The presence of the UPDF in South Sudan falls within Museveni's scheme of extraction and plunder of South Sudan resources, taking advantage of the political cleavages within the SPLM leadership. Like Kiir, Museveni has not disguised his disdain for Dr. Riek Machar. As soon as the violence erupted in Juba on 15 December 2013, he dispatched contingents of UPDF and helicopter gunships to engage the rebel forces in Bor in a manner that suggested he had a direct role in fomenting the conflict. The ministers of defence of the two countries signed the Status of Forces Agreement months later, to catch up with legal requirements in the Ugandan Parliament and to ensure that the GoSS paid the bill, which ran to hundreds millions of dollars. Uganda became the arms procurer from manufacturers and dealers for the SPLA. Because of the war, UN oversight prevented South Sudan's direct purchase from the manufacturers, which required government-to-government transactions; the GoSS had to pay exorbitant costs for the transfer of arms through arms dealers and intermediaries linked to some influential individuals in Uganda. The appointment of Gen. Paul Malong as the SPLA's chief of general staff fast-tracked those deals, which did not necessarily require correspondence or documentation.

I have tried to demonstrate that corruption was present from the time of the SPLM/A's formation. Corruption was able to develop and envelop the liberation movement because of a paradigm shift from the revolution to neo-liberalism and the neo-colonial socioeconomic and political engineering of the liberation movement. This produced an elite class completely isolated and alienated from the masses and liberation ideology. As a consequence of this alienation, this political military

---

[59] The search for LRA in South Sudan was a hoax to justify the UPDF's presence in South Sudan as part of the US's war on international terrorism. Museveni succeeded in internationally isolating and turning public opinion against Joseph Kony by ordering UPDF soldiers to commit horrendous crimes and blame them on LRA. In Western Equatoria, it was the UPDF elements rather than LRA that terrorised the civil population. As soon as the Arrow Boys formed, we no longer heard of these crimes.

elite evolved into the parasitic capitalist class that, in collaboration with regional and international comprador capitalism, plundered South Sudan's natural resources. This triggered internal political conflicts in the ruling party, the SPLM, which eventually erupted into violence and the civil war. This brings us to the crucial question of whether or not the SPLM/A-spearheaded war of national liberation was ever a revolution.

The SPLM/A: A Revolution that Wasn't

A revolution differentiates by its political programme and the ideology that underpins this programme. It also differentiates by its leadership and the relation it has with the cadres as well as with the masses. I have discussed in the preceding pages how an alienated political military elite evolved out of the national liberation movement; how iconic words like "comrade" and "liberation" acquired opposite meanings among the combatants and the civilian population. I have discussed how corruption and the theft of public resources led to the emergence of a parasitic capitalist class whose social economic and political views were averse to those of the masses of South Sudan. The people of South Sudan have inventoried and documented the scope of the physical and psychological damage this elite has inflicted on the country. They have also inventoried the theft of staggering sums of money in what was an apparent *betrayal* of the people. It is important to underline the word betrayal because the nature of this crime clashes with the image, planted in the minds of the people, of revolutionaries struggling to "liberate" the country.

This despicable attitude and behaviour of former commanders of the war of liberation betrays a salient truth that the SPLM/A was not a genuine national liberation movement. There was a general desire in the Southern Region to take up arms against Nimeri's encroachment on the democratic process. However, unlike during the rush to join the Anya-nya in the 1960s, the ambition for power and positions, both political and military ranks, seems to have driven the rush to join the rank and file of the SPLM/A. This stems from the fact that following the Addis Ababa Agreement many former Anya-nya combatants received positions in the army or in government, positions that they would never have dreamt of if they had not joined the rebellion because of the academic requirements normally attached to them. Therefore, many who joined the SPLM/A did so in the hope of becoming officers in the Sudanese Armed Forces, police, and other services. There were those who thought the SPLM/A was a place for social mobility and, therefore, used it to accumulate wealth in the form of cattle, money, or both in order to marry many wives.

I have noted that corruption and the theft of public money was something congenital with the SPLM/A's formation. In such a situation, when criminal action accompanies the emergence of a revolutionary organization, the revolutionary leadership should have problematized the moral implications of these criminal acts. If the crime transforms into a revolutionary act (i.e., robbing a bank to fund a revolutionary movement) it takes on an ideological justification.[60] The act of fudging the theft of army money in Bor, which triggered the mutiny, inadvertently informed the subsequent attitude and behaviour of SPLA officers and men in their interactions with themselves and with the civilian population. The SPLM/A operated in a manner that perpetuated the ills of the oppressive regime they had risen up against, making it difficult to distinguish or differentiate the revolutionaries from the colleagues they had left behind in the system. In fact, the SPLA general headquarters regularly announced and masqueraded as revolutionaries the criminals and fugitives of the Sudanese justice system after they joined the SPLM/A.[61] The neglect of social and ideological criteria in the determination of membership of the liberation movement rendered it a sanctuary for all kinds of social misfits, including regime spies and agent saboteurs.

SPLA leaders disparaged the Anya-nya leaders, characterizing them as people interested in hierarchical positions and jobs. However, the failings of the Anya-nya leaders would by no means compare with those of many who flooded into the SPLM/A purporting to have been senior executives in the Southern Regional Government in order to be given senior ranks in the SPLA. This suggests that many individuals, particularly those hailing from cities and towns rather than from the cattle camps, invariably were rent-seekers. Many had come to fulfil life ambitions they would never have achieved in the Sudan.

The SPLM/A was formed at a time when sharp and bitter political divisions were tearing apart the political class in the Southern Region along ethnic and provincial fault lines. This was fertile political ground

---

[60] Revolutionaries involved in clandestine and armed resistance often engage in criminal activities like bank robberies and kidnappings for ransoms, which they ideologically justify, but later on educate their cadres and activists against such practices.

[61] There were at least two cases: one indivdiual faked the robbery of his department's money, left the town's borders and reported himself to the SPLM command in the area. The people in Wau could not believe their ears when the SPLA announced the arrival of a "revolutionary." The other case was of an accountant working for the Regional Insurance Company. He ran away with the firm's money, forcing it into insolvency.

in which Field Marshall Nimeri cultivated his politics of "divide to rule", pitting Equatorians against the Dinka people of Bahr el Ghazal and Upper Nile. Nevertheless, the SPLM Manifesto did not draw attention to this situation, which bore serious implications on the future development of inter-ethnic relationships within the nascent movement. The manifesto neither contradicted nor dispelled the falsehood that the SPLM/A was an ethnic Dinka political enterprise. The Equatorian elites (Equatoria Central Committee), opposed to Dinka dominance, spun a narrative to support Nimeri's decision to abrogate the Addis Ababa Agreement and dismantle the Southern Region.

It was important, as early as that material time, and indeed imperative, that the SPLM leadership corrected the false notion that the formation of the SPLM/A was in response to Dinka having lost political control in the Southern Region. In fact, some intellectuals linked the numerical superiority of ethnic Dinka in the nascent movement to the notion that it was a Dinka movement. They deliberately rubbish any suggestions that the preponderance of ethnic Dinka in the nascent movement was coincidental to Dinka leadership. The failure of the SPLM Manifesto to speak to the objective reality of South Sudan in terms of its sociopolitical and cultural formations exacerbated suspicions that there were underlying political objectives. This makes it difficult to understand how the leadership of the infant movement, purporting to be national in character, became predominantly Dinka in composition.

It is worth noting that many politicians and political activists hailing from Central Equatoria believed that the SPLM/A was a deliberate challenge to the Equatoria Region they had just won. Thus, by its social and ideological architecture, particularly after the split with Anya-nya II in 1983, the SPLM/A could pass easily for a Dinka ethnic enterprise, the work of which was often conducted exclusively in the Dinka language rather than in Arabic or English, both of which were familiar to most southern Sudanese. In the absence of political awareness and ideological consciousness, it was not possible to convince the ordinary or average Dinka SPLA combatant from a cattle camp that the SPLM/A, or the liberation for that matter, was something different from being Dinka, or something that was not pursuing Dinka socioeconomic and political interests.

In its 21 years of existence, the SPLM/A vacillated between a Sudanese national enterprise and a southern Sudan (Dinka ethnic power project) political organization. Its national character appeared only with the formation of the National Democratic Alliance (NDA) in 1995 and the

New Sudan Brigade (NSB) deployed in Eastern Sudan. It is unfortunate that Dr. John Garang did live to witness how this project would play out in the CPA implementation. His tragic demise at that crucial time, just three weeks into office as the first vice president of the Republic of the Sudan, and as president of the government of Southern Sudan, left many gaps in the execution of the presumed ethnic agenda of the SPLM/A. However, faced with the stark objective reality of Southern Sudan, the Sudan, the IGAD region and the international situation, I would say that Dr. John Garang would have charted a different political trajectory that would have placed him and the SPLM above parochial ethnic socioeconomic and political interests. In this respect, his projection of Dinka nationalism was based on political expedience.

I can vouch, this was mere speculation. No one can know how matters would have played out. This is because only Dr. Garang knew the practical details of the liberation movement. The complete lack of institutionalized management of public affairs left every decision in the movement, both small and large, to his discretion. For instance, following the tragic helicopter crash, some of the movement's strategic information that trickled in to the new SPLM leadership suspiciously came from Dr. Garang's close relatives not his comrades in the SPLM Leadership Council. This suggests that a larger plan did exist and was awaiting execution at the level of the SPLM/A and in the government of Southern Sudan, which could have caused serious friction.

It is worth noting that the SPLM/A had no constitution although it purported to have formal organs of the state: the legislative organ, the National Liberation Council (NLC), and an executive arm, the National Executive Committee (NEC). Nevertheless, these structures did not function in a formal way. As shall be noted below, the SPLM/A functioned in command mode at the discretion of its chairman and commander in chief. The operation of the SPLM/A was so informal that Dr. Garang alone was in charge. Its new chairman and commander in chief, Cdr. Salva Kiir Mayardit, who indeed had not completely recovered from the Yei crisis eight months earlier, was at a loss. He wobbled between the SPLM/A "national power centre" and the emerging Bahr el Ghazal "power centre", both of which he headed.[62] The two groups

---

[62] The SPLM/A "national power centre" included members of the SPLM Leadership Council and the SPLA chief of general staff and his staff, as was constituted by Garang soon after he assumed the office of the president of the Government of Southern Sudan. The Bahr el Ghazal power centre comprised of SPLA commanders and politicians hailing from Aweil and Warrap who were vehemently opposed to Garang.

were antagonistic in a manner that exacerbated the difficulty of SPLM/A leadership's transition from Garang to Kiir.

President Kiir assumed the leadership of the SPLM/A at its weakest moment, having just lost its founding leader. The 2004 Yei crisis between Kiir and Garang had not been resolved before Garang's death. I noted earlier that Kiir has never forgotten nor forgiven his detractors. Lingering questions from the Yei crisis kept popping up between him and the so-called Garang's orphans. In addition to these internal challenges, the interim period was indeed a difficult time for the SPLM. This was due to factors related to its relationship with the NCP, in the context of CPA implementation, and its development as a political party in government. Emerging from a protracted and destructive war, the SPLM leaders had not trained for peace and the work of running government. There was no blueprint for managing the "transition from war to peace" except the peace agreement (CPA) itself, the Interim National Constitution (INC) and the Interim Constitution of Southern Sudan (ICSS).

The SPLM/A leaders in government and the military were, therefore, on a trial-and-error mission: they made do with whatever they knew or did not know. There was a general disorientation in the ranks, particularly after Kiir reversed some decisions and orders Garang had decreed before his tragic death. The new president's leadership style permitted the emergence of competing power centres within the SPLM, which only exacerbated the mutual alienation and apprehension.[63] The resultant intrigue, double-crossings, blocking of each other, gossiping, leader worship, and all kinds of unhealthy political brinkmanship produced an internal situation in the SPLM/A that heightened the mistrust among its top leadership and paralyzed strategic thinking and action. Nevertheless, President Kiir's "hands off the issues" posture, which allowed many problems to burn themselves out, somehow prevented a premature implosion.

This attitude of fudging matters rather than facing them directly to resolve them temporarily warded off tensions but could not prevent the eventual eruption of these differences. It also would not help the relationship with the NCP in pushing ahead with the CPA implementation, especially implementation of the three protocols (Abyei, Nuba Mountains/Southern Kordofan, and Blue Nile). It is to be remembered that the US administration pushed the three protocols

---

[63] The Bahr el Ghazal elders and the Garang "orphans" constituted a powerful lobby on account of their knowledge of the SPLM's political and diplomatic activities in the region and further afield.

down the NCP's throat. President Kiir and the SPLM's main political thrust, which to some extent lacked statecraft and realpolitick, was the holding of the referendum on self-determination. It determined all the dealings the SPLM had with the NCP in the Government of National Unity (GoNU). This completely dichotomised the SPLM and its political thoughts into "southern" and "northern" sectors at a very early stage, betraying a salient truth that the SPLM and its leadership concerned themselves only with matters that would lead to South Sudan's secession and little, if not nothing, to do with democratic transformation.

Democratic transformation of the Sudan polity concerned the SPLM as the second-largest partner in the GoNU. It was of the greatest necessity, both politicaly and morally, to push for democratic transformation. Garang would have used the CPA provision he personally negotiated to mobilize political support in northern Sudan against the NCP's reluctance to implement in full the CPA. President Kiir did not care about the ideological struggle against the NCP and, therefore, ignored the provision concerning democratic transformation. Moreover, internal cleavages within the SPLM leadership showed in the calibre of SPLM leaders and cadres deployed in the institutions of the GoNU, namely in the executive and legislature.

One could glean from the very beginning of the interim period that Kiir was interested only in Southern Sudan and the GoSS based in Juba, although the politics of CPA implementation were centred in the party head offices in Khartoum, the national capital. This affected the role of the SPLM as the second-most powerful party after the NCP in the GoNU. The fact that Kiir seldom attended the cabinet meetings of the GoNU in Khartoum suggested he did not care much about what happened there. It was a strategic mistake by the SPLM and this cast serious doubts about the SPLM's continued political existence in northern Sudan. Its political manoeuvring and engagement with the NCP required deployment in Khartoum, Blue Nile, and Southern Kordofan, states where there were politically astute leaders and cadres. From these areas, the SPLM received solid political support. There were also large SPLA contingents based there. In military terms, these were the SPLM's first line of defence against NCP recalcitrance and procrastination in respect to implementation of the CPA. But the SPLM deployed weak leaders and the three areas of Blue Nile, South Kordofan, and Abyei became vulnerable to the NCP's political machinations. Indeed, because of the SPLM's lack of strategic thinking and due to its political miscalculations fighting broke out in the three areas as soon as South Sudan became independent in 2011, leading to a complete rout of the SPLM.

The interim period was an opportunity for the SPLM to stamp its vision and concepts on the social, economic, and political reality of Southern Sudan, Blue Nile, and Southern Kordofan, if not the whole of Sudan. Unfortunately, it had no programme. Indeed, without an ideology it would not be possible to construct a political programme based on a theory of transformation. The SPLM relied on the CPA protocols to address the challenges of the interim period. The GoSS received its share of the oil revenues. However, this money, without a blueprint for its utilization, exposed the SPLM leaders' vanity and ideological and political vacuity. They began to use the money to reward themselves, what one minister in the GoSS called "payback time." This payback included awarding fictitious, inflated government contracts to friends and blood relatives. It also meant calling unqualified relatives and friends from the diaspora to take up appointments as senior civil servants. It was a situation where well-connected SPLA officers got employment in civil service institutions while still on active service in, and receiving salaries from, the army headquarters. The GoSS appeared to have a great deal of money at its discretion, but this was simply because the GoSS and its ministries had no development plans to implement. When poverty, ignorance, illiteracy, and a total lack of physical infrastructure were evident everywhere in Southern, this failure of the SPLM and its government to make development plans seemed quite unbelievable.

Southern Sudan had just emerged from a devastating war (1983–2005). The war had not only destroyed the physical infrastructure but also the social fabric of society, including its agriculture-based economy and culture. This required an urgent government intervention to address the transition from war to peace, in terms of an emergency socioeconomic programme, particularly in the agriculture sector to meet food security needs. It was also fortunate that the GoSS had the necessary economic and financial resources to meet this urgent task. In fact, the GoSS had the money to kickstart some of the economic development projects whose feasibility studies the HEC had completed before the war. The difficulties associated with the lack of organization or institutionalization of the SPLM's public authority showed up in the form of political paralysis immediately after the death of Garang.

President Kiir's leadership style exacerbated this political paralysis due to the emergence of power centres in the SPLM. Concerned only with protecting his position as SPLM chairman and president of GoSS, Kiir encouraged the internal SPLM power wrangling. However, he watched to see that certain individuals did not become powerful enough to challenge his power. This distracted the SPLM leadership and the GoSS from the task of providing development and social services. The SPLM leaders concentrated on, and indeed united their ranks around, personal aggrandisement and the primitive accumulation of wealth. In unison, these leaders, including the president, would complain about certain failures in the system, like the spiralling cases of corruption, nepotism, tribalism, and insecurity and yet, as government, they could not take action.

This takes us back to the rhetorical question about the SPLM/A's revolutionary credentials as a national liberation movement. At the risk of recycling an argument (Nyaba, 2000: 193) that the SPLM did not exist anywhere in the Southern Sudan realm except in the obfuscated configuration of the SPLM/A, it immediately became apparent when its leaders took over the helm of power in Southern Sudan in 2005. It proved that the SPLM/A was *only* Dr. John Garang, that without him it did not exist other than as an empty shell. This is exactly what it became, especially after December 2013.

That only a single leader could invoke awe in his colleagues and the public in a liberation movement, to the point that the life of the organization was contingent on him, could mean only one thing: the SPLM/A was not a revolutionary movement. Garang intended it as a personal power project and, indeed, he succeeded. The coincidence of being the only survivor of the original five-man High Command puts Kiir in a category of his own, one that combined strategy, cowardice, inferiority, and brutality to reach the top. There were times that Kiir acted the fool in order to get his way with his equally ruthless colleagues in the High Command (Kerubino Kuanyin Bol, William Nyuon Bany, and Arok Thon Arok), behaving as the obedient executioner of Garang's orders to arrest, detain, and/or physically eliminate pretenders to Garang's crown.

It was not by accident that Salva Kiir Mayardit inherited the leadership of the SPLM and the presidency of South Sudan. It was also not by accident that he copied Garang's methods as he pretended to be waiting for orders, even though he already was the leader. Thus, in the first two years of his presidency of Southern Sudan, Kiir did not demonstrate the presumptuous attitude and behaviour that come with power. He remained simple, accessible, and disposed to any idea, although he would hardly act except in cases that concerned privileges affecting Aweil and Warrap people, when he would act decisively. The opportunist and power-hungry elements that gathered around him exploited his outwardly benign character to create complacency and discourage strategic thinking. Matters seemed to slide without control, particularly in respect to corruption in the public service and the worsening insecurity and ethnic conflicts throughout South Sudan.

The SPLM leaders played the kind of politics internally and externally with the NCP that betrayed deep-seated internal cleavages. They were at each other throats, sometimes in a manner that resonates with the earlier referred to claims that southerners cannot govern themselves, but also reflective of the unsophisticated village backgrounds of these leaders. It was an extension and indeed perfection of the patronage system based on patrimonialism that existed in the liberation movement. Access to power depended on having the largest network of clients and subpatrons, and control of the means of violence (army, national security, and police). President Kiir had the advantage of numbers and money. He commanded the support of the Dinka elite and he distributed large sums of money to purchase political loyalty.

The same political patronage evolved around his deputy, Dr. Riek Machar, whose tribesmen and women held him in high esteem as their leader following the demise of Samuel Gai Tut, whom the SPLA killed in combat in 1984. The Nuer people formed the second-largest single ethnicity after the Dinka; relative here was the orally transmitted myth linked to Ngundeng's prophecy that a left-handed individual with a gap in his upper teeth would lead the Nuer. The Nuer elite worked and reworked this prophecy until the original description and its variations fit the person of Machar. These narratives were woven into the myth that has become important for ethnic Nuer political mobilization in response to Dinka hegemony and domination of power.

The other SPLM/A political leaders of note who are neither Dinka nor Nuer in this political fray are, in order of their former SPLM seniority: Dr. Lam Akol, James Wani Igga, and Pagan Amum Okiech. They were members of the SPLM's former Leadership Council, established on the eve of the CPA in 2004. Both Lam Akol and Pagan Amum hail from the Chollo (Shilluk) nationality. Cdr. James Wani Igga hails from Bari nationality; in the SPLM's popular language, he is an Equatorian. In all of the SPLM's unpredictability and intermittent political crises, James Wani has remained loyal and in Kiir's confidence. He readily accepted the embarrassingly upward or downward pushes in the SPLM power hierarchy.

President Kiir remained suspicious and apprehensive of Pagan Amum, but in 2008 he had to swallow his pride and accepted him as the SPLM secretary-general, but only after the SPLM's 2nd National Convention overruled him. On the other hand, Dr. Lam Akol, being the diligent, meticulous, and egocentric politician that he is, rubbed shoulders quickly with power, first with Garang and then later with Kiir, prompting his decamping (1991), re-camping (2003), and decamping again (2009) from the SPLM to form the faction called the SPLM-Democratic Change (SPLM-DC).

In the ethnic configuration of politics in the SPLM, the three leaders relied more on national rather than ethnic constituencies for their political work and survival. This is because hailing from ethnic minorities renders the national constituency of no consequence in the power and leadership contest, in questions of where and when politics organize, or power exercises based on ethnicity rather than political ideas and programmes. The tyranny of numbers decides the result of such contests. This is where the real triggers of the current civil war lie, the harbingers of South Sudan's self-destruction. In the social, economic, and political engineering of South Sudan, the SPLM leaders advertently followed in the footsteps of nationalist and independence-era African leaders who invariably promoted ethnicity and ethnic allegiance as their route to political power. These regimes invariably evolved into one-party totalitarian dictatorships under which flourished the political and economic empowerment of ethnicities in a system of political and economic patronage.

The current civil war in South Sudan is a direct result of the manner that the SPLM/A conducted the war of national liberation: outside its political and ideological context. As a revolution, the objective was to transform the conditions of socioeconomic and cultural backwardness of the people of South Sudan by developing and freeing their productive forces. This did not happen. The SPLM/A leaders took a neo-colonial path to development, which has now reduced the people to paupers. In this respect, the SPLM/A was not a revolution. It was at best, and remains, a power project. This explains the formation of different factions led by SPLM/A leaders who consider themselves historical founders of the movement and claim a stake in the name. However, what proves that the SPLM was a power project, whether in its original or variant forms, is the reluctance of these leaders to build institutions and structures of public power. Domesticating democracy would mean sharing power and decision-making with subordinates, who are loathed by all of these prospective leaders.

CHAPTER THREE

The Civil War was not Inevitable

At the end of it all, a question remains in everybody's mouth in South Sudan: Was the war inevitable? In fact, this is a compound question: it bifurcates into two important aspects. The first aspect of this question speaks to the skirmishes in the Tiger Battalion on the night of 15 December 2013, immediately after the closing session of the SPLM National Liberation Council. The Tiger Battalion housed the Presidential Guards unit. Strictly speaking, it was made up of soldiers from the Dinka (Kiir's bodyguards hailing from Warrap and northern Bahr el Ghazal states) and Nuer (the bodyguards of Paulino Matip Nhial and Machar, all hailing from western Unity State). These soldiers fought each other along ethnic lines. The second aspect speaks to the targeted massacre of innocent ethnic Nuer men, women, and children, which occurred in the residential suburbs of Juba between December 16 and 19. This searing incident, which also involved the killing of Dinka hailing from Agar and Padang Dinka because of facial marks similar to Nuer, occurred in full sight of the region, the UNMISS and the international community represented by diplomatic missions in Juba.

The split and developing hostilities between Kiir and his army chief of general staff, Gen. Paul Malong Awan, in the spring of 2017 began to unravel some of the intricacies, in terms of motivation and strategies, underpinning the decision to war that has raged since December 2013.[64] In fact, the unravelling began with the fighting in the Presidential Palace

---

[64] Gen. Paul Malong Awan has declared war on President Kiir and formed the South Sudan United Front/Army (SSUF/A).

(known as J-1) on 8 July 2016, which collapsed the Agreement on the Resolution of the Conflict in the South Sudan (ARCISS). By the end of 2017, the political tide had reversed, raising questions about the initial motivation. Nearly all of the political/military elements at the centre of the political cyclone in 2013 had shifted to take opposite sides of the conflict. Taban Deng Gai, Ezekiel Lol Gatkuoth — the main agitators on Machar's side — have since 2016 joined Salva Kiir; Paul Malong, Aleu Ayieny, and Telar Deng are now Kiir's enemies. The civil war has acquired a different character from what it was when it erupted in 2013.

An honest analysis of the civil war and the factors leading up to it would make interesting reading, including the agonizing humanitarian disruption, the immense suffering, and loss of life. I have discussed in Chapter Two the formation of the SPLM/A and the factors that give birth to its leadership and the crop of leaders that evolved in the context of the war of national liberation. I did not attempt to investigate the southern Sudanese political leaders who evolved in the Ingaz system; however, their time as ministers in the GoSS revealed their self-centredness. It is fair to say that the current brand of leaders in South Sudan, particularly the leaders of the SPLM and the SPLA, have shown that they are unable to make claims to represent national leadership.

The genesis of the war can be traced back to the formation, dynamics, and failure of the SPLM/A to become a national liberation movement. The political crises in the SPLM, driven by power and wealth, have mutated into an ethnically charged conflict pitting against each other the two largest ethnicities in South Sudan: Dinka and Nuer. An unfortunate combination of factors combined to set the stage. The sudden death of Garang triggered dynamics that led to the marginalization of the SPLM as the leading political force, including the emergence of an informal ethnic group called the Bahr el Ghazal Elders as a power centre around the president.[65] The SPLM institutions had not fully evolved or developed and, therefore, the emergence of a powerful power centre weakened and completely paralyzed the SPLM, which was still recovering from the tragedy of Garang's death as well as the Yei crisis, whicht remained fresh in the minds of many Bahr el Ghazal leaders who supported Kiir.

The SPLM did not have a blueprint for governing southern Sudan, even though it was effectively the ruling party in the subnational entity. Its institutions and instruments of public power and authority

---

[65] A group of politicians and intellectuals hailing from Dinka sections in Warrap, Aweil, and a few from Lakes whose agenda was to localize the SPLM power in and the economic empowerment of the people of Bahr el Ghazal.

were weak or nonexistent, save in the person of the leader during the war of national liberation. It had no unifying political ideology. The consequences of this were immediately evident after the demise of its founding leader in the form of contradictory positions that the different leaders adopted in their relations with the NCP and other political groups in southern Sudan. As a result, the leaders pursued individual personal objectives, thus accentuating the internal power struggle and the primitive accumulation of wealth.

The marginalization of the SPLM as the ruling party meant that politics were organized, power exercised, and resources and opportunities distributed based on ethnicity. The surge in Dinka ethnic nationalism, with its ideology of hegemony and domination, found expression in the formation of the Jieng Council of Elders (JCE), bringing together in organizational and ideological unity Dinka intellectuals from the different Dinka sections, including Abyei. This led to the further marginalization of the SPLM in the politics and governance of the state. The SPLM's power and authority shifted imperceptibly from the SPLM House and the General Secretariat to the Office of the President and the JCE. The JCE and related Dinka think tanks (Sudd Institute and Ebony Centre) provided policy briefs, which the president decreed into laws.

It is possible that there was no grandiose motivation for engineering and sparking the crises leading to the eruption of the civil war save the selfish ambitions for control of state power and resources. The whole affair is so irrational that any scientific investigation into the events leading to the eruption of violence in December 2013 forces the conclusion that the independence of South Sudan under the leadership of President Kiir, Machar, and Hon. James Wani Igga was a stillbirth. Their lack of political foresight and leadership to manage a country emerging from 21 years of destructive war made eruption of violence inevitable. Under the leadership of Garang they were on the periphery of decision-making processes and, more often than not, they were only concerned about personal issues. They pursued their personal ambitions to such an extent that they caused the social, economic, and political collapse of South Sudan.

The greatest personal weakness of Kiir was his Dinka ethnic chauvinism and inability to resist the JCE temptation to Dinka-nize the South Sudan state. He acquiesced and implemented JCE policies. The Jieng's political-military and business elite had twin objectives in the nascent Republic of South Sudan: to install absolute medieval-like Jieng power and to achieve the economic empowerment of its members. In this scheme, they saw a negative reaction from the Nuer as the only obstacle and, therefore, went about strategizing how to handle the fallout. The Dinka and Nuer can go to war because of rivalry for power or leadership of South Sudan; they can also go to war because of money or wealth in general. In an egalitarian environment, these two categories of power and wealth (as represented by cattle) can lead to destruction and death. Thus, in the process of achieving these objectives, the JCE created internal political disorder, a deep economic crisis, social fragmentation along internal ethnic and provincial lines, and the regional and international diplomatic isolation of South Sudan.

The JCE managed to monopolize the political process and dominate the economy, but the inherent irrationality of the scheme generated internal divisions and power struggles between Kiir and some of the people involved in implementing the scheme, including Gen. Paul Malong Awan, the former army chief of general staff. The conflict between the two leaders spilled over into their communities, leading to armed skirmishes and preparing the ground for the Jieng power edifice to collapse and crumble. The JCE are panicking at the prospect of losing their grip on power but have chosen the wrong way out of the multiple crises.

The egocentric nature of the two politically and demographically dominant ethnicities of South Sudan — namely, the Dinka and the Nuer — and their penchant to treat the state as their personal or ethnic property is the main source of South Sudan's predicament. Their almost mutual exclusivity constitutes the drivers of the current situation, although the root causes are structural, having to do with the lack of institutionalization in the SPLM power and public authority, and have little to do with the reality of their respective ethnicities.

Spinning Rumours into a Dangerous Narrative

Whether or not it was a deliberate plot requires further investigation to establish the truth. However, as mentioned above, the struggle for power could ignite a conflagration and working out a strategy for the absolute monopoly of power can entail physical and character assassination. The following lines are from a conversation the author had with Rev. Joshua Dau Diu, a senior member of the JCE:

> On a visit to Canada in 2010, a Nuer, an old friend, came all the way from Toronto to see me in Ottawa. He was very cordial and our conversation hinged on the social and political situation in southern Sudan as it prepared to conduct the referendum on self-determination.

Then, suddenly my friend blurted out, "We [the Nuer ethnicity] now constitute 65 per cent of the SPLA. Dr. Riek Machar must became the president of independent South Sudan, otherwise we are going to fight the Dinka to snatch the power from President Salva Kiir."[66] Back home in Sudan, I corroborated the conversation I had with my Nuer friend to another in which Gen. Taban Deng Gai had confided to President Salva Kiir that the Nuers will go to war if Dr. Riek Machar did not win the presidency of South Sudan come April 2015.

It is doubtful, however, that there was a Nuer intention, as a people, to go to war to install Dr. Machar. I told Rev. Joshua Dau that he was the trigger for the civil war and I was going to file a case against him at the International Criminal Court in The Hague. However, given Taban Deng Gai's relations with President Kiir then it was possible he could have concocted and told him this information in the context of a presidential intelligence briefing from his governor in Unity State. In fact, Taban was Kiir's man in the gubernatorial position in Unity State who worked against the political advances of Vice President Riek Machar and his spouse, Angelina Teny. In this respect, it must be credible that the JCE rolled the narrative into a toxic strategy involving Taban Deng Gai to rid President Kiir of his political nemesis Machar who, since 2008, had never hidden his ambition for power. I believe the unceremonial dismissal of Taban Deng as governor of Unity State therefore could have been a ploy to accelerate the military rather than political implementation of the strategy to get rid of Machar. It could also have been a case of killing two birds with one stone, given that Salva appointed Dr. Joseph Nguen Monytuil as governor of Unity state. This was done to neutralize and win over the Bull Nuer in case of any confrontation involving the Jagai (Taban) and/or Dok (Machar) Nuer sections. The JCE planted the narrative through gossips and innuendo to feed into the historical Dinka-Nuer ethnic rivalry and animosities over the division of state power and resources.

In a situation where state power and authority are personified rather than institutionalized, the political conflicts run along personal, ethnic, or provincial lines. These were sufficient grounds for the JCE to strategize and mobilize their Jieng constituencies under the clarion call of *dotku beny* ("Let's rescue the president"), suggesting that President Kiir was under siege by the Nuer. Ethnic hubris apart, the prospect of absolute

---

[66] Incidentally, many Nuer intellectuals incorrectly believe that Dr. Riek Machar was the first to introduce the concept of self-determination into the Southern Sudanese struggle for freedom and independence through the Nasir Declaration in August 1991.

control of power and wealth was a strong incentive for a Dinka-Nuer tribal war. This stems logically from the post-war power configuration and alignment in Southern Sudan, which placed Dinka, Nuer, and all other ethnicities within a hierarchy headed by the Dinka.

In a complex stratagem to entrench himself in power and at the same time clip Machar's wings, Kiir started to plan to reduce the number of ethnic Nuer in the SPLA. In a case in the Permanent Court of Arbitration (PCA) over Abyei, Southern Sudan lost Heglig oil fields to the Sudan because the framers of the Abyei case wrongly connected Heglig to the Abyei area. The PCA relied on the report of the Abyei Area Commission, which delineated the borders of Abyei area. Since the PCA rejected Heglig as part of the Abyei Area, the Government of Sudan immediately claimed that Heglig and the oils fields belonged to Southern Kordofan. The president blamed this loss on Machar, who led the GoSS delegation. In was in this context that Kiir engineered the border war with the Sudan, ostensibly to regain control over the Heglig oil field. He had maintained Taban Deng Gai as governor of Unity State, against the wishes of the people there, meaning that the president could be certain of Taban's loyalty and support against Machar.

President Kiir wanted the border war with the Sudan to serve some of his strategic political objectives, in anticipation of a final military showdown with Machar (read: Nuer). One objective was to expose Machar and Taban Deng as the drivers of the conflict with the Sudan. The idea, therefore, was to break beyond repair relations between the Nuer (formerly organised in a tribal militia) and their mentors in the Sudan. This would make the NCP government deny political and military support to Machar and Taban should they run to Khartoum if Kiir unleashed war on them. At the same time, Kiir would use the border war to drum up internal as well as regional political support, particularly military supplies from Uganda's President Museveni, who was so allergic to both Machar and the Sudanese president, Omar el Beshir. The other strategy relevant to this analysis was to deplete the numbers of Nuer in the SPLA. It is worth mentioning that President Kiir ordered the absorption into the SPLA of the Nuer militias allied to the SAF as a stratagem against some sections of the SPLA; it was also to win over Gen. Paulino Matip Nhial against Machar. The large numbers of ethnic Nuer in the SPLA became a concern, prompting the JCE to design a way of ridding the SPLA of them. The border war with the Sudan fought by these ex-militias exposed the Nuer as unreliable allies to their former mentors.

The civil war in South Sudan and the immense humanitarian disruption it caused speaks much to the attitudes of the political leaders, particularly the SPLM leaders and their dangerously inflated egos that have driven them into the inferno, although the root causes — the underlying fundamental contradictions, as in the war of national liberation — remain the socioeconomic and cultural backwardness of the people of southern Sudan. Nevertheless, the triggers, essentially secondary conflicts, are senseless and irrational as they revolve around the leaders' self-pride, machismo, and ethnic bigotry. It is mind-boggling that the power struggle between Kiir and his deputy Machar could spell doom for the people of South Sudan. These two leaders appeared at the helm as the SPLM's chairman and deputy chairman respectively in August 2005 following the death of Dr. John Garang de Mabior. It is true that Machar re-joined the SPLM/A in 2002, 11 years after the 1991 split within the liberation movement. While many people in South Sudan were upbeat about reunification of the SPLM/A following the return to the fold of the architects of the Nasir Declaration 1991, certain quarters inside and outside the SPLM/A, hailing mainly from Bahr el Ghazal, saw this political development in a different light. They saw it as entrenching in power the people of the former Upper Nile region.

Between Kiir and Machar, something definitely was amiss. They did not share a higher national interest, an interest for which an individual will sacrifice his own life, ignoring his ambition for power in order to save the country and its people. They could not save the highly hyped youngest country in the world from self-destruction. In this respect, this present war, and the failure to prevent it, speaks volumes about Kiir Mayardit, Machar, and the political and military elite that surrounded them after they assumed the leadership of Southern Sudan in 2005.

Leaders' Incompatibility Becomes South Sudan's Predicament

The political events that culminated in the eruption of violence in December 2013 have their roots in the SPLM/A, and indeed mirror its historical sociopolitical development. I discussed in the previous section the factors that contributed to the derailment of the SPLM/A from the path of national liberation. The political and ideological subversion of the SPLM/A inadvertently or advertently led to the evolution of ethnic ideologies in the national liberation movement, setting off the clash of Dinka and Nuer ethnic hubris and a distortion of the character of the war. I also discussed the explosive links between ethnicity and the wielding of state power because of the primitive accumulation of wealth and the unequal distribution of resources and opportunities. Combined with the SPLM's failure to build a national awareness based on common core values, ethnic and provincial sensibilities have prevailed.

In this respect, the discussion of the current situation in South Sudan ties up with the tragic and untimely death of Garang in that it enabled Kiir, Machar, and James Wani to assume leadership of the SPLM. They came in from a position of isolation. They were not part of the decision-making mechanism of the SPLM because Garang and a coterie of lieutenants monopolized the SPLM/A's inner workings, especially after 1998, when he suppressed the functions of the SPLM institutions formed after the 1st National Convention in 1994. By his nature, his ability to command the respect and confidence of the people, Garang would not have allowed the crisis to explode, or even reach the boiling point. Garang looked at the bigger picture of things and would have prevented an eruption that could destroy the edifice. This was unlike his successor, Salva Kiir, who acted on political issues based on personal, ethnic, and provincial considerations. Garang would have prevented any differences from taking on ethnic or provincial characteristics. The war would not have broken out at all. Garang would not have allowed foreign leaders, including his friends, to meddle in the internal affairs of South Sudan. In this connection, the diplomatic and political friendships demonstrated by some regional leaders towards Salva Kiir as a support for the people of South Sudan may epitomise what one could call cynicism or crocodile tear shedding. It is believed that crocodiles shed tears as they eat a person. The friendship that evolved then at the national and regional fora, in fact, may have an intimate connection with Garang's tragic demise.

President Museveni has on many occasions spoken of his resentment of Machar because of his relations with Khartoum following the Nasir episode in 1991. It is completely undiplomatic that a foreign leader invited to attend a national occasion would speak disparaging of some leaders. It should have been embarrassing for President Kiir that his guest, the president of a neighbouring country, spoke badly of his colleagues. It is a literal truth that the tribulations of South Sudan and its people began with the conspiracy to assassinate Garang, the SPLM chairman and commander in chief of SPLA, the first vice president of the Republic of the Sudan and president of the Government of Southern Sudan. No one in the SPLM or in the GoSS has ever investigated Museveni's role in the tragic crash of the presidential helicopter carrying

Garang while returning to South Sudan from a visit to Museveni's rural home in western Uganda. The "human error" concluded by the technical report of the helicopter crash could have been engineered for purposes which may be related to the rivalry for regional leadership in the Horn and Great Lakes Regions. In this respect, President Museveni had an important role in the death of Garang. The fact that Kiir refused to commission an independent inquiry, either by the SPLM/A or of the Government of Southern Sudan, speaks to this conspiracy.

Coming back to the immediate post-Garang situation in the SPLM, it was then that we began to see a strong ethnic and provincial jetstream that went on to rock the SPLM and the government of South Sudan. This occurred immediately after Kiir took the oath of office as first vice president of the Republic of the Sudan and president of GoSS. The violent political and social currents did not appear out of the blue skies. They were indeed part of the social and political engineering work that was meant to implement the Yei agenda. It is worth mentioning that the Yei agenda had multiple levels and dimensions. For the purpose of this discussion, the immediate scheme was to pull Kiir out and away from under the shadow of Garang's leadership canopy. Hitherto, some people would deny that Garang even had a deputy because Kiir was never in any way visible in the SPLM/A (Nyaba, 2010). Therefore, to become visible, Kiir required a complete demystification of Garang, undertaken simultaneously with the de-legitimisation and disempowerment of his lieutenants, disparagingly and collectively nicknamed "Garang's boys" or "orphans."

In the SPLM/A, nobody had the courage or audacity to openly speak ill of Dr. John Garang. However, in private conversations and group gossip, they demonized him. This spread like a virus, leading the new establishment to ostracize and marginalize Garang's former close lieutenants when it came to important decisions within the SPLM and GoSS. The ensuing witch-hunt against the Garang orphans was so intense that it visibly paralyzed the SPLM functions in the party, as well as in the Government of National Unity (GoNU) and in GoSS. The new team that now surrounded President Kiir included people who had never been part of the SPLM under Garang, leave alone its inner circle, and therefore they had no knowledge of the SPLM's inner workings. They threw out all the SPLM's strategy of transition from war to peace, making it difficult for the SPLM to start its political business.

As usually is such cases, conflict and infighting in organizations occur during times of relaxation and recreation rather than during times of crisis, when everyone is busy exerting efforts to contribute towards a common good. The infighting accompanying the change of guard in the SPLM, as well as the SPLA, commenced with Kiir's decision to reverse Garang's order to reorganize the SPLA command structure. Soon after taking the oath of office, Garang ordered the removal of some senior officers from active SPLA service. Salva Kiir reversed this order on account that most of the officers affected hailed from Warrap and Awiel. This action was in such political bad taste that it caused confusion in the army and eventually frustrated attempts by its leadership and top brass to carry out an effective de-politicization, reorganization, and professionalization. Kiir's attempts to endear himself to the other armed groups (Nuer tribal militias), integrating them with their inflated ranks into the SPLA, exacerbated the instability within the SPLA rank and file. The numbers from the militias surmounted the bona fide SPLA numbers, making the Nuer the single largest ethnic group in the army. This raised serious concerns among the Bahr el Ghazal political elite, who saw the Nuer dominance of the army as a threat to Kiir's (read: Dinka's) power. This kicked off the political struggle in the SPLM and the emergence of the Bahr el Ghazal Elders (BGE), the precursor of the Jieng Council of Elders (JCE) as a power centre around President Kiir.

This eased the witch-hunt against Garang's orphans as the attention now shifted to those within the system who were believed to threaten the new political and power architecture. It is worth recalling that Kiir intended to exploit the schisms within the Western Nuer community instigated by elements of SAF intelligence service, involving the personalities of Machar and Gen. Paulino Matip Nhial, which emerged during implementation of the Khartoum Agreement (1997). This led to skirmishes in Bentiu between the forces of Machar and Matip in which lives were lost. The intrusion of Kiir between Machar and Matip, by appointing Matip to the bogus position of deputy commander in chief, widened the split between the two Nuer leaders, and served to rein in Machar's ambitions for power.

While focused on Machar, President Kiir appeared to have eased his personal hostility towards Garang's orphans. In reality, however, he had passed that job to some ambitious anti-Garang elements from Bahr el Ghazal. In the space of only two years, Kiir engineered a realignment of political forces in the SPLM, bringing closer to him some lawyers who orchestrated his consolidation and personification of the SPLM's power and public authority. As I note in the coming lines, this was the beginning of the project to build a totalitarian dictatorship. Kiir started to make arbitrary political appointments and give out large sums of money to purchase and shore up his political support as the SPLM prepared for its 2nd National Convention.

There is something odd in the relationship between Kiir and Machar that may require further investigation in order to understand how in eight years of working together as president and vice president they ended putting the country in a destructive civil war. Kiir and Machar are both ethnocentric and represent the negative poles of their respective ethnic relations. They have a love-hate relationship. Both will deny any differences or conflict between them, although their actions speak to the contrary. They prefer to box each other in the shadows rather than face each other, whether in the party or in the cabinet. Machar likes to undermine his boss to expose his weaknesses to the public, instead of discussing face to face with him to rectify issues before the public is made aware. Machar was the virtual president of the GoSS during the early days of the interim period, when Kiir spent most of his time in Khartoum as first vice president of the Republic of the Sudan. It is true that some of Machar's shortcomings in government, including criminal overspending of his budget by a large margin without anything to show for that spending, was precisely because Kiir preferred not to discuss it with Machar either privately or in the cabinet. He preferred to act clandestinely to oust Machar from the office of the vice president as a means of solving the problem that existed between them.

This roundabout method of settling political and administrative difficulties in the SPLM and in the government had a disastrous effect on the functioning of the GoSS system. It would have been better to keep within the precincts of legitimacy and legality as circumscribed by the constitution and the law. This allowed for impersonality and objectivity in the functioning of the system. Afraid of confronting Machar on many of the flaws in the GoSS and in the state governments, Kiir designed a strategy of turning the SPLM's 2nd National Convention into a forum to impeach and vote out of office both Machar and Pagan Amum. It was not the breach of SPLM's order driving this decision but the urge to make things easy in both the party (SPLM) and in the government (GoSS) by bringing in James Wani as the SPLM vice chair, as well as vice president of the GoSS, and Taban Deng Gai as the SPLM secretary-general.

The clumsy manner that the president conducted the preparations to convene the SPLM's 2nd National Convention betrayed his real intentions, leading to the failure to achieve his objectives. Instead of the procedures provided for in the SPLM draft documents, President Kiir ordered the formation of a Convention Organizing Committee and appointed Comrade James Wani Igga to head it. This move circumvented the SPLM organs and instruments. By so doing, Chairman Kiir demonstrated he was not disposed to the party's internal democracy. He wanted to use his executive powers as the president of the GoSS to effect changes in the SPLM's leadership hierarchy, exploiting the mistakes and political differences/frictions both Machar and Pagan Amum had made or entertained with some of their colleagues in the SPLM and in the GoSS.

President Kiir ordered the SPLM's lawyers to insert an amendment into the SPLM Constitution. This gave the SPLM chairman (Kiir) powers to dismiss the first vice chair (Machar) and the secretary-general (Amum). As if this was not enough, President Kiir issued specific instructions to the SPLM States Congress supervisors to block delegates to the SPLM National Convention who were suspected to be sympathizers of Machar or Amum. The idea was to ensure an absolute majority in support of Chairman Kiir's objectives at the convention; namely, to endorse without political glitch or hitch the party's draft basic documents (removing the position of first vice chair) and to elect the National Liberation Council (NLC) to rubber stamp the decisions arrived at outside the party institutions and organs. Kiir sent James Wani, chair of the Convention Organising Committee, to tour the northern states to drum up support for the president and his strategy to restructure the SPLM leadership.

The Interim National Liberation Council (INLC) convened a few days before the national convention to draw up the agenda for the convention. Kiir's objectives, the intended thrust of the SPLM's 2nd National Convention, had been kept under lid until then. They surfaced during the deliberations of INLC, disguised as "constitutional amendments" to reduce to only one the three deputies to the SPLM chairman. Comrade James Wani was to be the only SPLM deputy chair; this amendment automatically removed Machar from the SPLM hierarchy and, by virtue of that, from the position of vice president of GoSS. The president would have achieved his objective of removing Machar through his trusted lawyers in the SPLM. The other part of the conspiracy, which was to surface only on the floor of the national convention, was the election to the position of the secretary-general. To this end, Chairman Kiir assigned Yasir Said Arman to mobilize the SPLM's Northern Sector to elect Taban Deng Gai as the SPLM secretary-general.

However, Kiir's plan ran into trouble during the deliberations of the INLC. The lawyers at the centre of this conspiracy failed to convince the INLC members as to why it was necessary to reduce the number of the chairman's deputies. This drew acrimonious debate and generated bad blood between some members, prompting Kiir to solicit the opinion of two veteran South Sudan leaders who were observers to the national convention. Both Abel Alier and Gen. Joseph Lagu advised against making radical changes that might cause friction and conflict within the SPLM. Therefore, afraid of an imminent split at the SPLM National Convention, which could have serious negative ramifications for the SPLM and Southern Sudan, President Kiir backed down in order to maintain the status quo within the SPLM.

The idea of personally targeting someone simply because one did not like him, unless undertaken democratically in accordance with the rules and procedures, could spell doom for the organization. It was not enough for Comrade Kiir to say he did not like Machar and ignore the regulations for bringing about his removal from the SPLM hierarchy. This smacked of ignorance of political processes and democratic practice, attributable to the militarized character of the SPLM/A leadership, which engendered in Comrade Kiir dictatorial and autocratic tendencies. This forced the drafting of the SPLM basic documents and the South Sudan Transitional Constitution (2011) texts with specific persons in mind. This was against the usual practice of defining duties, responsibilities, and roles, and only then electing the competent individuals to perform those duties.

The removal of Machar and Amum, if necessary on account of their individual mistakes and not because of any personal problems with the SPLM chairman, did not require changes to the SPLM constitution. In democratic practice, the office is separate from the person holding it, who then would be subject to disciplinary action in accordance with the internal regulations. The problem in the SPLM leadership was organizational. The idea of reducing the number of deputies to one would not have arisen at all had the SPLM constitution and internal regulations assigned roles and responsibilities to the three deputies commensurate with the party, executive, and legislative functions of the SPLM at the national, southern Sudan and state levels in the country. For instance, the first deputy chair would assume the responsibility of overseeing the SPLM's executive functions in the GoSS and in the ten states of southern Sudan. The second deputy would oversee the SPLM's legislative functions in the SSLA and in the states' legislative assemblies, while the third deputy chairman would oversee the SPLM's executive and legislative functions in the Government of National Unity and those of the 16 northern states. The lack of identification and definition of these roles and responsibilities generated incessant complaints by many people in the SPLM, including the chairman, that they had nothing to do. This betrays the personal rather than organizational nature of Kiir's case against Machar and Amum. Here, at the organizational peg, anchors the SPLM crisis and the predicament of the South Sudanese people.

The SPLM's 2nd National Convention was a defeat for autocracy and a victory for democracy in the SPLM and in South Sudan. However, this victory did not cultivate democracy in the SPLM in terms of improving its internal and external democratic governance. The beneficiaries of this victory — Machar and Amum — did not exploit it to organize and build democratic institutions inside the SPLM to prevent Kiir, or any other leader, from repeating the same thing. As persons who had survived a plot to remove them, they should have combined forces with other democratic elements in the movement to focus on building the organs of the SPLM. Instead, they allowed President Kiir to use his executive powers of the state to dodge and paralyze the functioning of the SPLM organs and institutions.

The first step following the election of the National Liberation Council (NLC) and the appointment of the Political Bureau was to form the NLC into committees corresponding to the standing committees in the SSLA and to the line ministries in the executive. Each member of the Political Bureau would then head each standing committee of the NLC. This is precisely because as the SPLM's policy-making organ, each standing committee generates policies which, once approved by the Political Bureau, the General Secretariat would transform into legislative and executive plans to be implemented by the respective institutions. I am not completely sure whether President Kiir would have suppressed the work of the NLC committees since he would only chair the plenaries of its session. It is obvious that Machar, Amum, and many others in the SPLM were not conversant with party organizational and democratic practice and, as a result, played in Kiir's autocratic tendency.

Democracy is a political culture and a way of life. Not all who chant and brag about democracy are necessarily democrats. Some people desire democracy just for political expediency and they will not travel the length and breadth of the globe to practice or to apply the democratic principles in their political realm. President Kiir remains more of a soldier and an intelligence officer than a practicing politician. He does not make any pretence to being democratic. Thus, in the context of what followed, in the aftermath of the SPLM's 2nd National Convention, President Kiir knew he would not again resort to meetings or conventions in order to realise his political objective of dealing with his detractors in the SPLM. Like a praying mantis, he would mark his time only to act at the appropriate opportunity to ambush and destroy his detractors.

From May 2008 until the end of the interim period, the Government of Southern Sudan had two important events to carry out as part of the implementation of the CPA. These were the general and presidential elections (April 2010) and the holding of the South Sudan Referendum (January 2011). If President Kiir was to succeed in completing both processes he would need to put a moratorium on his personal power schemes in order to minimize political friction within the SPLM. This was important, if for no other reason, to prevent an implosion in the SPLM, in the GoSS, and in Southern Sudan. He had to jealously safeguard the unity of the SPLM and the unity of the people of Southern Sudan to enable him achieve success in the conduct of the elections and the referendum on self-determination. Despite this, however, Kiir did not abandon his scheme. From the depth of his heart he believed, and indeed to date still believes, that the greatest threat to his power is from Dr. Riek Machar. This was partly because Machar has never hidden his ambition, and party because of the Nuer's superior numbers in the SPLA after the absorption of the Nuer militias. His attempts to use the national convention to remove Machar had failed miserably. Therefore, he needed to wrongfoot Machar by choosing him as his running mate in the elections for the presidency of the GoSS.

Kiir's indefinite postponement of Machar's dismissal was a clever move. There were many battles ahead with the NCP, specifically the referendum bill on self-determination, which required Machar's cooperation. It was a short time between April 2010 (the elections) and 9 January 2011 (the referendum), during which the National Legislative Assembly had to promulgate the Southern Sudan Referendum Bill, otherwise it would be impossible to conduct the referendum. There were no two individuals better suited for this task other than Machar and Amum. Thereafter, President Kiir engaged his main detractors in continuous talks with the NCP over the Southern Sudan Referendum Bill and the National Security Bill, among other issues pending in the National Legislature. In Kiir's scheme of things, this was to divert their attention do they would completely forget the internal SPLM power squabbles.

It was an open secret among SPLM members that Kiir neither forgets nor forgives his detractors. He would mark his time, scheming until an opportunity presented itself for him to ambush and destroy his enemy. Machar should have known better and acted more carefully when dealing with President Kiir. He tactfully and politely could have turned down Kiir's offer to be a running mate in 2010 on the understanding that Machar would contest for the presidency of South Sudan in 2020, when Kiir would have completed his two terms in office. Such a strategy would not have brought conflict in the SPLM or war in the country. On the contrary, Machar acted opportunistically and didn't hesitate to take up his position as Kiir's deputy president. In Machar's scheme of things, continuing as Kiir's deputy gave him the liberty to operate like an entity separate from Kiir's presidency. Thus, instead of operating in cooperation with each other, their efforts tended to cancel out each other.[67]

The internal crisis played out again in the run-up to the elections. Elections and preparations for elections were functions of the SPLM General Secretariat under the secretary-general. However, while Kiir feigned a truce with Machar, he had not completely relinquished his grudge against Amum. In the same manner that someone other than the secretary-general presided over the Convention Organizing Committee, Kiir would not allow the SPLM General Secretariat to conduct the preparations for the elections. He cowed the SPLM Political Bureau to allow him to have his way again in mutilating SPLM institutions, playing the same game as during the SPLM's 2nd National Convention. Kiir decreed the formation of a 45-member National Elections Strategy Committee (NESC), to be chaired by Comrade James Wani Igga, to manage the SPLM's elections process. This repeated the mistakes committed in the run-up to the SPLM's 2nd National Convention, but this time with devastating consequences for the SPLM.

Since Kiir was the only SPLM candidate contesting the seat of the president of GoSS, the Political Bureau cleared him unopposed. There were some members of the SPLM who Kiir did not want to contest

---

[67] The presidential and general elections in 2010 demonstrated this contradiction. Although a running mate of Kiir for the presidency of Southern Sudan travelling together the breadth of Southern Sudan, Machar campaigned against SPLM candidates by supporting the opposition candidates in Unity and Upper Nile states. In the Chollo Kingdom he was concerned more about the performance of the SPLM-DC candidates.

the elections in various electoral constituencies on the SPLM ticket. The Political Bureau thwarted the regulations, guidelines, and criteria, which the Candidate Nomination Subcommittee had designed for members who would contest on the SPLM ticket. They instead opted for a flawed process, an Electoral College System designed by James Wani to block the SPLM leaders whom Salva did not want to contest elections. The NESC recruited outsiders, mostly NCP operatives, on the basis of friendship and social relationships, to undertake an internal SPLM exercise to evaluate and vet for nomination bona fide SPLM members. This nomination exercise was so subjective that it turned into a fiasco. On flimsy reasons they rejected or deliberately failed to qualify for nomination some senior SPLM leaders and cadres. In Rumbek, the Electoral College disqualified Daniel Awet Akot on the grounds that he was not a committed SPLM member. This was considered a big joke because Daniel Awet was a member of the SPLM/A Political Military High Command and later a member of its Political Bureau. How could he have been appointed to these positions without a commitment to the SPLM? In Mundri, the Electoral College rejected Kosti Manibe's candidature on the false assertion that he did not possess a university degree. The truth is that Kosti is a graduate of Kampala's Makerere University.

These were absurd machinations to elbow out certain unwanted people. In this particular case, the machination was in favour of Dr. Richard Mulla who contested and won the constituency as an independent, leaving President Kiir to appoint Kosti Manibe to the Assembly. His aim, as mentioned elsewhere, was to weed out the SPLM of leaders and cadres who likely would not toe Kiir's political line. I was one of the victims of this discriminative selection. On the flimsy ground that I had not presented a birth certificate, I was disqualified to contest on the SPLM ticket the Upper Nile gubernatorial position. This was to give room to a cadre considered more loyal to Kiir.

At the end of the nomination exercise, more than 300 SPLM members defied the party and contested the election for gubernatorial and geographical electoral constituencies as independent candidates, and women and party lists. Where the returning officers stood their ground against intimidation, independent candidates trounced the official SPLM candidates. Machar opted to support his spouse, Angelina Teny, as an independent candidate against Taban Deng Gai, the SPLM nominee for the gubernatorial position in Unity State, even though Machar was Kiir's running mate for presidency of government of South Sudan. This was a clear demonstration of political bad faith. As a member of the

Political Bureau that discussed and decided on Taban Deng as the SPLM flagbearer for Unity State's gubernatorial candidate, Machar should have convinced his spouse to abide by the party's decision, or he should have supported Taban Deng to implement the party decision. Democratic principles and practice obliged Machar to implement the decision of the majority in the Political Bureau. However, by insisting on supporting the independent candidacy of his wife he acted undemocratically and, therefore, forfeited any moral authority to criticize Kiir for his dictatorial way of imposing certain candidates.

The same Political Bureau rejected the presentation of the subcommittee on candidate nomination guidelines, procedures, and rules that the author led, in which it was proposed that the key to resolving such disputes was to conduct primaries. These remain difficulties of democratic practice and processes, which all must work to overcome in the social and political engineering processes. However, this incident must be one of the reasons that Kiir was not happy with Machar. As earlier mentioned, Kiir still harboured a grudge against Machar, even though he had kept him as deputy president. The only problem was that he employed political violence to generate secondary conflicts and to take the matter outside its political context.

The Southern Sudan Referendum Bill sailed through the National Legislative Assembly and the referendum on self-determination was conducted on time, as required in the CPA and the Interim National Constitution. Once the results of the referendum on self-determination showed support for independence, Kiir re-energized his scheme for personal rule, albeit through a constitutional provision. A clause in the Interim Constitution of Southern Sudan (2005) provided that if the results of the Southern Sudan Referendum were in favour of independence, then the ICSS would automatically transform into the Transitional Constitution of South Sudan (2011), with changes in the text affecting only the name and other minor alterations.[68] It therefore required only a committee of lawyers to review and undertake the task of expunging the ICSS of those provisions incompatible with the new status of Southern Sudan.

It was obvious that President Kiir was not satisfied with this provision. He wanted a complete new constitutional text. He commissioned a

---

[68] Section 208.7 provides that if the outcome of the referendum on self-determination favours secession, this Constitution shall remain in force as the Constitution of a sovereign and independent Southern Sudan, and the parts, chapters, articles, subarticles, and schedules of this Constitution that provide for national institutions, representation, rights, and obligations shall be deemed to have been duly repealed.

Constitution Committee, made up of 90 per cent SPLM members, to write a draft constitutional text. Kiir wanted more power than that provided for in the ICSS 2005. To this end he appointed the same lawyers who bungled the SPLM's 2nd National Convention (2008), to draft, similar to the SPLM Constitution, certain provisions with specific persons in mind. Section 104(2) of the Transitional Constitution of South Sudan (2011) was drafted on behest of President Kiir in clear reference to Machar: "The vice president may be removed by the President, or by a decision passed by two-thirds majority of all members of the National Legislative Assembly."

The trend to totalitarianism, which Kiir exhibited during the entire period — the unbridled corruption in government, which saw unequal distribution of financial and economic resources of the country in favour of certain states, and many other concerns — triggered agitation for a federal system rather than the decentralized system of governance in South Sudan. A sizeable membership of the SSLA, mainly from Equatoria and Upper Nile, wanted the words "federal system of government" inserted into the preamble and defined in the new constitutional text. Members from Bahr el Ghazal and parts of western Equatoria opposed it, opting for "decentralized system of government." This threatened a deadlock. In order to avoid the risk of a divided house in the declaration of independence, Kiir called Machar to inform him that he would remain the vice president and, therefore, should not accept the insertion of federalism in the constitutional text. This was how the federalist bloc lost out, leaving a bitter taste in their mouths because Machar had ordered all the Nuer members in the SSLA to not support federation.

South Sudan became independent based on an undemocratic constitution. President Kiir achieved the powers he had wanted all along: to rule unfettered by democratic or patriotic pretence. He ordered the appointment of 60 new members of the SSLA and the absorption into the SSLA of 96 former members of the National Legislative Assembly in Khartoum. The SSLA became a parliament in which two or more members represented a single constituency. This was Kiir's deliberate policy to emasculate the institution and render it dysfunctional. He appointed a cabinet of 32 ministers, more than half of whom were from the Dinka ethnicity. Further appointments were not only exclusively Dinka but also hailing from his home area of Warrap. These included the chief justice, governor of Central Bank, inspector-general of police, director-general of national security, and director general of immigration.

It was obvious that Kiir had embarked on building a system that operated by presidential decree rather than legislative process. This was because the decisions leading to the decrees were decided not through the formal party institutions but in informal ethnic and provincial lobby groups created to bypass the SPLM institutions and organs. The JCE, which served as Kiir's power base, had the greatest influence on the president. In fact, Kiir implemented the JCE policies aimed at social, economic, and political empowerment of the Dinka elite and businesses that were mainly from Warrap and Aweil. Before Kiir would appoint leaders from other ethnic communities, they were vetted by the JCE to determine their attitudes towards JCE policies.[69] In only the first two years of independence, power had shifted from the Office of the President to the JCE, making the president a hostage of the tribal cartel.

It was an attempt to control the political developments in the SPLM that later turned toxic and traumatic. It did not take long before the independence euphoria died down and the reality of deep social, economic, and political problems caused by eight years of misrule started to show. It is permissible to pass a blanket judgement on the SPLM's political failures. Those who could have resisted autocracy chose not to. In a situation where institutions have been emasculated, responsibility for commission or omission must lie with the principal. Chairman Kiir, his deputies, the secretary-general, and the entire membership of the Political Bureau are culpable for the SPLM's political failures. However, Chairman Kiir takes the greatest responsibility because he used state instruments, directed from a tribal command post, to see to it that nothing functioned in the SPLM, all because he was opposed to Comrade Amum being secretary-general. The party's centre of gravity had shifted over time from SPLM House to the Office of the President. This happened so that Kiir could continue to wage his campaign against the vice president and the secretary-general, but also anyone else — including ministers rumoured or named by the National Security Bureau — considered sympathetic to these two SPLM leaders.

I was the minister for higher education, science, and technology in the first government of independent South Sudan and witnessed the demoralization in the ministry due to the deliberate sabotage of our plan for building a world-class higher education system. In one and half years in the ministry, we could not implement our budget

---

[69] The SSLA of Manasseh Magog Rundial (Nuer), the speaker in 2013, was a case in point; similarly, the election of Anthony Lino Makana (Azande) in 2016. Once the JCE had decided on a favourable individual they would inform President Kiir, who would then order the SPLM chief whip to twist the arms of the members in a SPLM caucus meeting.

because the Ministry of Finance, on direction from the Office of the President, would not release the funds. In this respect, it is necessary to contextualize SPLM failures. The SPLM system decayed from the top of its political system. The political failures occurred because the leaders acted tactically, protecting their power positions rather than strategically addressing the wider picture of social and economic development of the country. These failures fed into the power struggle at the top echelons, which aimed to change individuals rather than the faulty system itself. This was a misplaced strategy based on a false reading of the internal SPLM configuration. The responsibility for the SPLM's dysfunctionality rested not on individuals failing but on the absence of institutionalized power relations in the system. This triggered a disproportionate reaction that targeted individuals, and by extension their ethnicity. Although the president viewed it as an exit strategy from a relationship with Machar and Amum that had nagged him for a long time, it instead compounded the problems and plunged the country into a deeper social, economic, and political crisis.

How and Why Salva Kiir Did What He Did

The political space President Kiir traversed, after he assumed leadership of Southern Sudan in August 2005, to arrive at the decision to dismiss his vice president, Dr. Riek Machar, and the entire cabinet on 23 July 2013, could not have been possible without the collaboration, cooperation, and active participation of all those clamouring against him today. Dictators the world over invariably emerge from modest backgrounds, build themselves or are built into totalitarian despots through the steady and forceful monopoly of truth. Kiir has proven his adroit mastery of political strategy, allowing him against all popular expectation to survive at the helm of SPLM power.

When Kiir first became president of the Government of South Sudan and first vice president of the Republic of the Sudan he appeared uninterested in public grandeur. He feigned simplicity but continued his reckless lifestyle, spending time with dubious people, even street girls. He drank openly and publicly at "Home and Away", a Juba restaurant he owned with his business associates, sometimes in the company of known prostitutes. No one in Juba would have suspected but this was Kiir's greatest strength. As an intelligence officer, Kiir did not trust anyone with gathering information. He did it himself and indeed knew the nitty-gritty details about everything that took place in his realm. But he lacked the courage to take action, or did he just pretend to be a coward? Kiir knew who in his government slept with whom and who stole what. Indeed, he sometimes encouraged them to steal under the guise of "payback time" or, as he said to his Warrap people, "If you don't get rich while I am the president, you will never make it again." President Kiir encouraged the GoSS ministers and SPLA generals to steal money and amass wealth from their commands. He turned a blind eye and deaf ears to the over overindulgences of his deputy and the SSLA speaker, the judiciary, the police, and the civil service. Little did they know it was blackmail!

To acquire absolute power and build a totalitarian regime in South Sudan, Kiir constructed a system that essentially blackmailed everyone in the GoSS, the business community, and elements of civil society, many of whom he showered with expensive gifts. When the SPLM members who served in the GoNU came back to Juba complaining about their mistreatment in Khartoum, the president offered them luxury V8 Toyota Land Cruisers. This was only to whet their appetites. Kiir had the auditor-general's reports that showed how much money had been given to individuals in or out of GoSS, and the amounts of money that certain ministers couldn't account for. Therefore, everyone felt intimidated, so much so that no one in the executive, legislature, judiciary, or civil service could really confront the president over some of his fatal decisions, which bordered on treason. He emasculated these institutions through favours, blackmail, and outright cruel negligence. As mentioned above, Kiir, by all means, will avoid direct confrontation but will mark his time until he has an opportunity to humiliate the recalcitrant.

Therefore, to return to the questions above, no one attempted to stop the president from whatever he chose to do. This included the use of the military to twice in two years chase Machar away from Juba. He had essentially blackmailed everybody. He sanctioned the formation of the JCE and inflated their egos by allowing them to believe that the power belonged to them, thus becoming accomplices to his crimes. This was at least the impression elements of the JCE had when in July 2013 they came up with the idea of the *dotku beny* campaign and the recruitment of the Mathiang Anyoor militias. There were grounds for every one of the state institutions — the legislature, judiciary, Army, and National Security — to call Kiir to task for violating the Constitution and for the events leading up to the civil war and the present socioeconomic and political crisis in South Sudan.

Let us begin with the SPLM as the ruling party. SPLM members, whether leaders, cadres, or activists, watched in silence as Chairman Kiir slowly and steadily turned the SPLM into a hollow shell. He sabotaged its political functions at all levels. The reason is simple and is related to the SPLM's culture of self-preservation, indifference, conspiracies, favouritism, jealousy, double-crossing, and the lack of internal solidarity occasioned by extreme militarism during the war of national liberation. This culture generated such a sense of mutual alienation that one closed one's eyes to avoid implication if something did not directly concern one. Thus, no one in the Political Bureau, NLC, or in the General Secretariat would come to the rescue of the secretary-general when Chairman Kiir targeted him for the historical mutual mistrust. Sometimes, due to jealousy and envy, one was left to carry one's own cross on flimsy and false charges aimed at putting one in a negative light. In this environment it was impossible to criticise the leader. People met ugly scenarios with silence in order to keep the peace. Kiir did what he did because people felt extremely weak and isolated, and shared no common values to invoke solidarity.

When Kiir returned into the SPLA ranks redundant and corrupt officers Garang had demobilized, it was an indicator or precursor of the type of army he wanted. Many of these men, prior to their dismissals, had been senior to the SPLA's chief of general staff, which created an imbalance in the command structure. These commanders worked to sabotage the chain of command by disobeying or openly defying the chief of staff's orders and commands. Kiir may have wanted to prove wrong Garang's appointment of Gen. Oyay Deng Ajak. It is no wonder that indiscipline and corruption pervaded the army. Theft of soldiers' salaries by their commanders, who send to the administration fictitious lists full of ghost soldiers, was common in the SPLA. In the rush for the primitive accumulation of wealth, some commanders, now generals, also went into corrupt business associations with foreigners to earn quick money.

President Kiir did not respect his army, otherwise how could he as president of the republic and commander in chief of the SPLA recruit private armies — namely, Dotku Beny and Mathiang Anyoor — parallel to the SPLA? This was treacherous. In some countries it would have been enough to impeach him. In South Sudan it appeared quite normal that the legislature and the army top brass did not protest when President Kiir went to Luri Farm to pass out his private militia. The only protest they registered was to boycott the function, which was officiated by their commander in chief and the minister of defence and veteran affairs. The Transitional Constitution of South Sudan 2011 Art. 103(2) provides for the impeachment of the president of the republic in case of high treason, gross violation of the Constitution, or gross misconduct in the management of national affairs. There is a rejoinder in the same article specifying how to conduct this impeachment. Let us assume that no one in the SPLM system would dare to lodge a case for Kiir's impeachment. Why wouldn't the opposition parties, members, or non-members of the SSLA or the civil society request to impeach President Kiir for the gross misconduct of lying that there was a coup attempt on 15 December 2013? Kiir brought into South Sudan without parliamentary approval or authority the UPDF and Ugandan Air Force to engage the rebels in the territory between Juba and Bor.

High-sounding actions like the parliamentary impeachment of a president seldom occur in situations of ethnic politics, political intimidation, or self-preservation, or in a culture of submerged political consciousness. The SSLA teemed with ethnic chauvinists and individuals whose allegiance was *only* to President Kiir and therefore would not countenance his impeachment. But the greatest political disaster to have befallen the SPLM and the people of South Sudan was the wholesale incorporation into the SPLM of former members of the National Congress Party (NCP) who came in with their own culture of corruption, intrigue, sycophancy, and flattery, who outshone the SPLM's own in leader worship to win over President Kiir. Those people, unlike the bona fide SPLM cadres, would not make the mistake of publicly criticising the leader but would continuously praise him, even for obvious mistakes. Not only that but they also were regular attendants at his court, even at odd hours of the day, engaging in gossip and small talk. They took over the SPLM and the GoSS and elbowed out Kiir's comrades in the armed struggle.

This capture of the SPLM and state institutions by former NCP leaders and operatives made it easy for Kiir's decisions to sail through not only the SSLA but also the cabinet, where the individual sense of self-preservation was ever more pronounced. This was to maintain ministerial portfolios by towing the president's political line. In this manner, Kiir succeeded in building a totalitarian dictatorial regime. This was partly because of the weak political culture in South Sudan and partly because Kiir used corruption, blackmail, and outright intimidation to cow the people.

Preparation for Military Action Against Riek Machar

The "dangerous slip of the tongue" (Hilde, 2016:158), which set rolling the fireball of conflict in the SPLM leadership, was Salva Kiir's weather balloon to test the political climate in the SPLM and in the country. But the venue was not appropriate. If Comrade Deng Alor and the other SPLM members present at that conversation had not picked up Kiir's slip of the tongue as a serious concern warranting a SPLM Political Bureau discussion, it would have fizzled out there and then like an accidental fart. In a village setting, one would be seen as a notorious misfit if you commented on a public fart of the chief. These are matters discussed in whispers and gossip. It became Deng Alor's crime against President Kiir when he raised the issue of the "dangerous slip of the tongue" in another setting. This was enough reason for Kiir to stop the political processes towards convening the SPLM's 3rd National Convention, scheduled for May 2013.

The slip of the tongue was about power succession in the SPLM and by extension the presidency of the Republic of South Sudan. Kiir's mode immediately changed after Machar jumped into ring to submit his bid for the SPLM chairmanship, which meant positioning himself for the presidency of South Sudan come the elections in April 2015. It was not an easy matter for Kiir, who had spent 21 years enduring personal humiliation under Garang's shadow. The matter efficaciously raised the temperature and destroyed all the existing political and comradely relations. It almost acquired the dimension of a crime or "treasonable" offence. The imperial president that Kiir had become in eight years would definitely take the country to war to prevent his loss of power.

Power succession in the context of South Sudan's ethnic configuration, implying that the power centre was shifting away from Kiir, became a matter of great concern to the Bahr el Ghazal Elders (BGE) and the Aweil-Warrap business cartels. The machinery to defend Kiir's presidency ceased to be a national or constitutional concern. It became tribal (Dinka) and, indeed, a sectional (Rek Dinka) concern. The JCE went to work spinning a credible and explosive narrative about what Taban Deng Gai and the Nuer gentleman in Canada had said regarding the Nuer going to war with the Dinka in order to fulfil Ngundeng's prophecy in respect of Machar's leadership of South Sudan.[70]

The political atmosphere in the SPLM resembled the time just before a great storm. The rumour mill swirled, quietly gathering up every

---

[70] Only the Nuer people know Ngundeng's prophecy and they keep modifying it to suit the prevailing occasion. It only surfaced after the Nasir Declaration in 1991, when Dr. Riek Machar, Dr. Lam Akol, and Cdr. Gordon Koang led a rebellion against Dr. John Garang. Since then the Nuer intellectuals who hoped to gain politically and economically from Machar's political leadership have supported the fabrications.

element of the Dinka-Nuer animosity. In the space of four months in 2013, between March and July, no political energy flowed in the SPLM circulatory system. The time for convening the state congresses, as well as the 3rd National Convention, scheduled for May 2013, passed without notice. Chairman Kiir ignored repeated requests to call the Political Bureau meetings and refused to call to session the National Liberation Council. He paralyzed the SPLM organs, enabling him to effect changes without reference to or interference from either of his two deputies or the secretary-general. He removed the governors of Lakes and Unity states, Chol Tong Mayay and Taban Deng Gai respectively, from their positions. This move was quite spectacular because the president had no constitutional right to relieve an elected governor, save in an emergency situation. The case against them was that they were connected to Machar. And then, without warning, President Kiir on 23rd July dismissed Machar as his deputy and sacked the entire cabinet.

The political developments in the SPLM leadership must have been confusing for many people then in Juba. No one in the SPLM could explain the unfolding situation, which was shrouded in the typical secrecy of the SPLM/A where every message was classified "top secret." Kiir was not talking or making public statements; some of us who were in government received news of our sackings from the cabinet as a blessing in disguise. Machar did not show any signs of disturbance. It was Taban Deng who openly displayed hostility to Kiir for relieving him of the governorship of Unity State, a position that he had used only to amass wealth and wives. This reaction on the part of Taban Deng laid credence to the JCE narrative of an approaching Dinka-Nuer war and they started to prepare the ground. President Kiir paid visits to Aweil and Warrap where the mobilization and recruitment of Dotku Beny had commenced in earnest. The manner and speed at which this force formed suggested that the president was in grave danger, that even the SPLA to which he was commander in chief could not sufficiently protect or defend him.

The question of power succession, read as power shifting from Kiir (Dinka) to Machar (Nuer), raised to a high pitch the political temperature in the Dinka areas. However, this political tension was hardly felt in Juba except by the few people in the loop. The manner in which the Dinka and Nuer ethnicities exercised power, politically and economically marginalizing the other ethnic groups, must have contributed to this general indifference to the smouldering conflict between the Dinka and the Nuer. The SSTV broadcast daily reports on the president's visit to northern Bahr el Ghazal. It was clear Salva Kiir was mobilizing the people of Aweil and Warrap and yet no one, including the Nuer leaders, who were targets of this diatribe, took note of this development.[71] President Kiir ordered Gen. Paul Malong Awan, the governor of Aweil, to mobilize, recruit, and transport to Juba 3,000 young men. They trained at Kiir's Luri Farm, to the chagrin of the Army's chief of general staff, Gen. James Hoth Mai, who in fact did not protest or attempt to counter the president's unconstitutional action of recruiting and training a private army.

The flabbergasting aspect of this conundrum was the lack of corresponding suspicious political or military activities on the Nuer side that would point to any plans to unleash a war on the Dinka. If the narrative of Rev. Joshua Dau was correct, then there would have been a corresponding mobilization and hostile propaganda emanating from the Nuer side. This was not the case. The Nuer side seemed unperturbed by the hot political air emitted by the JCE, who were fine-tuning and accelerating the pace of their plans. The lack of preparation on the Nuer side betrayed a salient truth that the plot was a one-sided affair to serve the JCE's political and power agenda. President Kiir passed his militia out of the training centre before the D-day and time for action had arrived. The army command refused to integrate the Dotku Beny militia into the SPLA. This prompted the president to commission them in alignment with and under the command of the National Security Service, in terms of salary, uniforms, and armaments.

The president and the JCE had moved faster than was necessary. The anticipated Nuer declaration of war because of President Kiir's dismissal of Machar from the position of vice president did not occur. Kiir had passed out the force from the training centre and yet they had nothing to do. They drew up a plan dividing Juba residential suburbs into sections and engaged the force in cleaning up those suburbs, moving from house to house. This plan turned out to be a stratagem to survey, reconnoitre, and diligently map the areas populated by ethnic Nuer in Juba. This was in preparation for the plan to carry out a targeted massacre of ethnic Nuer.

The dismissal of Machar and the sacking of the cabinet passed without much noise. The political environment in the SPLM remained

---

[71] At one of the political rallies held in Akon, his home village, President Kiir, speaking in Dinka, had this to say: "This power I have now belongs to you but some people want to snatch it from me. Will you accept that they take it be force or should I leave it to them?" The crowd roared back, "We will not accept. We will fight to defend you and your power."

calm but tense. Attempts to set something moving in the party, after the formation of the new cabinet, the appointment of James Wani Igga as vice president and the election of Manasseh Magog Rundial as speaker of the SSLA, came to nothing. President Kiir adamantly refused to open the party to dialogue; its democratic processes remained paralyzed and timelines and schedules were completely disrupted, requiring political will to reset them. Kiir had already readied himself for military action against Machar, Amum, and Rebecca Nyandeng Garang. What was not obvious was how he would execute his plan. He was counting on the rumours that the Nuer would go to war to impose Machar as president. However, the political events after 23 July 2013, the day he dismissed Machar, only showed Kiir as the one on the political offensive. He was not waiting for Machar to make a move.

Machar's much-anticipated move did not come until after a lot of political sewage had passed under the bridge in the form of stupefying ethnic and provincial competitiveness. In fact, Machar came late into the game owing to the influence of Taban Deng Gai, Ezekiel Lol Gatkuoth, and Angelina Teny, Machar's wife. The initial efforts were to approach President Kiir to see how he could accommodate those who had lost out in the cabinet reshuffle. This was the completely wrong approach to the issues at hand; being a minister in government was not a permanent situation or a birthright. The debate then shifted from accommodation in the system to returning the SPLM to the driver's seat. It was clear that the former NCP operatives had informally taken over the SPLM leadership through their personal relations with Kiir, elbowing out its bona fide members, many of whom were members of the Political Bureau. It became imperative to involve Machar, the first vice chair, and Amum, the secretary-general, now restricted to his house, to make it an exclusive SPLM affair.

Our meetings, which bordered on social rather than political gatherings, shifted from the houses of Gen. Oyay Deng and Dr. Cirino Ofuho Hiteng, to the house of Machar and occasionally to the house of Rebecca Nyandeng Garang. It was during this time that the SPLM's internal dynamics began to change. There was a noticeable withdrawal from the group by three colleagues hailing from Bahr el Ghazal, whose names I don't want to divulge. Because of their absence, Machar assumed leadership of the group by virtue of his position in the SPLM. The objective of the group was reforming the SPLM system, not snatching power from Kiir. The group became more resolved to return the SPLM to its rightful place within the power structure. Meanwhile, the president was more adamant than ever in his refusal to let the SPLM organs function.[72]

The group decided to call a press conference to put pressure on Kiir to lift the embargo on the SPLM organs and to call the Political Bureau to session. On 6 December the members of the Political Bureau (Machar, Pagan Amum, Deng Alor, Rebecca Nyandeng Garang, Kosti Manibe, Alfred Lado-Gore, and others) held the press conference at SPLM House. The statement distributed to the press highlighted the SPLM grassroots' concerns about the party's deviation from the SPLM vision, corruption in government, tribalism and ubiquitous insecurity and ethnic conflicts, and the apparent regional and international isolation of the youngest state in Africa and the world. The leaders made an open request to the party chairman to call to session the National Liberation Council (NLC) but asked that he first convene the Political Bureau in order to set the agenda for the NLC session. The press covered the conference and even the ministers of interior and information and broadcasting attended.

President Kiir saw the press conference as an opportunity to implement his elaborate plan against his detractors in the SPLM. The Security and Intelligence Bureau blacklisted everyone who had attended the press conference. He immediately ordered the SPLM General Secretariat to prepare for convening the session of the NLC. It had not met for a little over five years, not since its election in June 2008. The General Secretariat had only to implement the orders from the chairman in terms of the agenda, the political and organizational materials to be presented at the meeting, the number of participants and the meeting timeline determined.

I believe Kiir was weary of debates and political discussion. Moreover, he did not want to repeat his experience at the SPLM's 2nd National Convention 2008, which overruled him. In order to circumvent the democratic channels required for removing his detractors, Kiir decided on a two-track plan. He formed a committee to investigate Pagan Amum on several issues pertaining to the management of SPLM resources. The committee had presented its report to him and, therefore, wanted the NLC to pass and endorse the committee's recommendation to dismiss

---

[72] Comprising Dr. Riek Machar, Pagan Amum, Rebecca Nyandeng Garang, Deng Alor, John Luk, Kosti Manibe Ngai (all of whom were members of the SPLM Political Bureau), Alfred Lado-Gore, Dr. Peter Adwok Nyaba, Dr. Cirino Ofuho Hiteng, Dr. Majak d'Agoot, Gen. Oyay Deng Ajak, Gen. Gier Chuong Aluong, Eng. Chol Tong Mayai, Hon. Madut Biar, Taban Deng Gai, and Angelina Jany Teny.

Amum as secretary-general, waive his immunity, and send him to court for other administrative and financial charges made against him.

The action against Machar was military in nature, but it required another trigger, one that Military Intelligence would invoke as soon as the NLC session ended. The president had prepared to pre-empt any violent Nuer action by raising his private army and now saw to it that he would be the first to strike. In order to trigger his military plan, Kiir was counting heavily on Nuer social psychology and traditional warfare, which does not require advance preparation. The Nuer more often than not do not investigate the reasons for a fight and do not hesitate to enter any battle (*wannae thinh*). They inquire about the cause of the fight only later, whether in defeat or victory. The Nuer fight without considering or calculating the balance of forces between them and the enemy and, indeed, unlike many other peoples, they are not much troubled about the prospect of being killed. This is the psychological makeup of the Nuer people, the knowledge of which Kiir's intelligence officers used to provoke the Nuer members of the Presidential Guards on the night of 15 December 2013. Little did they know that it was a trap. Its objective was to justify the mayhem that would follow.

Fighting in the Presidential Guards and the Massacre of Ethnic Nuer

The NLC convened on 14 December amid heavy and tight security. President Kiir was in the full camouflage fatigue of the Tiger Battalion Presidential Guards. Most of the guests who addressed the opening session advised caution and prudence in managing the political differences within the SPLM. It was clear from the body language of the SPLM leaders that things were about to tip over the precipice. The president made it crystal clear in his opening speech that the events of 1991 would not be repeated or tolerated.[73] The environment in the Nyakuron Cultural Centre, which housed the NLC meeting, was so tense that Machar and many of the other leaders who had held the press conference on 6 December boycotted the closing session of the NLC, which was held the following day.

SPLA Chief of General Staff Gen. James Hoth Mai had been away in Australia visiting his family and arrived back in Juba on 15 December.

---

[73] A naked reference to Machar's stint in the SPLM leadership in what the leaders in Nasir christened as the creeping revolution, meant to agitate the people of Bor, who bore the brunt of atrocities that followed the Nasir Declaration.

President Kiir had ordered the disarmament of Nuer elements in the Presidential Guards. Taban Deng had been busy the whole morning agitating Nuer officers and men in the SPLA to fight. According to Gen. Oyay Deng Ajak in a personal communication, which also formed part of his court statement during his trial, Taban Deng and Ezekiel Lol Gatkuoth were fuelling the crisis while he was trying to cool tempers. It was obvious that Taban Deng had not undertaken any preparations for military action. "I told Gen. Thomas Duoth Guet, the director of the External Bureau in the National Security Service, that he was the right person to inform the president about the situation developing in the Presidential Guards, and the urgent need to arrest it. Gen. Thomas Duoth did not go to the president, otherwise the fighting could have been avoided," said Gen. Oyay in a statement to the High Court.

By Sunday 15 December, political events in Juba were inching towards a catastrophe. President Kiir closed the NLC meeting at about seven o'clock that evening on a visibly hostile note, forcing the members to disperse hurriedly to their residences as if to avoid an imminent danger. In fact, the venue was about one kilometre away from the Army headquarters. The first bullet was fired at about nine o'clock and the whole area housing the Tiger Battalion Presidential Guards was immediately engulfed in gunfire, including heavy machine guns, artilleries, and tanks. This went on throughout the night, until about eight in the morning when the shooting shifted to other parts of the city, including the residential suburbs. Nothing was clear until President Kiir went on the air at about 12 noon the following day to announce that there had been an attempted coup spearheaded by Machar, Taban Deng Gai, and Alfred Lado-Gore. He announced that the plotters had been defeated and loyal forces were pursuing the mutineers.

The shooting in Juba did not stop until Thursday 19 December. At the end of it an estimated 20,000 people had been killed, mostly innocent civilian Nuer youth, the elderly, women, and children in a deliberate well-planned house-to-house search-to-kill operation undertaken by the Dotku Beny forces in collaboration with elements of the National Security Services led by known SPLA commanders. Looking back on these events, for some of us who witnessed them, it can clearly be stated that there was no coup against the state. It was the climax of an elaborate, long-prepared plan for President Kiir not only to rid himself of his detractors in the SPLM but also to assert his personal rule. This was the outcome of nearly eight years of misrule: the massacre of Nuer civilians through a meticulously planned operation that was executed with precision. However, by resorting to military action Kiir failed to achieve his political objective: he only strengthened the enemies he wanted to destroy. There was no hint, not even a slight one, to indicate that Machar wanted to contest militarily his dismissal from the government. From his attitude, Machar was not disposed to repeating his bid for power in South Sudan through bloodshed. This stemmed from three incidents that involved him personally.

The first was the apology to the Bor community for the atrocities committed in 1991 following the Nasir Declaration and the split in the SPLM/A, which Machar made in the residence of Madame Rebecca Nyandeng on 30 July 2011. Machar took responsibility for the atrocities committed against the Bor people and pledged he would never repeat such acts. The second was his benign attitude and lack of resistance to Kiir's decree on 23 July 2013 relieving him of his position as vice president. His composure demonstrated that Machar had accepted the president's decree and had resigned himself to the functions of the National Legislative Assembly, to which he was an appointed member. In fact, there was no basis for resisting the president's constitutional prerogative as discussed above. What could be asked is how it was possible that Machar and the other democrats in the SPLM did not perceive the danger of giving the president excessive powers in the Transitional Constitution of South Sudan (TCSS) 2011, even more than he had exercised under the TCSS 2005. Opposition to the excessive powers could have then been the beginning of the political struggle towards democratic transformation in post-independence South Sudan.

Third, Machar's reaction to the shootings in the Army headquarters, which housed the Presidential Guards, was that of a leader who did not want conflict. He repeatedly ordered the commander of his guards in the Presidential Guards to not respond to any provocation and to not fight. He maintained that there was no war and they should just keep to their positions. These incidents were clear indications that Machar was only interested in political struggle, not in war. However, what remains to be ascertained was whether or not that the eruption of violence on 15 December could have caught Machar completely unawares. It is true that Machar belatedly came into the political consultation, which had been going on among the ministers that Kiir dismissed from the government. The consultations revolved around the crisis in the SPLM and the need to institute reforms, and had reached an advanced stage by the time he agreed to participate. Some members of this discussion group insisted, for obvious reasons, on keeping Kiir in the loop. He definitely must have known the thinking of the president. What is surprising is why Machar did not gather intelligence about the activities of Kiir, especially about his visits to Bahr el Ghazal and the hostile speeches he made there.

A politician of Machar's stature would definitely gather information to strategize his political action. Moreover, it was then an open secret that Kiir had mobilized and recruited 3,000 young men from his village and was training them at his farm in Luri. It was thus unbelievable that Machar remained confident that the president would not plan something sinister. The burning issues in the SPLM were about democracy and institutionalization of the SPLM power. It was not uncommon in the SPLM/A for political struggles to turn violent along personal or ethnic lines. While Kiir had swallowed his pride and acquiesced to the dictates of the SPLM's National Convention in 2008, which had imposed Machar and Pagan Amum on him, it was less likely that he would do so a second time. This explains his unconstitutional, indeed, treacherous action of recruiting a private army.

Two years into independence and exercising sovereign power was too short a time for Kiir to contemplate leaving office. He was conscious of his political and leadership weaknesses and knew he could not guarantee both the numbers necessary to win the SPLM chair in the 3rd National Convention, scheduled for May 2013, and an endorsement as the SPLM flag bearer in the presidential elections scheduled for April 2015. This fear of losing power propelled his use of a military option to resolve the SPLM's political and democratic problems. Being a soldier more than a politician, he acted cautiously, starting with the paralysis of the SPLM functions to deprive Machar, Pagan Amum, and Nyandeng Garang of the political means to challenge his decisions, and pressed on until the point where he was in complete control of the process. The objective to finally get rid of his detractors dictated the decision to convene the NLC in a climate of extreme political uncertainty. Kiir had prepared the ground for that action, albeit in a clumsy manner. He did not arrest Machar, Taban, and the others he had wanted to harm. The coup narrative was difficult to sell, except to the regional leaders who counted on him for business opportunities. His chief of Military Intelligence refuted the narrative to destroy in court the government cases against Pagan Amum, Gen. Oyay Deng Ajak, Dr. Majak d'Agoot, and Ezekiel Lol Gatkuoth.

It was difficult to tell whether the president would have ordered the attack on Machar's residence if he hadn't already escaped on the night of 15 December. The attack on the residence on 17 December killed all the remaining residents, including women, children, and his few bodyguards who already had been disarmed. This was definitely a war crime and appears to have been on the orders of Minister of Interior Aleu Ayieny Aleu.[74] It was common knowledge that Machar had reluctantly agreed to leave his residence under the cover of night, and this was the right decision. However, once outside Kiir's dragnet, he had the opportunity to sober up and reorganize his thoughts, make necessary contacts, and by necessity make rational and correct decisions. Events were moving with lightning speed. The targeted massacres of ethnic Nuer in Juba between 16–19 December triggered revenge killings in Unity, Jonglei, and Upper Nile. The Lou Nuer White Army had mobilized and was on its way to Juba.

Riek Machar Declares a Rebellion

It was shocking that after re-establishing contact and communication with people he knew would assist in resolving the conflict, Machar then announced that he was leading a rebellion. This requires some inquiry and analytical digression to establish Machar's motives for taking over the rebellion that had been planned and executed by people with whom he had no contact. The SPLA generals Peter Gadet (Bor) and Gen. James Koang (Bentiu) who rebelled acted on their own volition, driven by the massacres of ethnic Nuer in Juba. Similarly, the Lou Nuer "White Army" acted on its own to mobilize and organize a force to avenge the murder of their people in Juba. The name "White Army" comes from its origins as local, community-based defence forces, the word "white" referring to "civilians." His decision, therefore, to take over the leadership of a rebellion did not come from a correct analysis and reading of the political situation. It was emotional and opportunistic.

On his watch as vice president, beginning in 2005, South Sudan had slid into a state of constant insecurity and anarchy. Independence came against a backdrop of low-intensity wars in Jonglei and the midwest of Upper Nile, linked, respectively, to Kiir's decision in 2009 to award Shilluk land on east bank of the Nile River to Padang Dinka, and the unresolved disputed election results in 2010. The regime had become

---

[74] On the morning of 17 December, Aleu gave Inspector General of Police Gen. Pieng Deng Majok 15 minutes to transfer all the arrested politicians, former ministers in the government, and the SPLM secretary-general, who were being detained in his compound to the residence of Machar, only a few metres away. Aleu had prepared a force to go and execute these politicians. This operation instead fired on different targets — mainly women, children, and the already disarmed Machar's bodyguards.

repressive, arresting and detaining members of the Communist Party of South Sudan who were on a recruitment drive in Rumbek, a right enshrined in the TCSS 2011. In December 2012, the regime security forces mowed down peaceful demonstrators in Wau who were protesting the government's decision to evict them from their ancestral lands. The Lou Nuer youth invaded the Murle land in revenge for Murle raids the previous year in which more than 800 people perished. The action of the Lou Nuer youths was in complete defiance of Machar who had flown to Likwangole, Boma State, to stop the youths, suggesting a complete breakdown in communication with the state. South Sudan was in a deep economic crisis after the border war with the Sudan and the slump in the world oil market.

Inside the SPLM, party matters were running amok. In August 2013, Chairman Kiir decreed some changes in the SPLM National Secretariat. The decree emanated from the Office of the President rather than the SPLM chair. The secretary-general challenged the order in the High Court, which had made no ruling to date. National Security confined Pagan Amum to a radius of only ten metres from his residence and so threatened his lawyers that one, Dong Samuel Luak, fled to Nairobi, Kenya, in August 2013. He was captured and abducted back to Juba on 24 January 2017. His whereabouts remain unknown. The combination of all these factors and many others were worrisome indications that the country was about to erupt. Therefore, to declare a rebellion because of Kiir's massacre of the ethnic Nuer in Juba was opportunistic and demonstrates Machar's real nature as a Nuer chauvinist and an ethnic bigot.

The explosion of violence on 15 December 2013 was therefore just the tip of the political iceberg. It requires deeper investigation to generate a strategic powerful response on the part of any politician who wants to make changes. Thus, apart from the immediate concern about his life, a political leader of Machar's calibre should have not responded in the manner that Kiir wanted him to. I believe that Machar, once safely outside Kiir's dragnet, should have first analysed the situation correctly and studied Kiir's motives for triggering the fighting within the Presidential Guards and his order to massacre ethnic Nuer. He should have also studied the reaction and response of other ethnic communities to the massacres and, whether or not those communities, or the other ethnic Dinka, would join the resistance to Kiir. His action was a case of not learning from one's experiences. He had tried this in 1991 and, as it turned out, only the Nuer and some Shilluk joined his "revolution." Indeed, as someone once put it, it was a case of leading without learning.

It was obvious from all the signs that Kiir wanted to consolidate and entrench himself in power after removing Machar. Therefore, he orchestrated the fighting within the Presidential Guards as a ploy for his power plan. The massacre of innocent Nuer was also a stratagem to hoodwink the Dinka, through the Jieng Council of Elders, into believing that Machar (read: ethnic Nuer) was a threat to Kiir (read: Jieng) power. A correct analysis would have enabled Machar to discover Kiir's power motives. A response to the aggression should have only followed a shrewd assessment of the balance of forces between Kiir and the opposition. It should also been based on a strategic political objective for the rebellion.

However, barely two weeks into the conflict, the Extraordinary Assembly of IGAD Heads of State and Government issued a communique after its summit in Nairobi (27 December 2013). It was obvious from the text that the regional leaders had bought Kiir's coup narrative and therefore justified the Ugandan military intervention "to protect strategic installations." Machar's statement on the BBC that he was "leading a rebellion" inadvertently laid credence to the coup narrative, implying that Machar's failure to achieve the objectives of the coup had now forced him into rebellion. The statement unwittingly rubbished the momentum set in motion by strong statements that Madame Rebecca Nyandeng and the author made to the press and on electronic media contradicting Kiir's coup narrative.

Instead of bragging about leading a rebellion, Machar could have used the opportunity to inform the world about the massacre of innocent ethnic Nuer in Juba that followed the mutiny in the Presidential Guards. Machar was on the run for his life after escaping from Juba and Kiir was pursuing him with helicopter gunships. He could have spoken about the attack on his compound on 17 December and the massacre of his bodyguards and the women and children who had sought refuge there from the killings in the city. This would have won him sympathy. However, due to the pompous way he announced his leadership of a rebellion he lost the sympathy and support of the region. News of the atrocities committed by Nuer in Bor and Bentiu, reminiscence of the 1991 incident, started to filter into Juba. This created a backlash against Machar and the Nuer in general. In his mishandling of his response to the unfolding crisis, Machar had unwittingly removed the rope from Kiir's neck and placed it around his own neck.

Machar had no compelling reasons to make such a hasty declaration of his intention to go to war. The situation was still fluid and unpredictable; the forces that had fled with him from Juba, and those that joined him in Bor, were only in a defensive mode; the rebelling forces had not yet grasped the scope of their rebellion. Members of the Lou Nuer White Army had their own motives, which were not necessarily linked to Machar's political objectives. The South Sudanese people, other than the Nuer and Dinka, were still in shock about what had happened in Juba. Before they had a chance to sober up the people were confronted with news of the brutal revenge killings of innocent civilians in Bor, Bentiu, and Malakal, where marauding hordes of Nuer White Army mercilessly butchered the elderly, hospital patients, and the disabled. It was sheer madness and showed the total lack of responsible leadership. Whether or not Machar ordered the massacres is immaterial. His responsibility still lies in declaring war without a clear objective and strategy for achieving that objective. As an ethnic Nuer he knows that Nuer warfare, in its traditional setting, is very repugnant, invariably about war booty — cattle, women, children, and the occupation of land. This was bound to create enemies rather than win allies for his cause. Because of these atrocities the initial sympathy for and solidarity with victims of Kiir's actions in Juba quickly ebbed and people's attitudes changed to anger and bitterness. The vengeance and counter-vengeance character of Machar's war immediately achieved President Kiir's primary objective: to transform the SPLM's internal political conflicts into a military campaign against his distractors along ethnic lines. In this respect, Kiir managed to neutralize or turn into his allies the other ethnicities against the Nuer.[75]

Not surprisingly, at least half of the Nuer officers and soldiers in the SPLA joined the rebellion, out of anger over the massacre of their innocent kith and kin.[76] However, it was the Nuer White Army — armed civilians hailing from Lou Nuer and Jikany — which constituted the bulk of the opposition forces that entered into combat with the SPLA in Bor and Terekeka, while the UPDF provided artillery fire, helicopter gunships and cluster bombs. The White Army was a formidable force; it managed

---

[75] Rebel forces under the command of Gen. Johnson Thubo (Olony) in the Shilluk Kingdom were observing an uneasy truce with the government when the conflict erupted in Juba. The Nuer's unprovoked massacre of Shilluk in Malakal prompted Olony to throw his support behind President Kiir, turning the tide against Dr. Riek Machar and the Nuer White Army.

[76] The military parade Gen. Peter Gadet gave Machar in Gadiang included 45,000 officers and men.

to inflict heavy casualties on the SPLA and allied UPDF. However, the use of helicopter gunships and cluster bombs was something the White Army, in its clan-based formations, had not anticipated. It quickly demoralized them, prompting their withdrawal; for them, there was no material incentive in fighting a helicopter gunship.

I believe that Machar's announcement that he was leading a rebellion was a bluff to present himself as the protector of the Nuer people, as well as to create political space after Kiir's dismissal of him as vice president. He was sending messages that had nothing with any rebellion. Machar was a successful SPLA commander and knew well that if he was going to fight it must be on his own terms, regarding timing and location. He could not declare war on an unfavourable ground. Moreover, there were matters of urgency to attend to before any announcement could be made. Primarily, Machar needed time to organize, train, orient, and form the forces into organic combat units. He needed to define the enemy or target as well as the political objectives of the war. He also needed to secure military logistics in terms of ammunitions and food for the army. In this respect, he would have had to reject outright or procrastinate on IGAD's regional intervention in the conflict. The delay in the IGAD peace process would have given Machar the time necessary to build his forces and prepare for war. There were legitimate reasons for him to refuse to send a delegation to Addis Ababa, Ethiopia.

Machar should have condemned IGAD's endorsement of Kiir's coup narrative in its communique of 27 December 2013. It was common knowledge that there had been no coup. If their intervention was to have meaningful impact, the IGAD leaders should have been evenhanded in handling the crisis. He could have questioned the role of President Museveni in the mediation, as he was already involved in the war on the side of Kiir. He could have also demanded the immediate and unconditional withdrawal of the UPDF ground and air forces from South Sudanese territory. He could have demanded that IGAD and the international community condemn Uganda for its use of the internationally banned cluster bombs. These and other demands, including the release of political prisoners, as conditions for participating in the peace talks, would have enabled Machar to engage the IGAD region and United Nations Mission in South Sudan (UNMISS). At the same time, the start of the peace talks could have been delayed until he was ready with his terms for negotiations.

Machar should have denied any connection with Gen. Peter Gadet and Gen. James Koang, the respective commanders of the Bor and Bentiu mutinies. He should have also denied having any connection with the Lou Nuer White Army on the grounds that he indeed had not mobilized them. This would have given him enough time to build his forces and acquire military support, particularly anti-tank and anti-aircraft rockets. These considerations appear to have not crossed Machar's mind at all. He acted in response to Nuer social psychology and war strategies and jumped onto the crest of a limited popular Nuer uprising that had been set off by the massacres in Juba. There were no political underpinnings and nothing beyond a desire for revenge. Machar now wanted to exploit this limited popular unrest to reclaim leadership of the Nuer and the position he had lost in government.

The formation of the SPLM/A-IO, as we shall note in the coming section, was not to fight a war but to use it as a means to negotiate Machar's return to Juba. The marauding White Army returned home, melting into their villages, with their war booty, which included abducted children and women, vehicles, furniture, and guns. Thus, by April 2014, the uprising by Nuer areas in Unity, Upper Nile, and Jonglei had lost steam, enabling the government to recapture all the areas the opposition had controlled with the exception of Lou (Waat and Akobo) and Sobat (Nasir and Maiwut).

The Commoditization of Rebellion

Starting a war or allowing oneself to be pushed into it without clear political objectives and a certain measure of preparedness is dangerous, to say the least. It is suicidal and destructive for the people. A good general goes to war only on his own terms. The general determines the timing and place to fight in order to assure victory or the strategic political objectives of war. One does not fight just because there are soldiers to lead into a battle. A leader fights when it is necessary and if there is no way of avoiding the war.

The contemporary history of the Sudan reveals that war sometimes creates opportunities for a variety of people. The political economy of war generates forces that make it a profitable business, perpetuating ad infinitum the conditions of war. Many leaders and pretenders have stepped onto the political stage because of war. The pretenders are those who have no knowledge of politics. A leader with no ideology or clear political objective will transform the war situation and its opportunities/potentialities into a commodity, which he will then sell or buy to shore up his political support at a price determined not in monetary terms but in the potential or inherent opportunity present during a stage of war.

When civil wars end, as they did in 1972 and 2005, in whatever manner, a potential opportunity is created for the political leaders as well as for the combatants. We saw this after the Addis Ababa Agreement; after the CPA, it was more dramatic. The opportunities came to the politicians in the form of government positions (the executive and Legislative Assembly) at different administrative levels (GoNU, GoSS, state, and county); and for the combatants in the form of ranks and positions in the military, security, police, and the prison and wildlife services. In this situation, the original drivers of the war tend to disappear. It will require more explanation and analysis to clarify this thesis of the commodification of war in South Sudan.

President Kiir had no good reason for unleashing war. He was in complete control of the state after dismissing Machar and the entire cabinet on 23 July 2013. It was his constitutional prerogative. Moreover, in the intervening period, until the eruption of violence on 15 December, there were no reports of security breaches in the country indicative of moves to snatch power. However, during that period a foreign leader twice visited Juba as a guest of the state: on 9 July, the second anniversary of independence, and on 30 July, the SPLA's Martyrs' Day. This important guest made insulting remarks, which were clearly referring to Dr. Riek Machar. These remarks did not come out of nowhere. In fact, they rang a bell of suspicion, suggesting that an invisible hand was behind Kiir's military actions.

Dismissal from a government position is not unusual. It should not have amounted in any way to political animosity between leaders. In fact, in similar situations, those removed from government can still function in the party. The ANC recalled both presidents Thabo Mbeki and Jacob Zuma from the presidency of South Africa; they remained committed members of the African National Congress (ANC). Why would the removal of Machar as deputy president create such political rancour in the SPLM and the country? He should have just gone and resumed his functions as the first deputy chair of the SPLM and continued the dialogue for reforms in the party. However, by ending all contact at such an early date, suggesting that they had drawn their swords and were ready to fight, the SPLM leaders allowed their inflated egos to control them. It enabled the rent-seekers to capture the political stage. Through the use of gossip, backbiting, and intrigue they heightened the political tension, leading to the explosion on 15 December. The response to Kiir's provocations should not have been reciprocal. Without his announcement of a rebellion, Machar could have averted the civil war.

But it was difficult for Machar to prevent the war. As I said above, a war situation generates a potential or opportunity for the acquisition of power and wealth. These two categories have proved potent drugs in the social, economic, and political engineering processes in South Sudan. This explains one interesting aspect of Machar's rebellion. I earlier wrote that he was not disposed to violence in his quest for power and, therefore, had not formed an army. Nevertheless, he declared a rebellion knowing that he was not prepared on the ground. The announcement that he was leading a rebellion and the subsequent formation of the SPLM/A-IO would appear to mark Machar's second violent attempt to lead South Sudan. However, following on from the above, his true intention was to put himself in a position to negotiate his return to Juba. This stems from the fact that he was not prepared for the war. Most of the lieutenants and leaders who had supported his bid for power in 1991 were no longer with him. In fact, most of the intellectuals and politicians who followed him into the bush were newcomers to the armed struggle and, therefore, did not know him in person. He was now in charge of everything in the nascent movement, including the choice of the name: SPLM/A-In Opposition (SPLM/A-IO). The greatest mistake he made was to insist on using the name of a movement and army — SPLM/A — that had become unpopular among many people in South Sudan, adding only "in opposition". The choice may have been made in anticipation of returning to Juba and mending matters inside the SPLM. But he acted without thinking about the sentiments of his Nuer constituency, which loathed the acronym SPLM/A.

The new movement was formed at a "consultative meeting" in Nasir among the "democratic forces for change", comprising "the SPLM, other political parties, civil society organizations, traditional leaders, church leaders, representatives of victims and survivors of genocide, and other eminent personalities and generally all those affected by the crisis." In all honesty, this event in Nasir was the theatre of politics catching up with the military action, replaying the drama of the SPLM/A's formation in Itang in July 1983 to catch up with the army mutinies in Bor, Pochalla, and Ayod. The only exception now comes in the "liberation" misnomer. This nascent political military outfit was not a liberation movement.

The consultative meeting in Nasir was led under the title of "Towards Consolidating Democratic Transformation, Good Governance, and Transparency to Achieve Peace, Freedom, and Prosperity." A statement was issued, listing as democratic principles the following: a federal structure of governance, security-sector reforms, judicial and legal reforms, public service reforms, an interim federal constitution, and peace agreement. These democratic principles would form the foundation on which to restructure the state in South Sudan and, thus, constituted the new movement's political objectives. Far from liberation idiosyncrasies, this list of populist slogans, christened "democratic principles", smacks of an attempt to strip the struggle against Kiir's regime of its political and ideological content. This is typical of liberal and right-wing politics in South Sudan. It betrays the reformist agenda that only a peace agreement can put in place. It would only confirm the doubts expressed above about the nascent movement's preparedness and capacity for war. The use of high-sounding words like "democratic transformation", "federal system of governance", and others were mainly for public consumption and political mileage.

The consultative meeting served two purposes: to legitimize and confirm Dr. Riek Machar Teny-Dhurgon as the chairman and commander in chief of the SPLM/A-IO, and to renew the mandate of the negotiating team under the leadership of Gen. Taban Deng Gai, who was the virtual second in the SPLM/A leadership hierarchy. Viewed from its statement, the new SPLM/A-IO wanted to sound out the people of South Sudan on its interest in peace rather than in the armed struggle. This can be gleaned from a series of political and military positions that the new movement adopted.

First, there was no statement to follow up on the initial announcement of the rebellion. That statement would have elaborated the reasons for the rebellion and the strategy for fighting the war. There was a deliberately muted response to the strong voices emanating from the Nuer people demanding that Machar not negotiate with the Kiir's government. The general feeling was that the new force should fight the war to its logical conclusion of defeating and overthrowing the Kiir regime. The people agitated for a strong, effective, and efficient political-military organization to accomplish this task. It seemed, until this material point in time, that it had not dawned on Machar that his rebellion announcement presupposed the acquisition and procurement of military supplies to prosecute the war. But he had not succeeded in securing supplies; this may explain his muted response to the people's agitation. However, it is possible that his pursuance of the peace agenda was part of his reluctance to procure military support. Put another way, he may have used his failure to secure military hardware as an alibi for pursuing the peace option.

The new movement needed sufficient external political and military support to enable it to match or outdo Kiir's army, which now enjoyed the combat support of the UPDF ground and air forces, as well as the Sudanese rebel armies operating from inside South Sudan. The new movement could not count on any friends in the region to upset the external support Kiir was receiving. This supports the argument, as I wrote above, that if Machar genuinely desired to fight Kiir he should have taken the time to solicit sufficient military and political support before announcing the rebellion. Looking at the region surrounding South Sudan, Machar had only two options in his quest for military support. The Federal Democratic Republic of Ethiopia would have been the nearest possible donor. Ethiopia is linked to South Sudan in terms of its shared border and people (Koma, Nuer, and Anywaa) in the Gambella region of western Ethiopia. However, it would not be easy to solicit support from the Ethiopia government, which was the chair of IGAD. It could not play a double game of being a mediator and at the same time a donor to a rebel movement. Moreover, Machar had not established any kind of contact with Ethiopia officialdom; the only contact was through the IGAD Secretariat.

In the regional and international configuration of issues then, the Republic of Sudan could provide support to the SPLM/A-IO on a reciprocal basis. President Kiir and President Museveni were in the business of supporting the Dar Furi and SPLM-N rebels operating from inside South Sudan. Therefore, the Sudan was expected to willingly support the new rebel movement in South Sudan. However, Sudan's economic interests in South Sudan outflanked its security concerns and this prompted its reluctance to support Machar. Sudan had higher stakes in the oil fields and the revenues accruing from the transhipment of South Sudanese oil to international markets.

In order to sacrifice its economic interests, there would need to be something in the domain of ideological solidarity for the Sudan government to support the rebels in South Sudan. Moreover, the NCP government's relations with Machar were far from cordial, particularly after he deserted the position of assistant to President Omar el Beshir over the non-implementation of the Khartoum Peace Agreement (1997). Nevertheless, Khartoum might take the risk of supporting Machar but for the fact that his delegation of Taban Deng Gai, whom Khartoum did not trust, created political unease. Further, there was nothing in Machar's political objectives that factored into Khartoum's economic and security concerns, nor had Machar presented credible strategies to keep Khartoum from being sanctioned by the international community. The NCP intelligence services' disillusionment with the Nuer militias' lack of secrecy was another hurdle, as Khartoum would not want itself be seen as interfering in the regional efforts for peace in South Sudan.

The SPLM/A-IO had no ready donor. This meant that Machar would have to find the money to finance the war, whether personal money from his savings or solicited from family friends. He needed to demonstrate that he was capable of financing the war, otherwise the project of leading a rebellion would remain stillborn. Machar had been the vice president as well as minister for physical infrastructure, which rehabilitated government buildings through a huge budget, between 2005 and 2007. As he harboured power ambitions, it was assumed that he had accumulated money to support his political struggles, including his rebellion.

On the other hand, Gen. Taban Deng Gai, the virtual number two in the new movement's hierarchy, had been the governor of the oil-rich Unity State for eight years. Many people in South Sudan, including the author, assumed that Taban Deng had accumulated a personal fortune from his time as governor. This is because there was nothing in the state or in Bentiu town to show for the five per cent of the oil revenues the state received over the period that Taban Deng was its governor. Both Machar and Taban Deng, with their stolen wealth, could easily foot the war bill. However, neither Taban Deng nor Machar was ready to invest his personal money in the war project. In fact, Machar said he had no money: if there was anything, he said, it belonged to his son. Taban Deng had business interests in Dubai and was definitely apprehensive about putting his personal fortunes into the war. This worsened the uneasy relationship between the two, prompting Taban Deng to boycott the third IGAD negotiating session in July 2014. Taban Deng therefore used the time in between negotiating sessions to run his business in Dubai, sometimes stopping over in Khartoum. On these trips he managed to secure some ammunition stocks but not enough to sustain the fighting against Kiir's forces.

The lack of military logistics showed quickly in the performance of the new movement, which really feeds into the argument that time must be taken to prepare before launching a rebellion. The nascent movement did not care to establish army barracks, which exacerbates the difficulty of procuring sufficient food for the combatants. The army moves on its stomach, goes the old adage, so without food it would be difficult to keep the combatants in one place. It was therefore not suprising that fighters and even officers returned to their communities and clans to form into units of the White Army under their respective traditional leaders. This completely changed the character of the war and negatively affected the morale and discipline of the combatants, and indeed marked the collapse of the organized military campaign against the regime.

Second, the procurement of military support was Machar's responsibility as the leader of the movement. He could not have left it to anyone else, no matter how close they were to him: the success of his war effort depended on the procurement of military hardware. He should have committed himself to arranging meetings with friends and potential benefactors. Instead, Machar spent most of his time in meaningless meetings with petty traders and commission agents who would not accept his financial terms. Investing too much time in Addis Ababa or at his headquarters in Pagak engaging in meaningless diplomacy was tantamount to sabotaging himself and his efforts to procure military support. He seemed to have decided to strengthen the SPLM/A-IO's support for the peace negotiations. But shopping for military supplies was as important, indeed more important, than engaging in diplomatic functions. This could have enabled him to negotiate with the government from a position of strength.

A leader needs to first secure his military support as a means of strengthening his diplomatic offensive. It was little more than a dream for the SPLM/A-IO leaders to expect President Kiir to agree to share power and reform his regime without a measure of military threat. The weak military strength of the nascent movement, because of the lack of supplies, definitely pushed the SPLM/A-IO leadership to accept the terms of any peace agreement imposed by the mediators. These terms would have been different had the SPLM/A-IO negotiated from a position of military strength. It became clear that Machars's acquiescence to the peace negotiations made a joke of his initial declaration to wage a rebellion. In this respect, a peace agreement was the cheapest means of regaining his position of vice president in a power-sharing arrangement.

The peace negotiations were by no means easy or straightforward. The negotiation modality that the IGAD's special envoys adopted was cumbersome, involving constant shuttling between the principals for consultations. The principals were divided in response to their respective national security, economic, and political interests in South Sudan. In the fourth negotiating session (August 2014), the special envoys presented three proposals to the negotiating teams. The first proposal was that both President Kiir and Machar not participate in the transition. This proposal caused a stir, particularly in the SPLM/A-IO ranks, given that President Museveni had torpedoed the proposal in support of President Kiir's incumbency.[77] The second proposal was that Kiir remain in his position while Machar would become the prime minister. The IGAD summit deemed this arrangement unstable.[78] The third proposal was that Machar would become first vice president while President Kiir and Vice President James Wani Igga would retain their positions. This proposal stuck and became the basis of power-sharing clauses of the ARCISS.

Another important point proved that Machar was not interested in regime change to transform the conditions that obtained in South Sudan. He lacked strategic planning for the war. Among the factors that create conditions for victory in a war is the sabotage of the enemy's economic installations. The SPLM/A-IO leadership did not require lectures on this important war strategy, and Machar is highly conversant with war and military literature. He was a successful zonal commander in western and northern Upper Nile during the war of national liberation. He knew perfectly well that the war against Kiir involved hitting strategic economic installations to deprive him of financial and economic resources for prosecuting the war. I believe Machar chose to block that knowledge, and this explains why he vehemently turned down the proposed strategy of attacking and shutting down the oil fields in Adar. Indeed, without the little money that trickled down from the sale or exchange of oil for refined fuel in Mombasa, President Kiir would not have been able to prosecute the war for so long: he would not have been able to pay the Ugandan and Dar Furi mercenaries. Therefore, the first step Machar should have done after announcing his leadership of the rebellion was to hit at the oil production, which remains the regime's sole source of foreign currency. In this respect, the political survival of the regime in Juba did not depend on its political and military strength but rather on SPLM/A-IO's military weakness, as well as its lack of critical and strategic thinking.

It was in the context of short-term thinking that Machar and Taban Deng conspired to defuse Johnson Olony's operations to take control

---

[77] It presupposed that Kiir and Machar would each nominate a representative to share power in the transitional period. In the SPLM/A-IO, the talk was more about Taban Deng than Alfred Lado-Gore for the deputy chair. Taban took this seriously, whetting his power appetite and generating political ripples, which became apparent in the July conspiracy he hatched with Kiir.

[78] The experience of the Grand Coalition established by President Mwai Kibaki and opposition leader Raila Odinga to address the violence that followed the disputed elections results in Kenya (2008) informed the proposal the special envoys presented to the IGAD Summit.

of the oil fields after he captured Malakal, Akoka, and Melut in May 2015.[79] The Chinese oil company operating in Unity and the Adar Yel oil fields demanded that Machar and Taban Deng put a moratorium on military operations. They agreed and stopped the SPLM/A-IO's march onto these fields in return for huge sums of money and 40 flats in a housing complex in Nairobi, Kenya. The failure to capture the oil fields was the biggest blow the SPLM/A-IO inflicted upon itself during the political and military campaign in Upper Nile. It left Gen. Olony and the Agwalek forces very bitter with the SPLM/A-IO leadership, which almost triggered a division and prompted Olony's refusal to send troops to Juba as part of the SPLM/A-IO contingent stipulated in the security arrangements of the ARCISS. The failure to capture the oil fields demonstrated not only the SPLM/A-IO's military ineptitude but also constituted a serious blow to its bargaining position at the talks with the government.

Third, the SPLM/A-IO did not organize nor did it function in the same manner as a political party or liberation movement. The movement laid emphasis on the military hierarchy and paraphernalia while relegating political work to the lowest of priorities. Machar concentrated on clans and community meetings where he discussed marginal issues of blood feuds and appointed members of the traditional authority. The clan-based meetings tended to speak to Nuer mythology, including Ngundeng's prophesies, especially the one that fits in with the war against the Dinka and Machar's long-sought leadership of South Sudan. These meetings were not about building a modern political military organization to address the immediate confrontation with the regime or the socioeconomic and political challenges at hand. These meetings were meant to imprint his image as a leader in the minds of his people. It is now understandable why Machar avoided at every opportunity discussing the organizational and political matters of the SPLM/A-IO. These discussions would have put him on the spot on the question of democracy and institutions in the movement. He believed that his leadership of South Sudan had already been declared through Ngundeng's prophecy.

---

[79] Gen. Johnson Olony rebelled against the government following the assassination of Gen. James Bwogo Olieu. He made contacts with the SPLM/A-IO and launched an attack that led to the capture of Malakal and surrounding areas, including Melut. He was surprised to hear that Machar had ordered the withdrawal and dispersal of the Nuer elements of his operation, leading to the failure to capture Paloich and Adar Yel.

Machar is very particular about representations based on province, ethnicity, and clan. He would spend long hours to achieve this, even at the expense of choosing individuals based on merit and knowledge. The selection of individuals into leadership positions based on clans, sections, ethnicity, or province rather that political experience and knowledge had led to the emergence of political deadwood at the top echelon of the SPLM/A-IO leadership, including in the National Liberation Council (NLC) and the Political Bureau. A colleague called these political upstarts "baby-class politicians." Their function was to give unqualified support for whatever Machar said and to jeer, boo, and oppose anybody in the leadership who disagreed with him. It was a perception of organization and practice of democracy that had been turned upside down. In fact, this perception speaks to the logic of maintaining absolute control over every aspect of the movement. As Young (2017: 36) puts it:

> The problems of Riek's leadership…he continues to totally dominate the movement, is unwilling to share power and has repeatedly thrown up obstacles to SPLM-IO institutionalization, which could undermine his authority. His lack of vision is manifest in the absence of convincing military and political strategies.

This kind of leadership cannot realise victory or political success. Machar preferred to work and engage with those who were politically mediocre, thus automatically making him appear to be the most knowledgeable just because he is the leader.

On the military front, the absence or inability of the SPLM/A-IO leadership to build military camps prevented the organization from being an effective and efficient combat-capable army. Most of the officers and men who fought the initial battles returned to their home villages, just as their kith and kin in the White Army had done. There was no organized front and most of the ensuing battles were mainly people resisting attacks by enemy forces as they advanced to occupy opposition positions. It took quite some time for Machar, the SPLM/A-IO's commander in chief, to appoint an army commander. The most senior officer was Gen. Simon Gatwech Dual, but Gatwech had joined the resistance somewhat late. In fact, Gen. Peter Gadet led the insurrection in Bor and was a more capable soldier than Gen. Simon Gatwech. Machar was not quite sure of Gatwech's loyalty and Taban Deng hated Gen. Peter Gadet. The presence of large numbers of non-commissioned White Army individuals and clan-based appointments and promotions within the rank and file became a great challenge to the organization of the army. In the end, Machar appointed Gen. Simon Gatwech as the army chief of general staff.

Machar prolonged his stay in Addis Ababa and travelled in the region and beyond, including going to South Africa for an ophthalmic consultation. He made the mistake of ordering the senior army generals and sector commanders to report themselves to Pagak. This was a tricky decision and indeed led to serious concerns among the generals. These generals operated in an environment where they had to fend for themselves and their subordinates because the general headquarters would not provide them with any supplies. It was not a wise decision to bring them to Pagak where there was virtually nothing for them to do. This led to a crisis of confidence that eventually saw the defection of some officers, among them Gen. Peter Gadet and Gen. Gathoth Gatkuoth, and the politicians Timothy Tot, Michael Mario Dhuor, and Gabriel Yual Dok, who have all decamped to Juba.

Internal ideological and political or even personal conflicts are inevitable in a political party or movement, especially when its leadership has failed to subscribe to organizational principles that are progressive and democratic in nature. Most of the conflicts in the nascent movement stemmed from the attempt to organize along the lines of Nuer traditional war formations and Nuer mythology linked to Ngundeng's prophecy, which is incompatible with the multi-ethnic character of South Sudan. Indeed, the SPLM/A-IO would have remained a purely Nuer affair without the conflicts the regime generated that led to the rebellion of Johnson Olony with his Agwalek forces in May 2015, and other military commanders in Equatoria and western Bahr el Ghazal, which gave the SPLM/A-IO a new lease of life.[80]

This brings me to the conclusion that the announcement of rebellion made by Machar made was vacuous, deceptive, and indeed a bluff except in the context of exploiting the opportunities it generated — what I categorised above as the commoditization of rebellion. In his recent publication on the Horn of Africa, Alex de Waal speaks of a "political marketplace" in the rebel-controlled areas (De Waal, 2015: 16). Machar's announcement of leading a rebellion against Kiir counters, in the minds of many Nuer, the failure of his 1991 bid to capture the leadership of

---

[80] Those from other ethnicities joining the movement were mainly individuals fishing for positions. It is difficult to believe that a leader like Alfred Lado-Gore came without a Bari runner: the Nuer had to carry him all the way to Bentiu where he was picked up to join Machar in Addis Ababa to become the deputy chairman. This was also true of Dr. Dhieu Mathok Diing Wol and others.

South Sudan. The rebellion once more has hooked the Nuer people to his adventure through a delicate but intricate balance of political patronage and the commoditization of rebellion. In this connection, dissent against Kiir generates "power potential." Machar is dishing out favours in the form of inflated military ranks in the SPLA and "ministerial portfolios" to be taken up in a future government after the peace agreement is finalised. The SPLM/A-IO has ceased to be a liberation movement and is now nothing more than a political marketplace in which the "power potential" inherent in rebelling against the government rather than money constitutes the means of exchange. One supported Machar in return for a rank in the army or a ministerial position, which would become valid once a power-sharing peace agreement was sealed and Machar became the first vice president.

Machar is exploiting this "power potential" inherent in the continued existence of the SPLM/A-IO despite its political and military weakness and his weak position as leader. Notwithstanding his incarceration in South Africa, Machar maintained telephone communication with the field, preferring to speak directly to junior officers instead of their senior commanders as a means of instilling loyalty. He also continued to make regular changes to the command, offering bogus promotions and appointments in the state structure in a bid to balance the representation of Nuer clans and sections. This created confusion, frustration, and demoralization in the ranks, enabling the enemy to make inroads into the SPLM/A-IO headquarters in Pagak and Waat in the Lou area.

The IGAD Peace Agreement and Its Collapse

The IGAD-brokered peace talks included nearly 18 months of intermittent negotiations and arm-twisting. Nevertheless, assured of President Museveni's continued political and diplomatic support, President Kiir refused to sign the imposed Agreement on the Resolution of the Conflict in South Sudan (ARCISS) on 17 August 2015. The SPLM/A-IO decided that Machar should sign the agreement. This is not because the agreement addressed the fundamental problems that underpinned the war. It was also not because it was the best alternative to a negotiated agreement but because Machar did not have the option of behaving in the same way as Kiir and rejecting the agreement. The SPLM/A-IO had no capacity to fight on. Further, internal conflicts and confusion generated by the triangular sociopolitical relations that existed between Machar, Taban Deng, and Madame Angelina Teny dogged the movement's leadership. Thus, to some of us in the leadership, the agreement was a better option because it provided an opportunity for political struggle in the absence of a military option. Furthermore, there was no strategic planning in the movement to give direction.

President Kiir signed the ARCISS two weeks later with reservations, some of which essentially amounted to its violation. It was clear, as I explained above, that Kiir did not want Machar to return to Juba, let alone share power with him. He did all he could to procrastinate on its implementation. On 2 October 2015, the president dropped a bombshell in form of a presidential decree that divided South Sudan into 28 states. Not only was Establishment Order 36/2015 a blatant violation of the ARCISS, it was a slap in the face for Machar's proposed 21 federal states. We had spent time debating the issue of states based on former colonial districts but Machar would not give up on the 21 states' formula. He did not care that it erased the two Dinka districts of Bailiet and Renk, which he wanted to annex to Nasir district and rename as Sobat and Adar states respectively. This infuriated the Padang Dinka, prompting their campaign for 28 states, which Salva Kiir decreed into law.

The establishment and operationalization of the ARCISS institutions and instruments was another difficult phase of struggle, renegotiation, interpretation, and manoeuvring between the parties. The pre-interim period elapsed without the establishment of the main ARCISS instruments. The IGAD special envoys, peace guarantors, the AU, UN, Troika, and newly appointed chairman of the Joint Evaluation and Monitoring Commission (JMEC), Botswana's former president Festus Mogae, could do nothing but only urge Machar to relocate to Juba, stressing that all other pending issues would be resolved while in the TGoNU.

The SPLM/A-IO went into another period of internal crisis. It had not completed its internal organization. There was no legislative authority to ratify the agreement. It did not have a secretary-general or an administrator to manage the different aspects of the movement's activities, which hitherto had been the prerogative of Machar. There was a struggle over the leadership and composition of the advance team. The seeds of disorganization started to cultivate and germinate, which were to produce the split in the leadership and eventual expulsion of Machar from Juba only two months after the ARCISS implementation. That Gen. Taban Deng Gai could lead the advance team in the presence of SPLM/A-IO Deputy Chairman Alfred Lado-Gore was something unusual but understandable as it reflected the earlier mentioned triangular relations that existed between Machar, Taban Deng, and

Madame Angelina Teny. This assignment enabled Taban Deng to cut deals with President Kiir. The deal surfaced on 8 July 2016 in the form of the fight in the Presidential Palace, known as J-1, between the bodyguards of Kiir and Machar.

The regional leaders, under pressure from US Special Envoy Donald Booth, refused to heed the concern of the SPLM/A-IO in respect of several issues that the advance team had failed to iron out with the government of Salva Kiir. These included the armaments and transportation of the SPLM/A-IO military force to be sent to Juba. The advance team could not agree on six points critical for incorporating ARCISS into the TCSS 2011 in order to produce a constitutional draft bill to enact into the Transitional Constitution of South Sudan (TCSS) 2016, upon which the Transitional Government of National Unity (TGoNU) would be established. At a meeting on 31 January 2016, JMEC Chairman Mogae could only tell the advance team that all the outstanding matters would be resolved after formation of the TGoNU.

The decision on the part of the peace mediators to leave these outstanding issues for to the TGoNU to resolve meant that the peace mediators, guarantors, and the international community were now running away from the responsibility of implementing and enforcing the agreement in its letter and spirit. One could read two things in between the lines. The first was that there was unveiled disdain for Riek Machar on the part of the regional leaders. In fact, many thought he had no case at all and therefore showed no sympathy for him. This explains why matters were left in such a state that Kiir had the upper hand in the ARCISS implementation. It left no options: there was no political or diplomatic space for the SPLM/A-IO to manoeuvre itself out of the impasse. Machar had to make a choice: reject the arrangement on the grounds that it was too dangerous or accept the risk and fly to Juba. On 26 April, Machar took the oath of office as first vice president and three days later, on 29 April, President Kiir swore in the TGoNU cabinet. This was before promulgation of the TCSS 2016 as the constitutional and legal grounds for the TGoNU, suggesting that it would then operate without a constitution or with the TCSS 2011, which had been amended in 2015 to extend Kiir's terms of office. It was obvious that the agreement could not hold. Anger, hatred, and mistrust still oozed from the faces and body language of all the leaders.

The advance team was already in turmoil owing to the secret deals that its leader, Taban Deng, had been cutting with the government side. This included squashing the procedures spelt out clearly in the agreement for the allocation of ministerial portfolios between the parties. Taban cut a deal with Nhial Deng to enable the SPLM/A-IO to select the petroleum docket because he wanted it for himself. In the appointment of SPLM/A-IO ministers, Machar denied Taban Deng the petroleum portfolio. This imploded the internal disagreements that had started to simmer in Pagak. Machar should have acted strategically, denying Kiir and Taban Deng the opportunity to scuttle the ARCISS by playing to Taban's desire for the petroleum docket. Had he prevented the creation of the Kiir-Taban alliance, Machar would have prevented the early collapse of the TGoNU and ARCISS. Taban Deng's unbridled power ambition and intense anger over being denied the petroleum docket heightened the conflict between Machar and President Kiir and accelerated the arrival of the impending catastrophe. In retrospect, it would have been cheaper to give rather than deny Taban Deng the ministry of petroleum as a means of denying President Kiir the opportunity to scuttle the ARCISS.

The fighting in J-1 on 8 July resulted in the deaths of more than 400 officers and men. The subsequent full-scale attack on the positions of the SPLM/A-IO in Jebel Kujur on 10 July marked the collapse of the TGoNU and ARCISS and forced the movement back to arms. It also marked the limit to which the liberal peace process could travel under the prevailing national and regional conditions. One would also assume that those events in Juba, the 40 days and nights that Machar spent under close military pursuit as he fled to the border of the DR Congo, would have ended Machar's faith in a peace agreement as the solution to the conflict in South Sudan. This was not to be the case: his belief in the need to make peace through negotiation remains unshakeable. And yet, despite his conviction about peace he still behaves like a warrior, releasing war statements, albeit without undertaking commensurate actions.

The decision of Taban Deng Gai to rekindle the war just because Machar had denied him the petroleum portfolio in the TGoNU is completely unforgivable. Taban Deng's name came up in the genesis of the conflict in 2013. With what happened in July 2016, it is easy to believe that he had a role in the agitation for a Nuer-Dinka conflict. President Kiir had earlier dismissed him as governor of Unity State. Whether the dismissal was in connection with what he had purportedly told the president, or the dismissal was a ploy and indeed a bait to trigger the war, requires further investigation. Either scenario suggests that Taban Deng is capable of doing anything to achieve his objectives.

The IGAD High Level Revitalization Forum

The renewed fighting between the SPLA and SPLM/A-IO forces began with dangerous provocations that triggered the J-1 skirmishes and quickly turned into a full-blown war involving artillery, tanks, and helicopter gunships. This was a clear indication that the ARCISS had collapsed and nothing short of a renewed agreement or wider conflagration would resolve the impasse. The presence of members of other parties in the cabinet — the SPLM Former Detainees (FDs) and the National Alliance parties — did not make the Kiir-Taban cabinet a national representative body. The insistence of JMEC Chair Mogae that the ARCISS was still alive did nothing to bring peace. The government continued its military offensive against the SPLA-IO, capturing some of its positions, particularly in West Bank Upper Nile. Had Mogae admitted ARCISS's collapse, due to its repeated violation, IGAD and the international community might have worked harder to salvage something out of ARCISS.

The SPLA was pushing for the total defeat of the SPLM/A-IO, leading to an escalation that engulfed the whole of South Sudan in an ethnic-based conflagration. Even in hitherto peaceful areas in Equatoria and Western Bahr el Ghazal, political and armed opposition emerged and proliferated. Amid the government's violations of the peace agreement, the humanitarian situation deteriorated still further. In June 2017, JMEC Chair Mogae admitted that ARCISS was fatally wounded but still contended that it was not yet dead. This could not be anything but malicious cynicism on the part of JMEC chairman. His mandate makes him the witness for IGAD, AU, UN, and the international community. He is obliged to report sincerely on whatever has occurred in South Sudan. This was at a time that the government forces were murdering innocent people and razing their villages and farms. One million people elected with their feet to walk to Uganda to save their lives. Nevertheless, Mogae proposed a programme to "revitalize" the 2015 agreement.

The so-called High Level Revitalization Forum (HLRF) between the government of the Republic of South Sudan and the opposition groups (11) was designed without clear concepts or a strategic framework. One of the Jieng think tanks — either the Sudd Institute or Ebony Centre — must have conceptualized it. President Kiir forced it down the throat of the IGAD special envoy, Ambassador Ismael Wais, who was unable to define what revitalization meant, to endorse and implement it. Neither IGAD nor the Troika was able to explain how revitalization of the ARCISS could occur without the participation of the principal signatory, namely Dr. Riek Machar. The parties, but more particularly the SPLA, have never implemented the resolution of its first session: cessation of hostilities. We may consider the HLRF second session a failure because the government delegation refused to append its signature to the principles. In the session held in May, the IGAD special envoys presented to the parties what they called a "bridging proposal." This was merely a copy of the government's position on the revitalization of ARCISS; the SPLM/A-IO and the opposition alliance (SSOA) rejected the proposal. Surprisingly, the government delegation also rejected IGAD's presentation of its position.

This came against the backdrop of President Museveni's visit to Juba (after a seven-hour meeting with the SPLM/A-IO delegation) to attend the meeting of the SPLM National Liberation Council, called specifically to discuss the SPLM reunification and the implementation of the Arusha Agreement. This SPLM reunification and its 45-day postponement was a smokescreen meant to scuttle the attempts of the IGAD Council of Ministers to release Machar from incarceration in South Africa to participate in the revitalized peace process. In this respect, it is possible to conclude that the SPLM reunification and the implementation of the Arusha SPLM are hurdles Kiir and Museveni erected to torpedo the success of the HLRF.

This brings me to the conclusion that the dire situation South Sudan and its people are in, the product of bad elite politics, needs South Sudanese leaders — real patriotic leaders, not self-serving politicians — to rise up and resolve its traumatising situation. Those who stand to lose from peace and stability in South Sudan are the very ones now running around in the guise of resolving the conflict. They will never bring peace to South Sudan because they stand to lose.

President Kiir and Machar Could Have Averted the Catastrophe

Theoretically speaking, war occurs between two leaders who represent two sides in a conflict. War erupts only after they have exhausted all avenues for resolution of their disagreements. To an observer of South Sudan's political landscape, it would appear that the current civil war started as a conflict between President Salva Kiir Mayardit and his former deputy Dr. Riek Machar Teny-Dhurgon. However, on closer scrutiny one is compelled to ask the innocent question of whether or not the two leaders represent two poles in the conflicts underpinning the war. I would answer in the negative. This is precisely because Kiir and Machar represent the same pole in the conflict that pits them against the people of South Sudan. The problem is ideological and is within the parasitic capitalist class, of which both Kiir and Riek represent the pinnacle of that class. The differences between them are simply personal but have been falsely represented as part of the historic rivalry between the Dinka and the Nuer nationalities. This is the usual right-wing mischaracterization of politics.

I believe that the two leaders are in a love-hate relationship, which makes each of them recognizes himself in the other, in a dialectical fashion of the struggle between opposites. Both Kiir and Machar need each other. President Kiir knows and is aware of Machar's pitifully pompous posture and jejune character. Because of this, Machar believed he was in less danger than other SPLM first-row leaders. Kiir wants, for psychological purposes linked to the history of war of national liberation, someone in the person of Machar with whom to shadow box. Perhaps Kiir wanted to demonstrate that he could also fight and win battles. It is noteworthy that as commander of the SPLA Kiir never won a battle: wherever he was posted to command was always a disaster for the SPLA.[81] On the other hand, Machar needs Kiir as his boss. Aware of his own political and leadership weaknesses, Machar desires to remain hidden behind Kiir's own weaknesses in order to survive in power. He does not want to be the principal because that would expose him to criticism, and he has always avoided blame for his failures. The two leaders represent the worst of political naivety and incompetence in the SPLM, and are ready to sacrifice the country in support of their ethnic politics. The civil war, therefore, is an expression of the two men's ambitions for grandeur and promotion of parochial personal ambitions.

The two have been in perpetual denial of any serious problems between them, although their attitudes and actions towards each other speak to the contrary. In the run-up to the SPLM's 2nd National Convention 2008 it was obvious to everyone that Kiir had decided to elbow Machar out of the SPLM hierarchy, and yet they denied that there was any problem between them. Again, in April 2013, President Kiir, in a dramatic turn of events, withdrew Machar's delegated powers. This sent people falling over each other to try to resolve the problem and reconcile the two leaders before things went out of hand. In a meeting with two archbishops and the venerated former leader Abel Alier, the

---

[81] Pibor (1984), Rumbek (1988), and Kurmuk (1990-91).

two leaders insisted that they did not have any problems with each other. Indeed, a problem can only be resolved if there is acceptance and recognition that it exists, otherwise it would be like chasing a mirage.

It was therefore imperative to separate the two men in order to save the people of South Sudan from self-destruction. However, this proved impractical, if not impossible, given the undemocratic character of the SPLM and the low level of political consciousness, which made it impossible to find a rational way to disengage them without triggering conflict. This put the party and the country in a precarious dilemma: put up with a failed SPLM leadership or risk conflict and war. This danger prompted some of us to debate this matter first with Machar because we thought, as an intellectual, he would appreciate, reflect deeply, and perhaps be the first to make a sacrifice in order to save the country. But it was not to be.

Years before, in December 2011, the Government of the Republic of Kenya offered to host a retreat for ministers in the four-month-old government of the Republic of South Sudan. Kenya had midwifed the consummation of the CPA and by extension the birth of South Sudan as an independent and sovereign state. Members of the Kenyan government of President Mwai Kibaki must have watched the poor performance of the subnational GoSS with horror. They took it upon themselves to try to correct the situation and help the young republic's government improve its performance. It was a good opportunity for the first government of South Sudan to learn of the intricacies of executive work. The retreat to Mombasa offered me an opportunity to meet and discuss with Machar a matter that some of us thought deserved more attention on the part of the SPLM's top leadership. Some of us who had been appointed ministers in the post-independence government of the Republic of South Sudan had spent the six-year interim period serving in the Government of National Unity (GoNU) in Khartoum. We therefore had had little opportunity to participate in whatever capacity in Southern Sudan.

One such important matter was the relationship between Machar and President Kiir. Of course, a good working relation between the principal and his deputy is of paramount importance for the harmony of a government and stability of a country. Given the history of the SPLM and the ethnic rivalry in Southern Sudan, it was important and necessary that Kiir and Machar cultivated and nurtured good working relations to enable South Sudan transition to stable peaceful statehood and nationhood. I therefore wanted to discuss with Machar the prospects of leaving the executive work in government to President Kiir, while he took over and concentrated on the political work of building the SPLM.

This was an attempt to streamline and define the roles of the SPLM top leadership. In this arrangement, President Kiir would concentrate on the executive functions of the party in the government. Comrade James Wani Igga would concentrate on the legislative functions of the party in the SSLA, as well as the legislative functions of the state assemblies. Machar would put all his energy into construction of the party and its organs at different levels of South Sudan. The secretary-general, Comrade Pagan Amum, would deal with the administrative functions of the party. This arrangement would minimize and ease the tension and friction Machar seemed to cause, carrying his pompous posture to every occasion, big or small, attended by the president. The idea was to reduce the domain that their respective egos would cross or rub in order to minimize the risk of a clash or conflict.

Unfortunately, Machar could not appreciate the serious concern we attached to their bad working relations. To my dismay, he could not stomach, and did not want to entertain, any of my talk. He had expected me to speak disparagingly against Kiir, which he could use in support of his bid for leadership. I have known Machar since our university days but came to know him better in the SPLM/A, particularly after the Nasir Declaration in 1991. I could not believe he would be averse to building the SPLM into a political party as the driving force in the socioeconomic and political engineering processes of South Sudan.

It was obvious that the condition that aborted the conflict in 2008 still lingered in the SPLM, as well as in society. Ethnic politics were polluting the social and political atmosphere and no one seemed to care. In such a situation, the senior leaders should take it upon themselves to avert a catastrophe. Therefore, it was up to Kiir and Machar to act wisely and avoid the eruption in 2013. In fact, Machar's dismissal from the position of vice president notwithstanding, whatever surrounded the decision in terms of personal enmity or otherwise, need not have meant the end of his political career. The country remained greater and more important than any individual or group of individuals. The people of South Sudan in their totality were more important than any person or group of leaders. Therefore, it would be unconscionable to sacrifice lives in war or conflict only to sustain an individual in power. In this respect, Machar, who considered himself aggrieved, should have taken the initiative to address the anger that forced Kiir to dismiss him from government. In nature as in society, it is the weakest who must surrender in order to save himself, or retreat in order to advance, paraphrasing Mao Zedong. I am convinced beyond any doubt that Machar could have prevented the conflict that erupted in December 2013 had he swallowed his pride and initiated a dialogue with Kiir at the level of the SPLM, or had he taken leave to travel outside the country to ease the tension.

There were veteran leaders, religious leaders, and friends of South Sudan who were ready to intervene to break Kiir's intransigence. But Machar also needed to restrain and neutralize Taban Deng Gai, as well as his own wife, Angelina Teny, who for various reasons were bitter with the president for playing them against each other in Unity State and had now dumped them all. Machar needed to save himself and South Sudan from the two greedy and heartless cousins, Taban and Angelina. Having differed bitterly over the leadership of Unity State leadership they now reconciled and drew their swords against Kiir. In fact, the people of South Sudan, the IGAD region, and the international community must blame the war that erupted in December 2013 on President Kiir, Aleu Ayieny Aleu, Telar Deng Ring, Paul Malong Awan, Taban Deng Gai, Ezekiel Lol Gatkuoth, and Angelina Teny.

It was again Kiir, Malong, Taban Deng, and Angelina who precipitated the July 2016 war, which saw Kiir and Taban Deng go to war against Machar and the SPLM/A-IO, leading to the collapse of TGoNU and the ARCISS. The fighting in J-1 and in the Jebel would not have occurred had Machar's intense fear of Angelina, coupled with his lack of strategic thinking, not denied Taban Deng the petroleum portfolio in the TGoNU, rekindling the bitter memories of their leadership wrangles in Bentiu. Had Machar had the integrity and tenacity to control both Taban Deng and Angelina, he could have initiated the dialogue with Kiir to avoid conflict and war. Unfortunately, Machar, like Kiir, who also was under the control of the JCE and Malong's Beny Bith (magicians), could not extricate himself, as a wise leader would have done. It is disturbing that the destiny of the people of South Sudan depended on the decisions of only a few individuals. This speaks to the objective reality of people's low level of social awareness and political consciousness. The majority of South Sudanese are yet to emancipate themselves from the grip of ethnicity, ethnic chauvinism, and bigotry. They are still submerged in ignorance, superstition, and mythology. Is it not weird that the most egalitarian and acephalous of our communities display the psychology and demagogy of feudal serfs? This is proof that the SPLM/A-led war of national liberation did not succeed in changing South Sudan society.

The people of South Sudan are the victims of this senseless war. We have lost lives and millions of the people are displaced. It was nauseating to watch President Museveni, whose country hosts over a million South Sudanese refugees and who is on perpetual mission to torpedo peace in South Sudan, telling the members of the SPLM National Liberation Council, "I sell my bananas and milk to you." The war is not only senseless, but it also has engendered a culture of indifference and apathy on both sides. It is about time to think of saving the people more than political power. The struggle for rights and civil liberties must now take centre stage in our political thinking. The armed struggle as a tool for social change in South Sudan has failed because it was executed outside its ideological context.

CHAPTER FOUR

To Fix South Sudan We Must Complete the National Democratic Revolution

> The essence of neo-colonialism is that the State which is subject to it is, in theory, independent and has all the outward trappings of international sovereignty. In reality its economic system and thus its political policy is directed from outside.
>
> — Kwame Nkrumah[82]

The political compromise that was the CPA of 2005, which IGAD brokered with the support of the Bush Administration, fell short of addressing the fundamental problems that underpinned the Sudanese conflict. The struggle to resolve these issues spanned six decades. The CPA, however, thrust the SPLM onto the hitherto unfamiliar grounds of government and running the state. As is always the case when an important stage in a process is bypassed, the SPLM leaders' stint at government and running a state was bound to result in serious mistakes and failures.[83] The process to prepare for this important task should have started with the formation of the SPLM/A itself, as a necessary stage of its development.

The 21 years of armed struggle seem to have been a waste of revolutionary energy. As Thorvald Stoltenberg eloquently put it,

---

[82] Kwame Nkrumah, *Neo-Colonialism: The Last Stage of Imperialism* (London: Thomas Nelson & Sons, 1965).

[83] A student who has not completed eight years of primary education cannot expect to do as well as the one who has completed the matriculation examinations.

"Leaders of war are seldom good leaders of peace, freedom and development. The South Sudanese experience is a tragic case in point."[84] It is a literal truth that the SPLM/A conceived the armed struggle and prosecuted the war outside its political and ideological context. The war of national liberation should have been part of the construction of the new social reality in South Sudan — a national state with social, economic and political systems that are different from the ones under the oppressive regime in Khartoum. South Sudan would have then been in a better situation, in terms of addressing the fundamental problems underpinning the war. Because it fell short of that political and ideological conceptualization, the people of South Sudan are now forced to endure another devastating civil war.

I discussed this fact in the previous section. The failures of the SPLM-led government showed up immediately after the signing of the CPA in the form of corruption and insecurity but, more dramatically, in the current civil war, which erupted barely three years into independence. It proved a salient truth that something fundamental went terribly wrong in the manner that the SPLM/A managed or conducted the war of national liberation. I also discussed the drivers of the current civil war and concluded that the liberal peace-making process and the resultant peace agreement could not address this fundamental contradiction. It was in this connection that I faulted Dr. Riek Machar's rebellion because he based the SPLM/A-IO and its struggle on the same premises of power sharing and a superficial reform of the system.

War breaks out to resolve the contradiction, or to pave the way for its resolution, in the words of Chairman Mao Zedong. The military action President Kiir took on 15 December 2013 did not come about because politics in the SPLM reached a point where they could not proceed, but because he did not want politics and the democratic processes involved in conducting them. That action not only prevented the maturation of the political conflict but also pointed people in the wrong direction of ethnicity and provincialism. In the same vein, Machar's rebellion failed to grasp the nature of the conflict. Instead, he acquiesced to Kiir's ethnic and provincial categorization of the conflict. He exacerbated the failure by brushing aside a proposal to organize and strategize differently from the manner that Garang had singlehandedly conducted the war of national liberation. That manner engendered the secondary conflict, which triggered the December 2013 violent eruption. South Sudan

---

[84] Hanssen (2016), "Introduction", p. 22.

needed a paradigm shift towards a national democratic revolution as an inevitable stage in its socioeconomic and political development.

Revolution is a process of change. In our context in South Sudan, revolution is a process by which the present condition of socioeconomic and cultural backwardness of the masses transforms through the development and modernization of their productive forces. There should not be any qualms about this modernization, although many people, particularly the right wing and the liberal/traditionalists, get frightened when they hear the word revolution. They perceive and indeed read violence in "revolution." This begs the simple question: what kind of violence are we talking of? The people of Southern Sudan have experienced violence in their long history. The most violent period was that of slavery and the slave trade, in which Arab and European slavers forcefully wrenched away from their homes many able-bodied people. The colonial pacification of the country was violent, forcing people to resist to maintain their very existence. They have also witnessed the violence of the two previous wars, and now they are in the midst of the worst conflict — fighting among themselves. Therefore, of what kind of violence are they shy?

However, there is need to contextualise violence; it has its causes and drivers. As is the case everywhere in the world, violence boils down to two forms. The first is the violence perpetuated by the oppressor against the people in the context of economic exploitation, social discrimination and political exclusion. This violence is oppressive, reactionary and, therefore, it is right to oppose it. There is then the violence that accompanies people's resistance against, or meted out to, their oppressors. In either case, violence is inevitable. The people do not have to fear or shy away from the violence they mete out in the context of recovering their humanity, dignity, and self-worth. Therefore, rejecting revolution simply because it begets violence is fallacious and a lame excuse. It is tacit support for the status quo and suppresses people's awareness.

The word "ideology" makes some extreme right-wing and liberal elements, particularly those with Christian education backgrounds, apprehensive and fearful. They say that ideology is bad because it is associated with communism or socialism. This again is a wrong perception attributable to ignorance and prejudice, or what in progressive literature is referred to as "mental blockage." While it is a truism that revolution as a process is ideological in context, nevertheless "ideology" is not peculiar to a particular philosophical trait; semantically, it connotes ideas packaged and expressed in a systematized and rationalized format. Therefore, revolution as a process must have an ideology that defines it. In the contemporary and recent past, the world witnessed the American Revolution, French Revolution, Bolshevik Revolution, and Chinese Revolution, with their corresponding ideologies. Revolution is inevitable when a system fails to reproduce itself; the new system that grows within its womb must be nurtured.

In theory and practice, revolution means that for meaningful change to occur, or in order to undertake change in the lives of the people, requires a set of ideas commensurate with the socioeconomic and political transformation that the people desire in their lives. The sum total of these ideas, packaged in a systematic and logical manner, constitutes the ideology of the revolution. They encapsulate its vision, objectives, strategies, and the desired outcome. Nothing in those two words — "ideology" and "revolution" — should frighten the right wing and the liberals in any way. Perhaps, in a way, by expressing their fear of "ideology" and/or "revolution" they echo the ideological position of the exploiting classes —the parasitic capitalist class — and their links to regional and international comprador capitalism which oppose revolution because of their interest in the extraction and plunder of South Sudan resources.

Having laid bare the baseless fears of the right wing and liberals about revolution to change the lives of the people of South Sudan, I come to the kind of revolution that the people of South Sudan stand in need of, or should undertake and why they should. First, let us take a critical look at the socioeconomic and cultural state of the majority of the people of South Sudan. The objective of a revolution is to address problems, mainly problems of social and economic development of South Sudan. A cursory view of South Sudan reveals a number of characteristic features.

The bulk of the people live traditional lives in rural villages or solitary settlements.[85] They have lived like this since time immemorial. They live by tilling land to produce food and other necessities of life, or rear livestock. There are a few towns, which initially were colonial outposts, district headquarters or trading centres. Few unpaved roads connect these towns, suggesting that the countryside is not easily accessible. In the towns, the socioeconomic situation is by no means better. There are

---

[85] Some traditional settlements (Shilluk, Otuho, and Toposa) are large, reaching the size of a small town. The Dinka and Nuer, as well as communities in Equatoria, construct individual homes. The Dinka and Nuer also have cattle camps, which bring together many clans.

few schools or medical facilities except in cities and larger towns. There are no industries, which means that the national productive forces are still underdeveloped. In this kind of situation, in which the social and economic indices are in the negative, our people are considered among the poorest people in the world. This sad situation, which should prick the conscience of every South Sudanese leader, is the fundamental problem, which manifests itself in secondary contradictions like the current civil war, triggered by a power struggle among the political elite, or the ethnic conflicts triggered by competition over land, water, pastures, and cattle rustling.

Nevertheless, agro-pastoralist communities like the Toposa, Didinga, Otuho, Mundari, Dinka, Murle, Nuer, and Shilluk have livestock. In fact, some count their herds in terms of hundreds or thousands of cattle, sheep, goats, and camels. Why is it that despite all this wealth the world considers them poor, or they themselves at times pose like hopeless people who need international humanitarian intervention? Yes, they have these resources and yet they are considered poor because they have not transformed these animal resources into wealth or values expressed in monetary quantities. That is to say, they have not developed their productive forces. The manner in which they own these resources cannot make them rich because they keep them as cultural assets, just to show social status and importance and, at best, as bride price in marriage. As long as these resources remain as cultural assets they will not give our people money to exchange with or purchase other necessities of life like clothes, cars, decent housing, etc. This explains why village folks will ask, as a matter of right, their kin working in government or private sector to give them money. They will never sell any of their livestock: they consider it shameful to sell livestock. A person owning 100 head of cattle cannot count as poor. The methodology of keeping the cattle renders him poor. It is "cultural poverty." We therefore have to transform the perception of this reality, and that is what we mean by revolution.

In trying to transform this reality, we come to realise that South Sudan also has enormous natural resource potential. Important mineral resources like gold, chromite, asbestos, and diamonds have been worked by people or recorded as present in parts of South Sudan. The petroleum deposits in South Sudan make up the only natural resource from which we extracted value in the form of oil revenues that flow into GoSS coffers. The land of South Sudan is predominantly savannah and tropical with natural forests and exotic tree plantations in parts of Equatoria and Western Bahr el Ghazal. The forests provide timber and acacia gum, along with being home to wildlife and having aesthetic values for tourism. The River Nile and its tributaries like the Sobat, Bahr el Ghazal, and Yei have huge fish and other aquatic life potential. This is over and above the fact that large swaths of fertile land suitable for mechanized agricultural production exists in South Sudan. These remain as only potential until they have been transformed to extract the economic value embedded in them.

The development of these resources to extract value or to transform them into economic assets falls within the responsibility of government of the Republic of South Sudan, in terms of policies, development planning, and legislation. This is a political matter and requires a clear understanding, which links to the struggle for independence and the war of national liberation. The essence of independence and sovereignty lies in the power and authority to control, or rather manage, the social, economic, and political life of the people. Independence and sovereignty means that our national government, as our sovereign representative, has the power and authority over everything within the territory of South Sudan. It exercises this authority through legislations, laws, regulations, and guidelines.

The SPLM constituted the Government of Southern Sudan (GoSS) in 2005. This marked the zenith of its struggle for national liberation. It had constitutional, political, and moral authority over the people of Southern Sudan. Annually, it received US $4 billion to US $5 billion in oil revenue. With this amount of money it could have undertaken the social and economic development of southern Sudan; to build physical infrastructure: schools, hospitals, roads, electricity, decent housing; and provide social services and economic development. The SPLM and its cohorts from the NCP and other political parties in the GoSS failed to provide socioeconomic development to the people of South Sudan. The reason for this failure is simple. Only leaders rooted in the revolutionary ideology of addressing the condition of socioeconomic and cultural backwardness of the masses can provide this development. I have mentioned above the ideological shift the SPLM/A leaders undertook that eventually linked them after the CPA to the Bretton Woods institutions (the World Bank and the IMF) for economic and fiscal policy, which has now left South Sudan and its people impoverished.

What does this tell us? In a nutshell, the SPLM leaders have deviated from the liberation ideology, the concept, and vision of the New Sudan. This deviation aligned its leaders to forces interested in extraction and plunder of South Sudan's resources but not in the social and economic development of its people. This explains why there is nothing in terms of development projects or physical infrastructure development to show for the more than US $50 billion that South Sudan received from the sale of its oil in ten years (2005–2015). This means that social and economic development that places the masses at the centre of public policy is a function of ideological orientation of the government and, therefore, touches on what I alluded to above, that South Sudan is ripe for revolution. Before embarking on explaining the relation between government and the social and economic development of South Sudan, I want to make a digression.

The People's Republic of China emerged from colonial occupation and feudalism only in 1949, with the triumph of the communists led by Mao Zedong over the nationalist government. Hitherto, most of the Chinese people were peasants and, just like our people in South Sudan, would have been considered poor. There were remnants of the feudal mode of production, like private ownership of land and the feudal relations of production, which the communist government liberated through agrarian revolution. China did not have big manufacturing enterprises; the industrial revolution had not come to China. However, under the leadership of the Communist Party, the Chinese embarked on social and economic development, starting with a revolution in agriculture and industry to address food security and other needs of the local market. Then, in 1966, the Chinese launched the Cultural Revolution to enable the Chinese people to benefit from advances in knowledge, science, and technology, and to create the Chinese person. Today, China is the second-largest economy in the world without ever having passed through the capitalist mode of production. This, however, is not to forget the staggering human costs and psychological trauma that accompanied the Cultural Revolution in China, noting that each nation must chart a revolutionary path that befits its people.

In Africa, the post-colonial state had a choice of taking either a capitalist or non-capitalist path for its socioeconomic development. But it could not have been a choice in the real sense of the word. The essence of the struggle for independence was to be free of foreign or colonial domination; that is, to consolidate sovereign right to public policy, control the national productive forces, and to enhance social justice and fraternity among the masses. Colonialism produced a national pseudo-bourgeoisie, which tied the post-colonial state to metropolitan country in an asymmetrical relationship: neo-colonialism, which perpetuated the exploitation, extraction and plunder of the resources. The neo-colonial state is the antithesis of a national democratic state constructed at the height of a national democratic revolution.

The United Republic of Tanzania pursued "Ujamaa socialism", based on African societal values. Made up of 124 ethnicities, Tanzania is the only country in Africa where the national petty bourgeoisie has evolved values rooted in the people; where ethnicity, by law, cannot be utilized in the quest for power or for political mobilization. The founding father of the republic, Mwalimu Julius K. Nyerere, used the magic of unified culture in the form of an indigenous lingua franca — Swahili —to build the Tanzanian nation. The socioeconomic development in Tanzania contrasts with that in neighbouring Republic of Kenya in terms of social awareness and national culture and cohesion. This is because although Kenya for much of its independent history had been a one-party political dispensation, politics were organized and power exercised based on ethnicity. As a multi-party liberal democracy, according to the 2010 Constitution, Kenya nevertheless has a polarized society due to ethnic political exclusion, economic marginalization, and social discrimination.

Coming back to the situation in South Sudan, on independence it resembled most post-independence sub-Saharan African countries, especially those that had to engage in protracted negotiations with the colonial powers. The SPLM leaders did not behave as if they and the people of South Sudan had conducted a revolutionary armed struggle. This was not surprising because these leaders, as we have mentioned elsewhere, had switched into an elitist class that was completely isolated from the masses, and were concerned with how they could accumulate wealth and get rich quickly. This attitude on the part of the leaders to get rich as quickly as possible is not compatible with working to address the socioeconomic and cultural backwardness of the people. This explains why instead of providing social and economic development the leaders engaged in self-aggrandisement, corruption, and looting of the state coffers.

The SPLM leaders and their cohorts from the NCP and other political parties had no idea of how to meet the aspirations of the people for freedom, justice, prosperity, and fraternity. For the SPLM leaders, this omission can be attributed to the paradigm shift away from revolution after the war of national liberation. As soon as they assumed power in the Government of Southern Sudan, the SPLM leaders began to pursue right-wing and liberal policies with free-market economic ideologies. This linked South Sudan's wretched subsistence economy to the world capitalist system, which presupposed the existence of a capitalist class that would be able to lead the social and economic development of the country.

The assumption was that this class, the national pseudo bourgeoisie comprising the political military elite which emerged from the war of national liberation, would have the capital to invest and develop and exploit the natural resource potential in agriculture, minerals, services, and industries. However, this class did not possess capital of its own because it did not control any means of production. It derived its power from its control of the state and its resources. Because of this linkage to the state and to the regional and international comprador capitalism, in the context of extraction and plunder of South Sudan's natural resources, this class remains parasitic in character. It can only survive by sucking the state resources and funnelling these resources outside the country.

The parasitic capitalist class, because it does not control any means of social and economic production, is incapable of leading the social and economic development of South Sudan. We have witnessed in the last ten years (2005–2015) the steady reduction in the South Sudan's socioeconomic indices, to the point that they are now all in the negative. It is true that the war, leading to the fall of oil production and increase in government expenditure, was a factor in this decline, but the main cause remains the bad economic policies that the SPLM-led government of South Sudan pursued after 2005, which ignored the development of agriculture and livestock sectors of the economy.

The failure to provide social and economic development led at the political level to competitions for power. The control of state power and its financial and economic resources was tied into a dangerous knot with ethnicity and ethnic politics. It is no wonder that South Sudan witnessed, immediately after the independence, an upsurge of Dinka ethnic nationalism and its ideology of hegemony and domination. This led to the formation of the Jieng Council of Elders as a power broker around Kiir's presidency of South Sudan. The JCE captured the state and transformed South Sudan into a totalitarian dictatorship. This has now plunged the country into deep social, economic, and political crisis, leading to the civil war and dire humanitarian disruption.

It will not be easy for South Sudan to come out of these crises as long as the political forces in the government and the opposition play the political game along the lines of power sharing and superficial reform to the political system set up since 2005. The system ignores the people and therefore generates conflicts in different forms and at different levels.

We must admit that a revolutionary situation obtains in South Sudan. It is represented by the apparent failure of Kiir to provide even for his government. It is worth mentioning that civil servants have not received their salaries for eight months while the government is prosecuting a war. That the civil war has engulfed the whole country and people have taken up arms is indicative of the widespread rejection of President Kiir's rule. This is true even in the Dinka areas of Lakes and Warrap in Bahr el Ghazal. The perennial wars between the Agwok and Apuk in Gogrial, between the Rek and Luany Jiang in Tonj, and among the Agars, in which thousands have perished, indicate that there is something wrong with the system. However, because of ignorance and an inability to perceive the reality in the correct perspective, the people have no way of expressing their discontent with the regime except by internalizing their dissatisfaction and fighting it out among themselves. Communities pick up the gun only to defend their existence as free people, thanks to the secondary conflicts that the Kiir regime is throwing up everywhere in South Sudan. This forces another rhetorical question.

On another level of this reality, there exists a strong separatist tendency among Equatoria's political elite, which is an expression of ethnic nationalism in a provincial perspective. It defines as one entity the nationalities in Equatoria, notwithstanding their different social and economic formations. The National Salvation Front (NAS) and the so-called Concerned South Sudanese (Eastern Equatoria, Central Equatoria, Western Equatoria and Western Bahr el Ghazal states) smack of this separatist tendency, driven partly by hostility to the SPLM/A-IO's presence as a force in Equatoria and reflecting their subjective attitude towards the Dinka and Nuer in general.[86] This separatist tendency stems from leaders who want short political cuts to power, avoiding the difficulties and exigencies of mainstream political struggles. They intend to acquire power through the narrow avenues of ethnicity and provincialism. The strategy of fragmenting the people along ethnic and provincial lines will not resolve the fundamental problems underscoring the civil war in South Sudan.

There are no fundamental contradictions between the people of South Sudan, organized socioculturally as ethnic formations. They have co-existed and co-habitated since time immemorial and, therefore, do not constitute a problem. There are no apparent issues between the

---

[86] A position paper on the revitalization of the ARCISS, 15 October 2017, which was published on the social media.

Nuer and the Dinka, or between the Dinka and the Nuer on the one hand and the Equatorians on the other hand. The fundamental problem is between the people of South Sudan, now organized in their social and political-military formations, the totalitarian dictatorship, and the parasitic capitalist class erected under the leadership of President Kiir. Therefore, such formations as above, which tend to isolate the people of Equatoria and Western Bahr el Ghazal from their compatriots in other parts of South Sudan, are driven by a complete lack of scientific knowledge of the objective reality on the one hand, and the intention to exploit the ignorance of people on the other hand.

Therefore, to address the current situation of war and prevent state collapse, an economic meltdown and humanitarian crisis, requires concerted efforts by all South Sudanese across ethnic and provincial lines. The attempts to divide the people's struggle in the manner of the so-called "Concerned South Sudanese" have tried to acquire political legitimacy by dividing South Sudan and its people into Equatoria and Western Bahr el Ghazal on the one hand, and the rest of South Sudan on the other hand. It is harmful and patriots should combat this tendency.

The Stage of National Democratic Revolution

With independence, South Sudan entered the stage of national democratic revolution in its socioeconomic and political development trajectory. This stage brings together all the social and political forces struggling to enhance and consolidate the country's independence and free the national productive forces. This may require some explanation. As part of the Sudan, the southern provinces became independent together with the rest of the country in 1956. However, the people of Southern Sudan rejected and resisted the transition — decolonization through assimilation (Islamization and Arabicization) — to become independent in July 2011.[87]

We have to point out that the failure of the Arab-dominated northern political elite to address the contradictions inherent in the racial, religious, linguistic, and cultural multiplicity of the Sudan, as well as the socioeconomic and political disparity occasioned by the colonial era's uneven development of the country of the Sudan, triggered wars and conflicts that ended in its dismemberment. The situation obtained because instead of pursuing the national democratic revolution the

---

[87] "Decolonization by assimilation" is borrowed from *Why Comrades Go to War: Liberation Politics and the Outbreak of Africa's Deadliest Conflict* (Oxford: Oxford University Press, 2016), by Philip Roessler and Harry Verhoeven.

dominant political elite, in collaboration with the national bourgeoisie, placed the country on a capital development trajectory. This defined it within the two parameters of Islam and Arab nationhood, leading to social discord, political conflict, and civil wars. The country therefore missed the opportunity to address the fundamental problems of poverty, ignorance, and illiteracy of the masses. The wars of liberation the people fought were, therefore, an expression of the conflict between the people and the ruling classes because the ruling classes had failed to align their social, economic, and political interests with those of the masses.

The national democratic revolution is made up of the social, economic, and political engineering processes that the political and social forces undertake to enhance and strengthen national independence and fraternity; to strengthen national symbols; enhance freedom of the masses and promote social justice. They develop and free the national productive forces from any kind of foreign control and domination. The task of the national democratic revolution is to address the fundamental contradictions reflected in the poverty, ignorance, illiteracy, and superstition that submerge the consciousness of the masses. Besides these, it also addresses the secondary contradictions inherent in the social, ethnic, linguistic, religious, and cultural multiplicities of South Sudan.

As things stand, only the revolutionary and democratic political and social forces can undertake and lead a national democratic revolution. This is by virtue of their ideology and revolutionary consciousness, knowledge of the laws of socioeconomic development of society, and high level of discipline and commitment to the people. The weakness reflected in lack of organization and ideological unity of these revolutionary and democratic political and social forces explains why the national democratic revolution has not kicked off, even though the objective conditions for its eruption have existed in Southern Sudan since the formation of the SPLM/A in 1983. The dominance of right-wing and neo-liberal forces in the national liberation movement was the biggest drawback, soaking the movement in reactionary and ethnic ideologies.

The eruption of violence in December 2013, notwithstanding its ethnic overtones, was nevertheless an opportunity to rekindle the national democratic revolution. It provided conditions conducive to the development of a revolutionary consciousness among the combatants and the masses. The massacre of ethnic Nuer in Juba, which triggered mass mobilization against the regime, was nevertheless a chain that straightjacketed the movement to the Nuer mythology linked to Machar. This prevented the development of the nascent SPLM/A-In Opposition into a social revolution capable of transforming state and society. As a result, its leadership could not pursue the struggle in a scientific way and had to opt for a peace agreement with the government through the IGAD mediation.

National Democratic Revolution Versus the IGAD Peace Mediation

The failure, or rather the refusal, of the SPLM/A-IO leadership to build its political and military forces forced it to negotiate peace with the government of Salva Kiir Mayardit. The vacuity of negotiating a peace agreement — a liberal peace — lies in the fact that it leaves intact the oppressive reality. Not only that, but also the refusal of President Kiir to sign the Agreement on the Resolution of the Conflict in South Sudan (ARCISS) demonstrated that the agreement was at the mercy of the dictator. He violated it at will until it finally collapsed following the fighting in the Presidential Palace (J-1) in Juba on 8 July 2016.

The fighting in Juba rekindled the war not only in Upper Nile and in Jonglei but also spread it to the hitherto peaceful areas of Equatoria and Bahr el Ghazal. An analysis of these dynamics shows that the peace agreement addressed only the question of power sharing between the two protagonists; it did not address the concerns of the people for inclusivity in the decision-making processes. One fundamental issue the people in Central and Western Equatoria and Western Bahr el Ghazal raised was the national character of the armed forces. Kiir's refusal to establish centres in those areas for the cantonment of their sons and daughters who wanted to join the armed forces, viewed as an expression of power, triggered their suspicion of anticipated marginalization and hence the call to arms. The national character of the army and security forces in a multi-ethnic setting such as South Sudan is significant as it is a condition for social harmony and peace. The inordinate dominance of ethnic Nuer in the SPLA following the absorption of the tribal militia created the imbalance in the power configuration that engendered and brought instability to the social and political levels, and eventually triggered the eruption of violence in December 2013.

It was obvious that ARCISS would not hold because it did not create the required social and political equilibrium. At the same time, it could not sustain the conditions created by the civil war. The resumption of war was therefore inevitable, never mind that the parties that forced its resumption (Kiir/Taban/Malong) did not have the political and military capacity to establish a clear-cut military victory. This led to its escalation, engulfing hitherto peaceful areas in Equatoria and Western Bahr el Ghazal and seeing the emergence and proliferation of armed and opposition groups.

The proliferation of political groups opposed to the ethnocentric, kleptocratic and totalitarian dictatorship speaks to a reality that the people of South Sudan need not repeat the experience of the SPLM/A during the war of national liberation. The eruption of violence in Juba in December 2013 created conditions for social revolution in South Sudan. It will not take long before these opposition groups have merged into a wider coalition aimed at social transformation in South Sudan. Therefore, the emergence of different social and political groups struggling for social change shows that the emerging national and democratic character of war is the best condition for a national democratic revolution. This is a departure from the SPLM/A methodology during the war of national liberation, and also from the SPLM/A-IO, which had no clear political objective but wanted everyone to fall under its tutelage. Therefore, the IGAD high level revitalization (HLRF) of the ARCISS is an attempt to undercut a national democratic revolution. This is because instead of giving the opposition forces time to organize, align, and unite themselves into a front capable of forcing change, the HLRF is dangling in their faces positions in the transitional government of national unity it hopes to form.

The evolving social and political context calls on the national democratic revolutionary forces, armed and political opposition, to forge a unity to enable a collective and concerted effort against the regime. There is a need for mutual recognition and acceptance of each other as equal stakeholders, notwithstanding political and ideological differences. This will accelerate consensus building around social, economic, and political development processes to address the issues of poverty, ignorance, and illiteracy afflicting the people of South Sudan. This is the bottom line of political action, which involves peasants, workers, petty business people, and intellectuals formed into a front, the National Democratic Revolutionary Front (NDRF), armed with a political programme encompassing all aspects of the social, economic, and political life of the people of South Sudan.

The strategic political objective of the national democratic revolution is destruction of the totalitarian, ethnocentric, kleptocratic state that Kiir has erected in South Sudan, and the construction in its place of a national democratic state. The national democratic state will emerge in the context of the struggle for freedom, social justice, equality, and prosperity, reflecting the highest expression of South Sudanese fraternity. Citizenship is the basis of relation, where there is respect for and promotion of fundamental human rights and political and civil liberties, as enshrined in the Constitution.

This development will be a radical departure from the classic evolution of state. Historical materialism provides that the state evolved from society to rise and hang above it in hierarchical relationship with society. This model of a state's emergence and its development has been the source of human suffering. The present state in South Sudan, as in many other countries in sub-Saharan Africa, is a legacy of this construction. It is an oppressive state and, therefore, the national democratic revolution is a deliberate and conscious process of its deconstruction. The national democratic revolution erects a state that comprises all the social strata that construct it and, therefore, are or remain in horizontal relationship to each other. In this case, once the NDRF defeats and takes over power from the oppressive state it will begin implementing the national democratic revolutionary programme to address the primary and secondary contradictions that have afflicted the masses over the years. The national democratic state epitomizes the highest aspirations of the people of South Sudan; it enables them to realise freedom, justice, fraternity, and prosperity through their own efforts.

I established above that the emergence of ethnic nationalism is one of the drivers of the current civil war. This negative ethnicity issue is a contradiction inherent in the ethnic, religious, and sociocultural reality of South Sudan. It has become explosive because President Kiir promoted the apparent dominance and hegemony of Dinka ethnicity in the distribution of political and economic power in South Sudan. We must remind ourselves that 67 nationalities or national groups in different demographic weights and at varying levels of social, economic, and cultural development inhabit South Sudan. This means that social harmony and peace obtains only when political dispensation factors these nationalities and national groups into the socioeconomic and political engineering processes of the state. The contemporary history of the Sudan and South Sudan reveals that political exclusion, social discrimination, and economic marginalisation and exploitation were factors in past conflicts and war.

One of the imperatives for transforming the civil war into a national democratic revolution is the disturbing aspect that both Kiir and Machar ethnicized the internal political conflicts of the SPLM, which turned ethnic communities against each other. They hail from the same socio-ideological formation and that makes it easy for them to explain their political differences in terms of ethnicity. The recruitment of Dotku Beny and Mathiang Anyoor to fight the Nuer on behalf of the regime, and the Nuer White Army to fight the government on behalf of Dr. Riek Machar proves the point above and definitely remains a disturbing aspect of the current civil war. It has destroyed not only the social fabric of marriages and social interaction, but also erased the social capital that bound these people together for decades and enabled them to ward off their common enemies. The ethnicity question in South Sudan is, therefore, a serious national problem that warrants quick attention at the social, economic, and political levels.

The programme of the national democratic revolution approaches the ethnicity question from a scientific premise to correct historical injustices, false perception, and other psychological images that inform and influence the current social and political relations in the country. This approach is anchored in the application of the principle of justice, which translates into equality and equity in the distribution and the even development of the natural resources to generate wealth. This is at the economic level but it also occurs at the political level because, as they say, economics is concentrated politics. A decision to undertake an economic development project in a particular location is also a political decision to develop the area and to transform the lives of people. This reminds us of the decision of Abboud's regime to place the cane sugar factory in Gunied in Buthana, northern Sudan, instead of Mangalla in Equatoria, where feasibility studies indicated production would be cheaper. This economic project was a political decision of the oppressive regime to deny socioeconomic development to the Bari, Pari, and Mundari areas, notwithstanding the economic feasibility of the project. The national democratic state will undertake equitable socioeconomic development of the country.

It is imperative and of paramount importance that the national democratic state accords each ethnic group its right to participate in the national social, economic, and political life of the country. This is in addition to any particularistic projects to enhance its visibility and audibility in the power configuration of the state. The ability of each group to benefit from the material and cultural resources of the country removes the ground for discrimination, domination, and hegemony of the larger nationalities. The national democratic state ensures that everyone is provided with the necessary material and technological resources to develop their languages and cultures to enable them compete with others at the national level. In practice, this means that the national democratic state, alongside the construction of physical infrastructure throughout the country, shall embark on a campaign of enlightenment and political education to raise people's social awareness and political consciousness, leading to changes in their attitudes and perception of social reality.

A change in people's attitudes and their correct perceptions of objective reality is fundamental for emancipating the masses from ignorance and superstition. This is necessary not only for the conscious development of the national productive forces but also for combating archaic beliefs, customs, and practices that lead to social discrimination. It enables the people to conceive the common bonds that tie them together as South Sudanese, and definitely trump the excessive attachment to clan, tribe, or province. This strengthens their common identity together with fraternal and patriotic attachment to each other as equal citizens. Therefore, addressing the nationality/ethnicity question up front is the central objective of transforming the civil war into a revolution. It would end historical ethnic hatred and animosities, which the totalitarian regime has exploited to fragment the people along ethnic lines. The targeting of innocent people based on ethnicity is a direct result of the regime's ethnicized politics. The resolution of the nationality/ethnicity question is, therefore, an important condition for the success of the national democratic revolution. It is key to peace and social harmony, and to "unity in diversity" as a cornerstone of state formation and nation building in South Sudan. This will consign to the dustbin of history certain practices in society and state based on primeval relations and patrimonialism.

The national democratic state also addresses the ethnicity/nationality question at the sociocultural level by combating archaic traditions, beliefs, and practices embedded in social reality: that is, practices and traditions that discriminate against and dehumanize other members of society, in particular women and the girl child. It is common knowledge that among our communities a woman is considered as a commodity to be exchanged for cattle, camels, or pigs, or money in the form of dowry. This practice interferes with certain rights of the woman as a human being, particularly the right of the girl child to receive an education and to choose her partner in life. It also interferes with her political and civic rights to leadership. Thus, the so-called affirmative action that gives certain percentages for political and social representation is a form of patronage not linked to the assumption that women are inferior to men and therefore need special treatment. The presumed differences between men and women are constructed socially and politically in a male-dominated society. One of the priorities of the national democratic revolution, therefore, is the emancipation of society from the repugnant traditions that discriminate on the basis of gender.

To transform the way people relate to each other requires more than changing their material conditions; it also requires a strong political will to combat ignorance, ethnic bigotry, chauvinism, and religious narrowmindedness. This will not, however, be easy. One of the methods by which the national democratic state addresses this problem is through knowledge dissemination and introduction of compulsory universal primary education in addition to a campaign of alphabetization and adult education as an important component of the national democratic revolution. It provides the people of South Sudan, in which illiteracy is about 70 per cent, with the rare opportunity to benefit from the experiences of the Cuban Revolution and that of the Derg in Ethiopia in eradicating illiteracy in their countries. We are aware that literacy enables the people to develop skills to harness technology and techniques, which leads to transforming the quality of their lives.

The measures above must accompany legislation to criminalize ethnic or provincial profiling of citizens. As they say, it is not easy to abandon bad habits. It may take time for people to abandon their bad habits or to erase from their minds the use of derogatory words and names. We had an experience in the Bahr el Ghazal Youth Development Association during the war of liberation. We made a decision that the youth should take the lead in prohibiting and combating ethnic or clan profiling using words or names deemed derogatory, like *fertit* or calling people by wrong names.[88] In this way, the Luo and the Biele refused to respond when the Dinka called them Jur. The Dinka use of the word *jur*, literally meaning "foreigner", insinuates that the Luo and Biele were recent migrants to the areas where they neighbour the Dinka. The opposite is true: it was the Dinka who migrated to that land. The reason behind this discussion is that people name themselves, and in re-humanizing ourselves, we give ourselves and/or place the appropriate name. In this respect, the Bahr el Ghazal Youth Development Association criticized the SPLM leaders for

---

[88] This word lumps together the about 25 small ethnic communities in the western Bahr el Ghazal districts of Wau and Raga.

aping colonial occupiers by changing the names of places, as they did with "New Kush" and "New Site", replacing the original Didinga names of Heiman and Natinga respectively.

The importance of addressing the ethnicity/nationality question on the economic and sociocultural levels is paramount. It links organically to the social awareness and political consciousness of the people and therefore mediates and moderates contradictions at the political level. We have noticed in political cultures in developed economies that power contests seldom translate to violence, as it does in many of African countries. Ignorance and lack of political awareness on the part of the masses, weak institutions, and the commoditization of ethnicity in the political marketplace by the political elite renders explosive the power contest. Literacy and the ability to read, write, and understand printed text is connected to the people's social awareness and political consciousness as it relates to and increases citizens knowledge of their rights and duties. Therefore, addressing the ethnicity question and combating ignorance are interrelated and lie at the core of the national democratic revolution.

This brings us to the issue of addressing poverty as an impediment to human happiness in South Sudan. Poverty is a condition of extreme deprivation of food, clean water, decent housing, medical services, education, and clean environment. Poverty makes life miserable and is characterized by a short life expectancy. It is an expression of socioeconomic and cultural underdevelopment, reflected in the negative socioeconomic indices of the country. The majority of the people of South Sudan are predominantly rural and agrarian, living as peasants, agro-pastoralists, and pastoralists. Thus, agriculture is the economic mainstay of the people and the means by which they generate wealth. This means that underdevelopment of agriculture is the driver of poverty in South Sudan. It is crucial that we investigate and determine the scope and drivers of poverty in South Sudan.

Poverty in South Sudan is an expression of colonial underdevelopment of the southern provinces, as well as its policy of uneven development of the different parts of the Sudan, a policy the Arab-dominated national governments deliberately perfected to prevent the secession of southern Sudan. In 1947, the colonial administration established the Equatoria Project Board to develop the agricultural potential of Central and Western Equatoria. By the time the Sudan became independent, the Nzara scheme was already producing woven cloth, soap, sugar, edible oil, and timber. It was a model of socioeconomic development that improved the conditions of life in the Azande land. It introduced cotton plantations to feed the ginning and spinning sections and this really changed the Azande economy through monetization. It was in the same context that the Mangalla Sugar and agro-industrial complex were conceived.

Poverty obtains in South Sudan because of underdevelopment of the means of production in terms of proper utilization of land and implements for tilling that could support sufficient production of food or cash crops. Many parts of the country experience a perennial "hunger gap", suggesting that the yield from the annual crop production does not carry people through to the next harvest. This is because agricultural practice depends on natural beneficence or the vagaries of weather, manual labour, and traditional seeding, which renders subsistence agriculture unpredictable and precarious. This means this type of agricultural production cannot generate a surplus that the peasants could market for other necessities.

Thus, during the hunger gap the peasants must either sell their animals or rely on their relatives in the towns in a perpetual, vicious cycle. To address this problem, which translates into addressing food security of the country, it is imperative to introduce modern agricultural implements to enhance production in food and cash crops. It is feasible to introduce largescale rain-fed and irrigated mechanized agriculture in all parts of South Sudan for the commercial production of food crops: sorghum, corn, rice, barley, and beans, as well as cash crops like sesame, sunflower, cotton, and groundnuts. This modernization of agriculture must of necessity begin with simple mechanical tools (e.g., ox plough) that the peasants understand and could manage by themselves in family smallholdings (up to ten acres) of land.

The use of the ox plough in agricultural production could be a tricky affair, particularly for those communities that revere or glorify possession of the cow. However, necessity created by famine and extreme food insecurity has, in the past, forced the use of cattle in agricultural production. In 1998, following the ruinous famine that killed tens of thousands of people in Bahr el Ghazal, peasants who hitherto were reluctant or hostile to the use of cattle in agricultural production voluntarily provided bulls to train for use in the fields, and indeed they found it profitable. They produced surplus crops, enabling them not only to sell the surplus but also to use that surplus to replenish their herds. It only requires conscientisation: arriving at the truth of food security by learning together and enabling the pastoralists, who are seldom disposed to using their animals in agriculture, to change their attitudes.

The revolution in agriculture takes advantage of developments in science and technology to increase productivity and stimulate the surplus potential inherent in this economic sector. This modernization of agricultural production through the use of technology and introduction of irrigation techniques in some dry areas will definitely reduce vulnerabilities caused by the vagaries of weather. This can assure the farmers of increased yields, necessitating access to domestic, regional, and international markets. In this way, South Sudan could benefit from the huge potential in the production of oil seeds (simsim, sunflower, cotton seeds, shea, and groundnuts), gum arabic, timber, sorghum, maize, and other crops. The most important aspect of the revolution in agriculture is linked to the introduction of processing technology in order to add value. This would mean constructing agro-industrial installations to process raw materials for the manufacture of products for local and export markets. This provides employment and at the same time leads to the evolution of a developed and conscious working class capable of promoting development and participating in the social, economic, and political engineering of the state.

The pastoral and nomadic sector, throughout the world, is the most underdeveloped, conservative, and resistant to change. The national democratic revolution must pay sufficient attention to this sector. Estimates indicate that South Sudan has over 12 million head of cattle and millions of sheep and goats, which this sector manages traditionally as cultural rather than economic assets. The revolution in agriculture must therefore address this sociocultural dimension in order to transform this enormous livestock wealth into economic and commercial resources through the introduction of modern and scientific methods of animal husbandry. This will require a complete break with the traditional animal husbandry through the creation of cooperative large-scale ranches designated for zero grazing, which has the benefit of reducing the impact on the environment. The development and modernization of the livestock sector of the economy has an added revolutionary value that could resolve and address some of the negative traditional practices among the agro-pastoral and nomadic communities that adversely affect the fundamental rights of women and the girl child. The peasants and nomads are not keen on sending their children, especially the girls, to school.

South Sudan lies within the tropics and has large swaths of natural forests and plantations, mainly exotic hardwood trees like teak, mahogany, and cedrela, particularly in Western Bahr el Ghazal, and parts of Eastern Equatoria; while natural forests of acacia senegal can be found in Upper Nile, northern Bahr el Ghazal, and eastern Equatoria. Northern Upper Nile produces nearly 45 per cent of the world's output of gum arabic. The development and conservation of forests is therefore important as part of the environmental protection programme of the revolution but also as a source of wealth for the country. The forests and wetlands double up as wildlife habitat and add value as a tourist attraction and source of revenue for the country. We cannot overemphasize the importance of the linkage of tourism and wildlife to environmental conservation and protection, particularly in respect to climate change. This would be the revolution's contribution to reducing environmental degradation.

The Nile River, its tributaries and the wetlands, including the Sudd region, have huge potential in aquaculture: fish, reptiles, and vegetation, which contribute to food security not only for the riverine population but also for other people. It is imperative that this sector is developed and modernized in order to transform the lives of the people living along these watercourses. Scientific methods and technologies should be introduced, including fish farming and reptile farming. Because the Nile River and its tributaries provide transport and communication, it is necessary and of paramount importance that their basins are dredged to reduce siltation and water hyacinths, which periodically block their channels.

Transportation to and communication in different parts of South Sudan remain a bottleneck due to the lack of paved road networks. This means accessibility to the country's different parts is difficult during certain seasons of the year. One of the priorities of the national democratic revolution is to construct road networks, bridges, and dykes in order to connect the country and make it easier for the populations to access social and economic services. Linking up the country has the political dimension of connecting the people and promoting national cohesion and peace. It is important to note that development and construction of the physical infrastructure must be in place as a precursor to industrial revolution. The production of energy as a vehicle for the industrialization of South Sudan is a priority. There is huge potential in hydroelectric power in the rivers and streams throughout South Sudan, which the government should harness and distribute through the construction of power transmission lines to different parts of the country. Other energy sources include solar, wind, and biogenic resources, which would augment hydroelectric power. Electrification of the country is one important project of the national democratic revolution.

Linked to the development of physical infrastructure is the provision of decent housing for people in urban and rural settlements. It will be necessary to alter the dispersed solitary settlements practised by some communities through a programme of villagization and urbanization as an important programme for improving people's quality of life. The programme of villagization blends with and indeed drives the cultural revolution, leading to emergence of a progressive national culture.

Higher education, as the main driver of socioeconomic and cultural development through knowledge generation and transmission, fits into the scheme of the national democratic revolution. There will be a need to democratize and make higher education accessible to the masses. It is imperative to construct world-class university campuses, technical colleges, and polytechnics to provide quality higher education, produce professionals and a specialized workforce, particularly in the productive enterprises, to undertake rapid modernization and industrialization of South Sudan.

The national democratic revolution must organize politics based on ideas and a practical programme rather than personality and political patronage, as has occurred in South Sudan for the last three decades. The significance and relevance of ideology in the social, economic, and political engineering of South Sudan will be made apparent in a nation-building process that emphasizes the principles of freedom, social justice, prosperity, and fraternity and such values as respect for basic human rights and fundamental freedoms. This will assist in combating tribalism, corruption, and licentiousness.

The national democratic revolution is a process involving many different stages. I discussed in another part of this book the failure of the SPLM/A-IO to transform the civil war into a national democratic revolution. This failure stems from the fact that the agenda of the SPLM/A-IO leadership was not social change but power. President Kiir transformed the power struggle in the SPLM Political Bureau into military action and, hence, the civil war. What Machar refused to do was to transform this military aggression into a revolution involving the people of South Sudan across ethnic and provincial lines. This explains why the war stalled, forcing him to negotiate peace with the government.

The peace agreement signed in August 2015 could not hold because President Kiir refused to share power with Machar. The standoff in the implementation rekindled the fighting, leading to the collapse of the ARCISS. After nearly two years of procrastination, foot-dragging, and opportunistic fence-sitting, in the hope that the Kiir would militarily annihilate the SPLM/A-IO, the IGAD mediators designed the so-called High Level Revitalization Forum (HLRF) of the ARCISS. Its objectives included restoration of the permanent ceasefire, full and inclusive implementation of the ARCISS, and a revised and realistic timeline and implementation schedule towards democratic elections at the end of the transitional period. These are unrealistic objectives, particularly the 30-month transition period after which the Transitional Government of National Unity (TGoNu) would conduct democratic elections. This gives President Kiir a lease of life since his tenure of office as president of the government of southern Sudan expired in May 2015. He is in office because of the war he unleashed in December 2013; therefore, without a radical transformation of the ethnocentric, totalitarian, and dictatorial regime it will not be possible to conduct a peaceful transfer of power whether by democratic or liberal elections.

The significance of the HLRF, however, lies in the possibility of enforcing a permanent cessation of hostilities to enable politics, and democratic politics for that matter, to take centre stage in engineering the post-conflict dispensation. We consider the HLRF as a means of easing the country out of reactionary armed resistance, which has produced warlords, into an era of political struggle in which cerebral (intellectual and knowledge) rather than muscular (violence and military) energies will be relevant. However, we should be vigilant and mindful that the HLRF and whatever agreement that emerges from it could recreate the same conditions as those that triggered the fighting in July 2016.

We should view whatever agreement the social and political forces achieve in the HLRF as a phase in the struggle for democracy, freedom, justice, and prosperity. It has reached this point because the SPLM/A-IO failed to build its military forces and to create a political programme that would have united behind it, or in collaboration with it, all the social and political forces struggling against the ethnocentric, kleptocratic, and totalitarian regime. The successful conclusion of the HLRF and the return of law and order will enable the social and democratic political forces to regroup, reorganize, and replenish their ranks, and realign themselves to continue the struggle to complete the national democratic revolution. The revolutionary forces, the forces of the national democratic revolution, will not down their tools for struggle but would instead sharpen them for the final assault on the regime. The revolutionary forces should make use of the intervening period to study and learn, organize, set strategies, and design new tactics for the struggle. It is clear from the recent experience that the people are ready to sacrifice for the cause of freedom and justice.

The immediate task is to work for the organizational and political unity of the opposition forces and build a consensus around a wider coalition for democracy and to save the country. The coalition, which calls itself the National Democratic Revolutionary Front (NDRF), is made up of all the social, democratic, and revolutionary political forces in South Sudan. It is an entity with a manifesto, a political programme, and a constitution. It is disposed to legal and constitutional methods of struggle. This means that each constituent member must have a legal existence registered with the Political Parties Commission.

The organization of society and the economy is the revolution's raison d'être in order to transform the conditions of social, economic, and cultural underdevelopment. The primary objective of the national democratic revolution is construction of a modern state in South Sudan, implying the evolution of a knowledge-based, cultured, peaceful, and harmonious society in South Sudan, a society characterized by the efficient and effective automation of agricultural and industrial production through the effective application of knowledge and advances in science and technology. The agricultural, industrial, and cultural revolutions will be linked up as inseparable components of the national democratic revolution led by the revolutionary and patriotic elements of the petit bourgeois. It is important to underline "patriotic elements" because the petit bourgeois by its nature is not a stable class. In the words of Amílcar Cabral, for the petit bourgeois to lead the masses it must commit class suicide and rise in the guise of revolutionary peasants and workers. It cannot be anything less. Thus, when we proposed transforming the civil war into a national democratic revolution, it was precisely to revolutionize and legitimize the SPLM/A-IO because it was created during a different circumstance of ethnic massacre, vengeance, and counter-vengeance. It was necessary to draw a line between a reactionary war and a revolution in terms of ideology, strategic political objectives, organization, and methods of struggle, including rules and procedures.

The revolution actually began in areas where the SPLM/A-IO was in physical control of territory and population. The dominance of the reactionary right wing in its leadership, however, stymied the growth of social and political awareness in the masses. Thus, the war was fought on flimsy political objectives of power sharing and superficial reforms in the system. The political mobilization was based on militarism and militarization of the population without raising their political awareness. In this context, the SPLM/A-IO failed to construct a counter-society that was different from the tribalized and oppressed society under the totalitarian regime. The national democratic revolution would not be about fighting to take power in Juba but about changing the society, corresponding to a down-up sociopolitical engineering process.

The shared values, attitudes, and common culture do not obtain of their own. They are consequent to the development and organization of the social forces of production. The importance of the national democratic revolution under the leadership of progressive democratic forces lies in an ideology that anchors and promotes common ownership of the means of production, giving the democratic state control over the major means of production. The people would be trained to internalize these concepts and start practising them as early as possible. The leadership of the national democratic revolution should then chart out these ideas in a political programme and policy framework with strategies for achieving the political objectives of the revolution.

The programme, in its social, economic, political, and military contents, would be time-bound. The strategic importance of the military action would be to weaken and eventually destroy the base of the totalitarian regime and its oppressive military and security apparatus. However, it would be necessary to align the military action and victories against the enemy with the social and political processes, in terms of raised levels of social awareness and political consciousness. The combatants and the masses must forge a relationship of solidarity and a sense of unity across ethnic and regional lines. This will correct the mistakes committed during the war of national liberation, when the SPLA turned against the very people they said they were liberating. The common struggle against ethnocentric totalitarian dictatorship leads to the evolution of a national culture that frowns on sectarianism, parochialism, chauvinism, and bigotry. We will never again hear people thumping their chests as "liberators" for all will have participated in the social, political, and military processes leading to the destruction of the regime, suggesting that it was a common enterprise.

Common Ownership of Means of Production

The idea of common ownership of the means of production, suggesting a socialist economic formation, is something that puts off many right-wingers, the neoliberals and the apologists of capitalism in South Sudan. It is imperative to explain this concept and the underlying philosophy. South Sudan is socioeconomically and culturally underdeveloped. This is the objective reality of our people and the country at large. There are no privately owned manufacturing plants, large-scale agricultural schemes, railways, or electrical generating plants. These do not, and will not, exist in South Sudan simply because no one has the necessary capital to construct them. Those South Sudanese, the parasitic capitalists, who accumulated money through corruption and outright theft from the public coffers have, instead of ploughing into and investing in the national economy, stashed this stolen money far away from South Sudan.

It is a fact that the parasitic capitalism in South Sudan is at a stage of primitive accumulation, extraction, and plunder, without care of replenishing what it has extracted or plundered; while global comprador capitalism with its regional proxies are interested in grabbing huge profits at minimum costs. This means that they invest where the country had reached some level of social and economic development in terms of existent physical and financial infrastructure (banks and ICT) to enable quick returns on investments. No investor, no matter how rich he/she may be, will come to spend money in South Sudan when he has to build roads and generate his own electricity. Investors will go elsewhere, to places where these amenities are in place and are not expensive. No investor has come for the huge limestone deposit in Kapoeta because of the lack of power. This means that only a people-centred government of South Sudan can and must invest in physical infrastructure (roads, power generation, and transmission lines) to enable the development and exploitation of these deposits for the production of cement and other natural resources.

Ignorance and prejudice blocks people from understanding certain concepts and consequently generates frictions and disunity in the ranks. It is therefore important that we contextualize the concept of common ownership of means of production. Common ownership of means of production means ensuring the dominance of the South Sudan state, and not the parasitic capitalist class and its imperialist connections, in the process of transforming the conditions of socioeconomic and cultural underdevelopment of the people of South Sudan. This is the task that the forces of the national democratic revolution have assigned to themselves to undertake, being the revolution's raison d'être as opposed to liberal economics and free-market ideologies, which perpetuate poverty and ignorance, the underlying fundamental reason for the South Sudan conflict. This conditions of poverty and ignorance has endured since the colonial period because the dominant petit bourgeois that inherited the neo-colonial state is incapable of developing the economy. Not only that but it has also tied the country to the regional and international comprador capitalism through the extraction and plunder of South Sudan's natural resources. This explains how in 12 years this class has squandered the more than US $50 billion South Sudan received in oil revenues.

A clear knowledge of imperialism as a historically constructed asymmetrical relationship between the poor (South) and rich (North) countries is essential in this discussion of common ownership of the means of production. The salient feature in this relationship of concern to national liberation in South Sudan is that it allows the rich and powerful countries of the North to control and influence in their favour the socioeconomic policies of South Sudan, particularly in the development and exploitation of their natural resources. This becomes obvious when we consider the role of the World Bank and the IMF in directing the fiscal and monetary policies of the GoSS between 2005 and 2015, the cumulative result of which has pauperized the people and left the country bankrupt. The parasitic capitalist class provided the link to the Bretton Woods institutions and the regional and international comprador capitalism, on account of its control of state machinery and the evolution of the totalitarian, ethnocentric, and kleptocratic regime under President Kiir.

It would be correct to say that the links to imperialism through the parasitic capitalist faction of the petit bourgeois only reproduces condition of poverty, ignorance, and illiteracy in South Sudan. This class has demonstrated its incapacity and lack of interest to lead the social and economic development of South Sudan in order to lift the masses out of abject poverty. Therefore, only the state control of major economic development projects would enable South Sudan and its people to get out of this condition of poverty. The state would provide the financial and economic resources for providing social services like health, education, transport, and communication, as well as extension services in agriculture and livestock sectors. It would provide the necessary physical infrastructure for modernization of agricultural production and animal husbandry.

Common ownership of means of production, especially largescale industrial and agricultural enterprises, is a political and ideological decision of the revolution. It is out of the consideration that South Sudan and its people, now at the bottom of the ladder of human development, can be raised up only through the agency of the state being at the centre of social and economic development. This decision, therefore, places the tools and instruments of strategic planning for social and economic development in the state agencies. This would enable equitable development of all parts of the country, unlike in the capitalist development paradigm where certain areas remain unattended to because the capitalists are interested only in reaping profits, meaning that the capitalist will invest only where he is assured of having a profitable business.

The most critical means of production is land. The question of land and its ownership is a central part of the national democratic revolution. The Transitional Constitution of South Sudan 2011 confirms the communal ownership of land, meaning that many communities frown on the private ownership of land. By way of example, in the Shilluk Kingdom, the king owned the land in public trust of the Shilluk people. Nevertheless, there is a potential conflict in the question of the use of land resources and ownership, especially in rural agro-pastoralist areas. In order to avoid conflict within the communities and between them and the state, where large economic installations exist the national democratic state should promulgate laws that promote a revolution in agriculture and rational utilization of land, keeping in mind ecological and environmental concerns.

In summary, South Sudan is ripe for a national democratic revolution. The objective factors are already in place in the form of the socioeconomic and cultural backwardness of the people, as reflected in their abject poverty, ignorance, illiteracy, and superstition. These conditions have suppressed their awareness and prevented them from a correct perception of the reality that oppresses them, thus further compounding the problem. The current civil war has forced the people to arm themselves to fight for their very existence as free people. This is an important objective factor for the revolution.

IGAD, HLRF, and the National Democratic Revolution

As discussed elsewhere in this book, the SPLM/A-IO-led armed struggle had stalled by April 2014. This situation of military stalemate has continued, even after the fighting in J-1 in July 2016. Recognizing the military weakness of the armed opposition, the government nevertheless failed to achieve total military victory, forcing the SPLM/A-IO into some kind of guerrilla warfare. The other opposition groups that emerged after the collapse of ARCISS added no value to the opposition save in-fighting and confusion. They were poaching men and arms from the SPLM/A-IO. The lack of unity and a common agenda against the ethnocentric totalitarian regime summed up the general weakness of the opposition.

The weakness of the opposition led the region and the international community supporters to tacitly allow Salva Kiir to militarily defeat the SPLM/A-IO; this included the incarceration of Machar in South Africa. But instead of a clear defeat of opposition forces, the war escalated, engulfing hitherto peaceful areas and worsening the humanitarian crisis. Without recognizing the mistake of supporting a dictator, IGAD proposed the HLRF as a means of putting back on track implementation of the ARCISS. It was preposterous for the IGAD leaders to speak of the revitalization of ARCISS while still recognizing the Transitional Government of National Unity (TGoNU) led by Kiir and Taban and pretending that it was implementing ARCISS.

The greatest weakness of the IGAD mediation was the divisions among its leaders with some, like President Museveni of Uganda, decidedly on the side of President Kiir. The HLRF designed by the Jieng think tanks was meant to extend Salva Kiir's legitimacy as president of South Sudan. Kiir's legitimacy rested on the ARCISS, which he rejected in 2015 and finally abrogated in July 2016 with the assistance of an SPLM/A-IO mole. The ARCISS, even without its implementation, expired on 17 May 2018. What the IGAD mediation does not seem to realise is that Kiir will never accept any kind of power sharing because he is committed to an ethnic project of hegemony and domination. This entails creating immense humanitarian disruption of other ethnic communities and their pauperization by destroying their economic base.

The HLRF's declared objectives include inter alia restoring the permanent ceasefire at a time when it is the government that is on the offensive in all war zones. The government has never stopped fighting since 15 December 2013. It has been on the offensive against the SPLM/A-IO through its different affiliated tribal militias and Sudanese rebel forces. Moreover, President Kiir is not interested in a peace agreement in which he shares power with Machar or any other rebel leader. This is a precondition for the ad infinitum continuation of the war. The IGAD mediation aimed at achieving full and inclusive implementation of the ARCISS, whatever that really means, but in essence it was covering Kiir's back for all the treacherous and heinous crimes committed by his regime. For instance, the parties were already in the process of implementing ARCISS when President Kiir attacked Machar and the SPLM/A-IO positions in Juba. As the head of the government delegation to the HLRF, Nhial Deng Nhial, in his opening statement at the start of the process, said, "We can ill-afford to reinstate that power configuration whereby the former first vice president deputizes the president again, otherwise December 2013 will surely pay us another visit." This was an unveiled threat that war would break out again if the IGAD mediation imposed Machar on Kiir once more, as they had in 2015. IGAD's expectations of the HLRF were unrealistic, asserting that the state should achieve full and inclusive ARCISS implementation.

In the same vein, it was not feasible to develop a revised and realistic timeline and implementation schedule towards democratic elections at the end of the transitional period. The idea of democratic elections in an environment where the parties are unable to achieve a permanent ceasefire is obviously unworkable. It means that the IGAD mediation had no independent strategic thinking about the situation in South Sudan save what the government presents to its diplomats and bureaucrats. In fact, the IGAD special envoys did not base their consultations with the parties on an intelligent analysis of the situation or with a clear idea of what they wanted to achieve with the HLRF. A clear knowledge of the context should have prompted the IGAD mediation to request the parties and stakeholders to provide ideas about how to resolve the dire social, economic, political, and humanitarian crisis in the country. Thus, instead of discussing the issues of governance and power sharing, the meeting in Addis Ababa would have been about implementing a political programme put together by the parties.

What next after the HLRF? This question is central to the phase South Sudan is entering, whether or not there is a peace agreement following the conclusion of the HLRF. The IGAD mediation has made the conclusion of HLRF contingent on a face-to-face meeting between President Kiir and Machar. The political struggle for power had been the central theme since 2013. The right wing in the SPLM/A-IO, by their sheer numbers, has strangled the struggle for social revolution. Nevertheless, the struggle does not end here simply because the leadership truncated the debate. As long as the problems driving the conflict are active and reproducing themselves, it means that a national democratic revolution remains on the agenda for progressive and democratic forces in South Sudan. It will definitely appear at the centre of social and political discourse sooner or later. The HLRF and the pressure of the international community will create conditions for détente in the form of a peace agreement in which the belligerents will respect the cessation of hostilities and form the Transitional Government of National Unity (TGoNU).

The anticipated détente will enable progressive social and democratic political forces to regroup and organize to continue the struggle for social change. The subjective factors, the determinants, of a national democratic revolution are still weak and leadership is lacking. Nevertheless, the internal political dynamics in South Sudan and the changing regional and international environment will sooner than later make inevitable the emergence of a leadership that will push the revolutionary process a step forward. Therefore, the need for social and economic development to transform the conditions of poverty, ignorance, and illiteracy will create social and political awareness that enables the people to demand not only better living conditions and sufficient social services but also to determine the governance system in the country. In the course of development of the national productive forces, leading to strengthened ties of freedom, justice, and fraternity, the ethnic bonds will loosen and dissolve as people relate on a different, more progressive and impersonal basis.

What Should We Do?

The struggle for social change is by no means easy, especially in a situation like that obtaining in South Sudan, where a primitive right-wing cartel holds sway over the state, society, and economy. The widespread poverty and ignorance of the masses favours the right-wing cartels because they can exploit this poverty, ignorance, and illiteracy to fragment and divide the people along ethnic and provincial lines, weakening their cause and turning them against themselves. We have witnessed this in the schools and universities, where the system promoted and encouraged, indeed financed ethnic, clan, and provincial associations among the students to divide them and scuttle their solidarity. The fighting in the University of Juba, which saw the

Dinka organise against the Equatorians, was part of this policy. This also occurred at the Bahr el Ghazal University in Wau.

The Southern Sudan Legislative Assembly, one of the pillars of the state, is not immune to ethnic sensibilities. The mindless power struggle in the SPLM has made it impossible to develop a governance system that recognizes merit in education, professional experience, or good practice. The leaders have always sought shortcuts to power and hence would scuttle any system that encourages or promotes transparency in the public domain. The SPLM leadership in 2009 rejected the guidelines to determine SPLM cadres to the SSLA. As a result, illiterate individuals whose mental and intellectual horizon hovers near their villages were elected to the SSLA. Out of ignorance and outright ethnic inclination, they defeated the SSLA's function of maintaining oversight of the executive. Indeed, as mentioned elsewhere in the text, had the SSLA leadership and honourable members been diligent enough to keep the executive and the president accountable for their actions the civil war would not have erupted.

Members of the political elite in South Sudan, like in other countries, have exploited the ignorance of the masses for their selfish interests, especially during election contests. People will sacrifice whatever they have, including their lives, for the so-called "our son." This son turns out to be son of a parasitic capitalist class that feeds on the lives of the people. The petty bourgeoisie as a class never cares about the people, the poor, and downtrodden. They care about their equals in knowledge, power, and wealth. This class will send the people to their graves under the guise of ethnicity but in reality only to protect their positions and wealth. In a turn of events against Machar, Taban Deng Gai, who on 15 December 2013 urged Nuer soldiers in the Presidential Guards to fight against the Dinka, is now the first vice president of President Kiir. This is because they are all birds of the same feather. They have forgotten about the tens of thousands of innocent Nuer women, children, and the elderly killed in the inferno. So it is that the elements of this class quarrel among themselves and kill the innocents.

The current social, economic, and political crisis afflicting South Sudan is not peculiar to it. They stalk situations where there is a sharp division in the distribution of wealth and opportunities. They are characteristic of conditions where there are few "haves" and a corresponding many "have nots." The political elite tries its utmost to blur this sharp distinction by using the ethnic agenda to gain power. It is "our turn to eat," they tell the people who have been made gullible by poverty and ignorance. They will not notice that it is a lie: they eat alone in posh hotels far away from the masses they have ensnared to fight their battles. The petty bourgeoisie in government behaves in the same way as those in the opposition, employing the art of deception as they aspire to power.

A cursory look at the opposition groups reveals the lack of a clear agenda for change. All their programmes speak about is power and how best they would manage the country presumably once in power. How could they manage the post-conflict situation when they have very little or no understanding of the social and economic context of South Sudan? It is obvious that because the petty bourgeoisie lack ideology and an understanding of the nature of the problems in South Sudan only the left-wing of the petty bourgeoisie (Marxist, communists, socialists, and social democrats) can lead South Sudan in a socioeconomic development trajectory that puts the masses at the centre of social, economic, and political engineering processes of the state. This is the essence of and their role in the national democratic revolution.

This brings me to the rhetorical question: What should we do? There is a big and difficult task for the revolutionary democratic forces in South Sudan. The first important thing is to undertake intensive social and political awareness raising. It is impossible to undertake a revolution without erasing from the minds archaic customs and reactionary ideas. This must be undertaken through enlightenment and political education of the masses, and as a means of combating ethnic chauvinism and bigotry to unite the masses of our people across ethnic and provincial lines. The success of this enlightenment drive is contingent on peace, stability, and rule of law to enable the people to exercise their freedoms and enjoy the rights enshrined in the Constitution. As agents of social change, we must undertake this task with commitment and diligence.

The second most important task is organization. It is impossible to undertake political work without political organization; it is central to the success of a revolution. We should understand organization in the context of being a vehicle for action in which the different parts — women, youth, farmers, pastoralists, and intellectuals — organize in their respective trade and professional domains to work towards the common goal of emancipating our people from poverty, ignorance, illiteracy, and superstition. This represents and, indeed, reflects "unity in diversity", in which dialectically the parts constitute the whole and the whole is a reflection of its component parts. The importance of organization cannot be overemphasized. It is the foundation of ideological unity and discipline in a movement or social and political formation. These in turn inspire commitment and readiness to sacrifice.

The struggle to execute the programmatic elements of a national democratic revolution is not separate or different from the daily struggle of our people for their social, economic, and political rights and freedoms, as enshrined in the Constitution. It was not possible to struggle for social change in the environment of armed struggle and militarism. This underpinned the failure of the SPLM/A leadership during the war of national liberation because it projected militarism over and above ideology and politics. In South Sudan, the elite have transformed the armed resistance into a power ladder not aligned to the social, economic, and political interests of the masses. Anyone who appears on the political stage first makes himself a chairman and commander in chief, whether or not he has forces behind him. However, it must be clear from the word go that the anticipated détente created by the successful conclusion of the HLRF must institute a political system that allows freedom of organization and speech and, therefore, we should strive to exploit this opportunity to struggle in a legal environment. This will be the correct meaning of abandoning the armed struggle in favour of political struggle.

Crucial to the possible successful conclusion of the HLRF is the prospect of its failure due to Kiir's intransigence and obstinacy against Machar's participation in the transitional government, which will allow the situation of war to persist ad infinitum. It will be necessary to study this situation and adopt appropriate strategies to meet its exigencies.

EPILOGUE

My Journey to and From the SPLM/A-IO: A Personal Account

> The ultimate measure of a man is not where he stands in moments of comfort and convenience but where he stands at times of challenge and controversy.
>
> — Martin Luther King Jr.[89]

Political activism is about change. The struggle for positive social change can be both a personally addictive and inspiring political undertaking. For an activist, the defining issue is not one's personal position or material gain, but scenes of injustice that steer one into action with the aim of transforming that condition. It is not justifiable to remain indifferent in situations that spur human passions and, indeed, it would be off the mark to blame or criticize those who act against injustice.

This is a personal account of joining Riek Machar's rebellion. I will not accept any rebuke because the events of December 2013 were searing to the soul, so much so that it was impossible to remain indifferent. The sight of tipper trucks carrying the bodies of thousands of innocent Nuer who had been massacred was a turning point for me. There are no official figures for the numbers killed, but I am certain that they are well beyond the few thousand that are usually referred to. From the surviving relatives and speaking with witnesses, I believe the number of people killed in Juba was more than 24,000. I know that

---

[89] Quoted from James Comey, *A Higher Loyalty: Truth, Lies, and Leadership* (New York: Flatiron Books, 2018).

many of my fellow tribespeople, the Shilluk, including my nephew Gen. James Bwogo, whom the Padang Dinka militia killed in 2015, refused to countenance my decision to support the SPLM/A-IO. They reminded me of my two elder sisters, Piero and Ciro Nyaba, who, like many innocent Shilluk, were massacred by the marauding Nuer White Army in Malakal in February 2014. I looked at the bigger picture of South Sudan and its destiny. It was also a decision that contradicted the self-criticism I later made about my joining of the rebellion against Dr. John Garang's leadership of the SPLM/A following the Nasir Declaration in August 1991 (Nyaba, 1997).

When certain stressful situations arise, like that which obtained between December 16 and 19, 2013, it is difficult to behave rationally, or with caution, caring about oneself and family. It did not occur to me that I was exposing my family and myself to extreme danger, even as I continued to write and conduct radio interviews about the terrible events. State security almost refused to permit my then six-month-old grandson, Nyaba, to board a plane to Kenya as South Sudanese stampeded to leave Juba. I learned later that President Kiir had ordered his forces to spare Madame Rebecca Nyandeng de Mabior and me. We had been under security surveillance ever since the press conference Machar and members of the SPLM Political Bureau held on 6 December.

On Monday 16 December, the police rounded up and detained all those comrades who had participated in the press conference. In fact, some of them, like John Luk Jok, turned himself in at Buluk Police Station after learning that the police were looking for him. Meanwhile, Machar, Angelina Teny, Taban Deng Gai, and Alfred Lado-Gore were all on the run. I remained free and communicated with the world through the Internet, social media and sometimes even did interviews with the BBC, until on Christmas Day, as I was being interviewed by the Washington-based National Public Radio, four Toyota pick-ups mounted with heavy machine guns, under the command of two police major generals, surrounded my house. The commanding officer tried his best to restrain the unruly police and so there was no commotion inside the house. I came out to hear what they had to say.

"We have been sent to pick you," said Maj. Gen. Said Shawoul, as he saluted me.

"Why do you salute a prisoner?" I asked.

"You are a minister," he said.

In fact, Minister of Interior Aleu Ayieny Aleu had phoned four days earlier to tell me that I was under arrest and the police were coming to pick me up. But the police did not come. I was to learn later that it was Aleu's own personal initiative and intention to have me arrested or eliminated, just as he had wanted to murder the others. He is said to have gone to President Kiir and told him that I wanted to be detained like the rest of my colleagues. "If Adwok wants to be a martyr, I will not be the one to commit that," President Salva is reported to have replied to Minister Aleu. I spent Christmas evening in the company of my former colleagues in the now-dissolved cabinet. It was something of a political picnic. We spent a nice time.

It was a picnic in both a figurative and real sense. This was because sometime in the afternoon of the following day the security officer came to alert us that some important guests were coming to visit us. It turned out that the important guests were Ethiopia's Prime Minister Haile Mariam Desalegn and Kenya's President Uhuru Kenyatta, together with their foreign ministers and security details. The ministers Dr. Barnaba Marial Benjamin (Foreign Affairs) and Aleu Ayieny Aleu (Interior) accompanied the VIPs. They must have brought an invitation for President Kiir to attend the Extraordinary Assembly of IGAD Heads of State and Government scheduled for December 27 in Nairobi. In that context, I believe they must have requested to see the "coup plotters." President Kiir granted them permission to visit us in the detention centre.

The two IGAD leaders spoke of how disturbed the region was about the volatile political situation in South Sudan. They promised to do their best to resolve the issues and return the country to normalcy. They also assured us that our ordeal would not take long. On our part, Pagan Amum, Deng Alor, and John Luk spoke of our innocence, the sad and unnecessary loss of life and destruction of property, and that we looked forward to the region helping to resolve the conflict. We spent that evening in a jovial mood, thinking that the intervention of the region would accelerate an end to the conflict.

At about ten o'clock the next morning, on Wednesday 27 December, Police Maj. Gen. Said Shawoul came to inform me that he was taking me back to my house. My arrest was a mistake but he had to take me through the office of the minister. Aleu told me he was under instructions from the president to return me to my residence, and so I was a free man.

"Why was I arrested in the first place?" I asked the minister.

"You attended the press conference on 6 December. That conference was the preparation for the coup against the state," he said.

"If that was the case, why was I not arrested at the same time as the rest of the colleagues?" I asked.

"The police did not know your house," he said.

So simple! That the police did not know where I lived in Juba was a rather strange excuse. I thought arguing with Minister Aleu further would not take me anywhere. I decided to take leave and the police drove me to my house in Hai Jebel. The story of my house, on a 20-by-20-metre plot in Hai Jebel, is one that I will tell one day. More importantly, I want to say that three days after the encounter with Aleu Ayieny in his office, a security officer ordered me off a Dubai-bound flight, where I was intending to live after receiving a three-year residence and work permit from the Sharjah Emirate. They seized my passport and formally told me that I was to remain under house arrest because I was communicating and writing against the government.

As part of the intervention by the IGAD leaders, President Kiir released seven of the 11 detained politicians: Deng Alor, John Luk, Kosti Manibe, Dr. Cirino Ofuho Hiteng, Gier Chuong, Madut Biar Yel, and Chol Tong Mayay. He allowed them to travel to Kenya, where the government hosted them in Nairobi. Four comrades — Pagan Amum, Gen. Oyay Deng Ajak, Dr. Majak d'Agoot, and Amb. Ezekiel Lol Gatkuoth — remained in detention. The government had decided to open a case against them. It was a confusing moment for me: I was not part of the political detainees and yet was under house arrest. The four detainees were taken to court but it soon became clear that the government was losing and therefore decided to withdraw the case. Pagan, Oyay, Majak, and Lol Gatkuoth were released and allowed to travel to Kenya. At the airport, where we all went to take the flight to Nairobi, I was told by the Kenyan government officials accompanying the four men that I was not part of the deal to allow the political detainees to travel to Nairobi. My colleagues left me at the airport, wondering about my status and what I could do to extricate myself from house arrest.

I decided that I would defy the orders to remain within the confines of my house in Hai Jebel and at times went out to different parts of Juba to meet friends or attend funerals and funeral rites of relatives and friends, or have a meal at Central Pub, where the elite go for a beer or two. There I met people who would ask, "When did you come back?" to which I would retort, "I did not go anywhere." One day somebody who did not believe my answer said, "Peter, do not lie. You have been speaking on the BBC, and writing those provocative articles in the social media from your house. Salva Kiir must be a good person." It was amazing that difficult circumstances could so quickly change people. It was clear from people's attitudes that if Salva Kiir decided to kill me because of my verbal and electronic protests then, definitely, it would have been my own mistake; or, in other words, I had called for my own destruction.

The part of Hai Jebel I stayed in was one of the most polluted areas of Juba. The city council never cared about its environment. The garbage, smoke, noise and stench were unbearable. Even though I was a minister in the national government, the Juba City Council would not respond to my protest against the pollution in the area. Following the fighting on the night of 15 December, the situation improved. The area within shooting range of both the army headquarters and the National Security Bureau was abruptly "sanitised." The shacks that oozed loud jazz and gospel music, the smoke and noise from the brothels and unlicenced drinking places surrounding my house had disappeared by the next day. The Ugandan entrepreneurs had packed up and gone home.

I convinced myself that I would be my own killer if I allowed stress, depression, hopelessness, and anger to defeat my spirit. That is how I spent the six-month incarceration in Hai Jebel, where only real friends would risk coming to visit me. I remember one day at Central Pub when a former colleague virtually ran away from me: he did not want people (security) to see him in my company. In three months, I was able to write a small book detailing what had happened in the period leading up to the eruption on 15 December. In the preface of *South Sudan: The Crisis of Infancy*, I said I would be lucky if I was alive to read it when it came out in print. This was because we had already survived three incidents of intense shooting in the area: the first was on the night of 15 December; the second was between the SPLA soldiers alone; and the third was when the SPLA attacked the three Nuer generals, Simon Gatwech Dual, Thomas Mabor Dhal, and Gabriel Gatwech Chan (Tangginye). The recurrent bouts of gunfire, throughout the night and day, and the sight of a T-72 tank parked just a few metres from my house punctuated the boredom of house arrest.

This constant danger heightened my desire to get out of Juba. The director general of National Security refused to give back my passport; I had wanted to travel to attend to my wife's operation in a Nairobi hospital. Although I was able to leave the house for a few hours, to take a walk or move around in town, this would nevertheless not take me out of Juba. I loathed going the UNMISS protection of civilians site. One day, listening to an FM radio station broadcast in Juba, I learned about the passing of a colleague and a comrade in the struggle from our university days. Prof. Bol Kolok had died in the United States. His remains were being flown to Juba, en route to burial in his hometown of Rumbek. I went to attend the prayers for his soul in Juba, and was given a chance to speak. At the end of my speech I asked the family for a seat on the plane taking the body to Rumbek. They agreed to this: the entire Agar community in Juba knew how close Bol and I had been.

They scheduled the flight to and from Rumbek for Friday, 27 June. My wife had returned from her treatment in Kenya so I discussed the trip with her. She graciously supported my going to Rumbek. I then rang a friend in Nairobi to inform him that I would be travelling to Rumbek. He thought for a while and then said that if I wanted to leave the country, he could arrange for a plane to pick me up in Rumbek. He gave me a name to contact as soon as I was in Rumbek.

I arrived at the airport carrying a travelling bag, which suggested that I was going for a long stay in Rumbek, despite the fact that the flight was to return to Juba that same day. I tried to explain that it was necessary for me to carry certain items in the bag. People would not believe my story. I felt forced to tell them of our experience in the SPLA, saying it was the rainy season and the unexpected could happen. We took off a bit late. After I arrived in Rumbek I proceeded to the burial site, completed the process in good time and returned to take the plane back to Juba. The plane took off as scheduled but just 15 minutes outside of Juba, the plane turned back to Rumbek. The airport in Juba had closed for daily repair work: the journey would resume only in the morning, announced the pilot.

We spent the night in Rumbek and in the morning I could not extricate myself from the group because it would then be obvious that I had a different plan. I had to pretend until morning, when I said I would not travel back on account that I had nothing to do in Juba, and that I preferred to come back the following day. I was not sure if anyone in the government of Lakes State knew I had jumped my house arrest in Juba. I spent the whole Saturday indoors, coming out only to have a meal, until I had the plan finalised with my friend in Nairobi. We avoided audio communication, using Skype instead, until I had all the details about the plane registration number and the name of the pilot.

Sunday is a good day for clandestine activities. I believe it is the day the Government of South Sudan and its institutions do not wake from sleep until after 11 in the morning. Moreover, when they get up they go straight to church. My real worry was whether the security officer at the airstrip would be there. It turned out he cared only about the fees the pilot paid and nothing more. We took off without a hitch on our five-and-a-half-hour flight from Rumbek to Wilson Airport, Nairobi. This journey was by all measure illegal, and indeed treasonable, having breached the security of South Sudan. I had defied Kiir's travel ban. I later learned that the security organs unleashed their anger and embarrassment on the poor Kenyan pilot and his Ukrainian manageress, who spent about two months in the cells.[90]

It would be cynical to think that I travelled to Rumbek to evade or dodge the NSIS dragnet. That is impossible because they should be everywhere in South Sudan and one would expect that a person taken off a Dubai-bound plane would have his biometrics distributed to all its units throughout the country, suggesting he should be apprehended if he tried to cross a border without a permit. In all honesty, the NSIS exists but does not undertake the functions for which it was established: protecting the country from internal and external political, economic and social threats through the diligent collection and analysis of information. The national security in South Sudan, unlike its counterparts in many countries, is a service for the protection of the president and operates unto itself in the capital. Outside Juba the system does not operate or indeed does not exist, and this may explain how I could travel from Rumbek to Nairobi, begging the question of how many nationals and foreigners have escaped the country in this manner, breaching national security.

Many people will say that the function of national security is to intimidate and extort information and resources from their victims, both nationals and foreigners. They enjoy free accommodation, meals and sometimes illicit sex in the hotels and lodges, and are present on every private or public project, and always they make it known that they are security officers, perhaps to cover the large-scale financial scams that occur under their watch. In most cases they are agents of corruption and therefore constitute "national insecurity", considering the number of cowboy contractors who have disappeared with millions of dollars in bank notes. The trip to Rumbek was made as a gesture of respect to my departed friend and colleague but I also exploited it to embarrass those who took me off the Dubai-bound flight. Nevertheless, I lost my three-year residence permit and had to change my plans.

---

[90] Gen. Lazarus Sumbeiywo, the IGAD special envoy to the South Sudan peace talks, informed me of this in a conversation when we met in Addis Ababa.

The Decision to Join the SPLM/A-IO

Beyond the reach of Kiir's security apparatus, it was possible to implement my plans. I made the decision to join the opposition long before leaving Juba. I remember arguing with a German friend who came to visit me during the house arrest against the Troika's decision to form the political detainees into an independent group to counter both Kiir's SPLM and Machar's SPLM/A-IO at the peace negotiations in Addis Ababa. This was because the political detainees were not involved in the war. My argument was that to arrive at a peace settlement it was better to limit to only two the parties involved, suggesting that the political detainees could contribute better to the search for peace by joining forces with Machar. Furthermore, they were with Machar until 15 December 2013. I thought the Troika was creating a rift that would complicate the peace process.

However, my reasons for joining the SPLM/A-IO even while still under house arrest in Juba was not driven by a desire for a peaceful resolution of the conflict through the IGAD mediation. Far from it: I joined the SPLM/A-IO because I saw in it the opportunity to complete the SPLM/A's failure to wage a war of national liberation. My analysis of the situation in South Sudan remains that the current crisis arose from the SPLM/A's leadership failure, or rather refusal, to pursue the agenda of a national democratic revolution in order to address the socioeconomic and cultural backwardness of south Sudan. The civil war, therefore, is not a Dinka-Nuer war, as some people view it. Nor is it a war between Kiir and Machar, as a reflection of the power struggle in the SPLM's top leadership. The civil war is a battle between the SPLM-NCP parasitic capitalist class and the people of South Sudan.

The resolution of this contradiction therefore required a complete paradigm shift in the political thinking of the SPLM/A-IO leadership and the political detainees. Without this shift, they would not be able to have a correct understanding of the objective reality and to design a political programme that addressed that contradiction. This meant political and organizational unity of all the social forces opposed to a totalitarian regime that sought the use of force to resolve political conflicts within the party. The refusal of the 11 former political detainees to join up with Machar, preferring to go it alone because, according to them, they did not have the blood of innocent South Sudanese on their hands, constituted a big obstacle to the unity of the opposition. This inadvertently played into Kiir's strategy to fragment the opposition.

I decided to travel to Addis Ababa to meet Machar, the leader of the SPLM/A-IO.

While in Juba I had maintained contact with Machar and the negotiating team. I insisted that the only way to bring pressure to bear on Kiir and his government was to deny him financial and economic resources to prosecute the war. I suggested that the SPLM/A-IO take over the oil fields instead of fighting battles, which had no strategic values. This fell on deaf ears. I came to understand later that a rift had emerged between Machar and his wife, Angelina Teny, on the one side and Taban Deng Gai on the other side. Whatever was the cause of the rift, it was clear they were pursuing different agendas. In fact, when I arrived in Addis at the beginning of the third negotiating session of the IGAD-mediated peace talks, Taban Deng, the SPLM/A-IO's chief negotiator, was not even in town. My arrival and joining the SPLM/A-IO coincided with the desertion of one of the former political detainees. It is possible that ethnic politics overwhelmed Ezekiel Lol Gatkuoth and he decided to throw in the towel and abandon the former detainees in order to join the SPLM/A-IO.

It is important to note that the SPLM/A-IO was predominantly Nuer in composition, understandably so because of the events in Juba in December 2013. Ezekiel Lol Gatkuoth and Taban Deng Gai count as the triggers of the fighting in the Tiger Battalion on the night of Sunday, 15 December. Had he not been arrested and detained, Lol Gatkuoth naturally should have joined the SPLM/A-IO. It was then a matter of avenging the massacre of ethnic Nuer in Juba, though vengeance or counter-vengeance would not resolve the underlying fundamental problems in South Sudan. The idea was to organize the war to pursue wider national objectives through a national democratic revolution. This paradigm shift towards a revolution, therefore, did not need a peace negotiated with Kiir. It required better organization, in terms of defining the political objectives of the war, and building the army, structures and institutions of people's power. It was important and necessary that the SPLM/A-O planned a protracted struggle to enable change in the rural environment, through a programme that provided social services, and build an economic base for the revolution. I believed the peace negotiations with the regime would leave intact the regime and would not address the fundamental problems of South Sudan and its people. It would only perpetuate those conditions, further fuelling the conflict.

It became clear to me in the first few weeks of my stay in Addis Ababa that the SPLM/A-IO leadership had no idea more than the wish for a peace agreement that would enable a return to Juba to share power with Kiir. I began to understand a few things, including why Machar had chosen the name SPLM/A-IO, even though he knew very well that his Nuer constituency loathed the name. I also understood why he surrounded himself with political upstarts and why he refused to build an army: Machar wanted the IGAD mediation to negotiate his return to Juba as Kiir's vice president. So when he asked me to draft basic documents for the SPLM/A-IO — manifesto, constitution, internal regulation, and members' code of conduct — I knew he just wanted to keep me busy in order not to engage him in ideological discussions. He procrastinated on discussing the content of the documents and instead embarked on reworking the documents, expunging from the draft texts particular words that did not resonate with his right-wing ideology.

In any struggle, only ideas — not the colour of one's skin or facial marks — unite people when they debate and discuss them in order to arrive at a consensus on the objectives of their common struggle. This was my impression when I drafted the SPLM/A-IO's basic documents. In reworking my drafts, Machar and Henry Odwar erased the movement's strategic political objective before the members even debated the draft. I had defined the movement as a section of the national democratic revolutionary forces, the strategic political objective of which was the overthrow of the regime in order to construct a national democratic state in South Sudan. The erasure of this clause incensed me. If the SPLM/A-IO was anything other than a revolutionary force what need was there then for a revolutionary democrat like me to remain in it? Many of the young men and women, particularly those who had been involved in the student movement in the Sudan, supported the idea of transforming the civil war into a national democratic revolution to correct the fatalistic notion among the Nuer White Army that the SPLM/A-IO had emerged to avenge the massacre of ethnic Nuer in Juba.

The first SPLM/A-IO conference convened in Pagak in November-December 2014. More than 5,000 people, including individuals from the diaspora, attended. This was an opportunity for Machar to present to the conference his political message and explain the root causes of the war as well as its objectives and strategies. Surprisingly, Machar did not use this opportunity to speak about the factors that had triggered the fighting in Juba. He instead ordered the conference to break into provincial, regional and ethnic/clan mini-conferences to discuss appointments and the filling of positions. As a result, the enthusiasm of the conferees dissipated and many went back home disappointed with the SPLM/A-IO leadership. It is difficult to tell if the SPLM/A-IO's first-ever conference had an objective apart from confirming Machar's leadership. The conference dispersed without discussing or adopting the basic documents, which makes questionable Machar's confirmation as the leader given that the movement's constitution was not adopted. This was a travesty of democratic principle and practice.

It is worth mentioning that the SPLM/A-IO conference convened after the Arusha Agreement on the SPLM reunification invited the three SPLM factions: namely, the SPLM in Government (Kiir), SPLM in Opposition (Machar) and SPLM Former Detainees (Pagan Amum). The conference was openly against the idea of SPLM reunification as that would mean continuing Kiir's leadership. The nexus between the reunification and the IGAD peace mediation smothered this hostility. The idea of SPLM reunification was Kiir's brainchild. Without a clear understanding of the motives behind this reunification, Machar agreed to send a delegation to Arusha, tasking Comrade Duer Tut Duer and me to lead the SPLM/A-IO delegation. He refused to answer our questions about the end game of the reunification process.

On the sidelines of the UN General Assembly in September 2014, President Kiir asked the president of the United Republic of Tanzania, Ndugu Jakaya Kikwete, to help reunify the three feuding SPLM factions. President Kikwete obliged and tasked the secretary-general of Tanzania's ruling party, the Chama Cha Mapinduzi, with this daunting assignment. I call it daunting because Kiir was not sincere about the SPLM reunification and, as it appeared, he wanted to insult his Tanzanian peer.[91] This is because even after the factions signed the SPLM reunification agreement on 21 January 2015, like the Agreement on the Resolution of the Conflict in South Sudan (ARCISS), Kiir refused to reinstate Comrade Pagan Amum to his position of SPLM secretary-general. The importance and usefulness of the SPLM reunification, if there was political goodwill on all sides, lay not in the reunification itself but in moderating and easing the passions between the factions to enable them to negotiate and sign the peace agreement in good faith. Short of that, it served no useful purpose.

---

[91] The EPRDF and the ANC had tried to support SPLM reconciliation and reunification before the IGAD-mediated peace talks. Machar rejected this initiative, however, on the grounds that the war was raging and, therefore, he preferred the peace talks to the SPLM reconciliation and reunification talks.

It is not easy to mediate peace between parties with a wide disparity in the balance of their military strengths. Admittedly, it was a difficult task for the IGAD special envoys to mediate an agreement about sharing power. It would have been easier had the SPLM/A demonstrated its military capacity, but this would have threatened Kiir's incumbency. The special envoys' introduction of an inclusivity principle involving all the stakeholders rendered untenable a negotiated agreement. The idea of a transitional government of national unity involving all the stakeholders complicated the negotiations and, indeed, shifted the focus to the power-sharing ratios. The IGAD leaders were divided according to the dictates of their respective competing national security, economic and political interests in South Sudan. This left the special envoys with no viable option other than to impose a draft agreement on the parties.

It took time for the parties to implement this imposed peace agreement. By the time the Transitional Government of National Unity (TGoNU) was formed on 29 April 2016, the SPLM/A-IO was in disarray. The loose manner with which Machar managed the movement, coupled with his lack of strategic thinking, enabled Kiir, through the agency of Taban Deng Gai, to cut inroads into the SPLM/A-IO. In just under two months of the TGoNU's formation, the war had erupted again. The coordinated attack on the SPLM/A-IO positions in Juba exposed its political, intelligence and organizational weaknesses. The gallant SPLM/A-IO forces fought bravely and were able to inflict major damage on Kiir's forces, in terms of soldiers killed in action and equipment destroyed.[92] The problem was leadership and the lack of strategic planning. This weakness showed up during the withdrawal from Juba. The SPLM/A-IO forces suffered heavy losses on the way to the DR Congo border due to a grotesque blunder committed by Machar: he communicated with Michael Chiengjiek Geay, his military logistics officer in Khartoum, unaware that Chiengjiek had shifted loyalty to Taban Deng Gai. Every time Machar transmitted the coordinates of his location, in the hope of receiving an airdrop of supplies, Chiengjiek relayed this information to Taban Deng in Juba, who passed it to SPLA Military Intelligence. Instead of receiving airdrops, the SPLA's gunships and drones attacked his locations. Even after this happened several times, Machar still had not realised that he was dealing with the enemy.

The Sudan government, on humanitarian grounds, picked up Machar and a few of his bodyguards from the Congo and transported them

---

[92] The number of Mathiang Anyoor killed was estimated at about 3,000; 12 tanks and APCs were also destroyed in and around Juba.

to Khartoum. It was under condition that he not undertake political activities, including meeting people or speaking to the press while in the Sudan. He was under strict national security protection. The SPLM/A-IO Political Bureau did, however, meet in Khartoum, in September 2016, but by then the SPLM/A-IO had completely disappeared from the regional radar. It was resolved at the meeting that the movement undertake some spectacular and strategic action to attract regional and international attention. Despite the fact that these resolutions were classified and strategic material, Machar gave an order for the resolutions to be posted online through social media sites. Against our advice, he decided to travel to South Africa for an ophthalmic consultation he could have had in Khartoum. Given that President Kiir had not given up on killing him, it was risky for Machar to travel as a regular passenger. He also did not read correctly the attitude of the Obama administration when Secretary of State John Kerry forced the IGAD region to recognize Taban Deng Gai as the de facto first vice president. In South Africa, neither President Jacob Zuma nor Deputy President Cyril Ramaphosa wanted to meet him. In November 2016, a confusion occurred in the travel plans of Machar, which led to his deportation from both Khartoum and Addis Ababa, followed by his arrest and detention in South Africa. It was a major move on the part of the US administration and IGAD regional leaders: they had exiled Machar from South Sudan.

The SPLM/A-IO in a Deadly Dilemma

The incarceration of Machar in South Africa not only placed the SPLM/A-IO in a very awkward situation, it also removed the veneer of democratic pretence in its political operations. The movement now had no one to make a decision, or guide it in the face of growing uncertainties. Machar had survived his escape through the bush in South Sudan, with Kiir in hot pursuit, deploying Erik Prince's Blackwater drones, SPLA helicopter gunships and battalions of infantry to track and kill him. But now he was under the control of South Africa. The movement's deputy chair, Gen. Alfred Lado-Gore, and its secretary-general, Dr. Dhieu Mathok Diing Wol, had defected to Taban Deng Gai and were now part of the Juba government.

The fighting in Juba found me and six other members of the SPLM/A-IO Political Bureau in Nairobi. We decided to form ourselves into a working group to continue executing the political and diplomatic functions of the movement, as well as to sound out the IGAD region and the international community about the evolving situation in

South Sudan. However, Machar did not appreciate, indeed, treated with contempt, the movement's political and diplomatic functions undertaken in Nairobi while he was on the run towards the border with Congo. The SPLM/A-IO had virtually no leadership so what we tried to voluntarily undertake was to provide leadership and fill the gap created by Machar's absence. Unfortunately, there were some members of the Political Bureau who did not want anything political or diplomatic done in the absence of Machar or which he had not sanctioned. They reasoned that taking such a step was tantamount to a coup against Machar. They torpedoed a suggestion to form a five-member committee within the Political Bureau to conduct the movement's functions, in collaboration with the Military Command Council under the chief of general staff. In this way, the absence of Machar would not affect or retard the political, military, and diplomatic functions of the movement.

What happened to the SPLM/A-IO in Juba, and the plight of Machar was something to be expected as long as the elements of the fundamental contradiction remained active. It is a situation that often occurs and arises when the enemy incapacitates part or all of the leadership of a rebel movement in a surprise military operation, or an opposition party through a police swoop in which its operational centre is overrun. In such a situation, those who remain at large continue with the struggle. By way of example, the Communist Party of the Sudan (CPS) at times had its leaders, including the secretary-general, arrested and detained, yet the party continued to function, albeit clandestinely, to direct the mass movement. The African National Congress (ANC) leaders who remained at large inside South Africa or abroad did not stop the struggle and wait until Nelson Mandela and his colleagues held on Robben Island were released. In fact, this is the meaning of being organized and disciplined as a party, or as a liberation or resistance movement. The struggle outside the prisons built up the mass support inside South Africa and throughout the world until the apartheid regime released Mandela and his colleagues. Even with the huge international solidarity for his release, it took time to persuade elements within the organization, coupled with Oliver Tambo's poor health, after which Mandela agreed to take over the leadership of ANC. This is the meaning of the principle of collective leadership in a democratic organization, where any individual is a leader among equals. Leaders walk from prison cells or return from exile to become presidents or prime ministers simply because their constituencies had won the struggle.

The decision we made in July 2016 in Nairobi to form into a working group in order to keep the SPLM/A-IO flame burning was the correct one. We managed to send delegations to sound out the AU meeting in Kigale, Rwanda, about the new situation in South Sudan; to the JMEC meeting in Khartoum; and the IGAD meeting in Addis Ababa, Ethiopia. This was normal political practice: when faced with a climate of extreme passivity those at large must continue the struggle by all means available. We wanted to repeat the same exercise during the government's extensive military and diplomatic offensive, which saw the recapture of most SPLM/A-IO positions, including its headquarters in Pagak. But it soon became clear why Machar had elevated some individuals to the Political Bureau: they were there only out of personal loyalty and were ready to obstruct any ideas that had not originated from Machar.

The situation in the SPLM/A-IO speaks generally to relations between political power and democracy among South Sudan's political elite. A fascination with personal power renders irrelevant democratic principles and practice known the world over. The elite extend this personification of power to the point of absurdity. This is evident from Machar's manner, his "commoditization of loyalty", behaving as if the political survival of the movement is contingent on him as a person. He insisted on managing the rebel movement from house arrest thousands of miles away. Machar is the chairman and commander in chief of the SPLM/A-IO, using electronic communication with members of his movement in the field, inside the PoCs, East Africa and in the diaspora. He contemptuously brushed aside a proposal to constitute a committee of the Political Bureau to run the movement ad interim, considering it an attempt to snatch his power.

When the life and survival of a political party or movement is contingent on an individual leader or group of leaders, when their temporal absence could spell the death of the party or movement, we must be sure such a movement has not reached the level of impersonal organization. This describes the situation in the SPLM/A-IO, which operates on wishful rather than strategic thinking. Through social media and WhatsApp fora, Machar has his grip on the movement from a dead ground (militarily speaking), dishing out bogus appointments, promotions and appointments of state governors, county commissioners and movement representatives abroad, as well as naming people to other administrative functions. He manages all political, diplomatic and military functions of the SPLM/A-IO, communicating directly with junior officers in the field and outside the chain of command. In this way, Machar frustrated efforts that could have seen him released from detention.[93]

Exploiting Machar's incarceration, the movement's lack of logistics, general demoralization and apathy in the ranks, the government managed to recapture most of the SPLM/A-IO territories, including its general headquarters at Pagak. This triggered desertions among the troops. In the Shilluk Kingdom (Sector One) some senior officers deserted out of frustration over the lack of strategic planning, joining the enemy. In Equatoria, with the formation of the National Salvation Front (NAS) and Southern Sudan National Movement for Change (SSNMC), many Equatorians deserted to join the new Equatorian-based opposition movements. By the end of 2017, the movement was hanging onto its continued political and military survival by only a tiny string of a few committed commanders and Kiir's ethnocentric politics, which virtually made it a Dinka war against other ethnic communities in South Sudan. This was to the chagrin of those in the region and in the international community who had written off the SPLM/A-IO as a viable political military force. It was a self-inflicted paralysis that had led to the proliferation of political and armed opposition groups who preferred to run their own separate and independent movements instead of joining together with the SPLM/A-IO.

Managing Relations with Other Opposition Groups

The SPLM/A-IO was by all measure the largest of the armed opposition movements. However, it had the disadvantage of being predominantly Nuer in composition and led by Riek Machar. This can be linked to the analysis we made before. The fact that those who rebelled later did not join the SPLM/A-IO must be viewed in light of Machar's leadership in general and how he managed the SPLM/A-IO like a family enterprise. The SPLM/A-IO forces, mostly Nuer, were dispersed throughout Equatoria and Western Bahr el Ghazal. Machar communicated directly with them, appointing their commanders in a manner that marginalized the local military and political leadership.

This raised the question of relations between the SPLM/A-IO and other opposition groups in the political and military domains. It was the

---

[93] The SPLM/A-IO forces required military logistics. A written authorization from Machar would have enabled the committee of the Political Bureau to make the necessary contacts to acquire the required military logistics to enable it to capture strategic targets, including the oil fields. An operation of that nature would have defeated the reason for detaining Machar in South Africa, resulting in his release.

height of naivety to assume that the emergent opposition groups would join the SPLM/A-IO just because it had deployed forces in different parts of South Sudan. Each politician decided to operate independently. This later led to the loss of life in northern Upper Nile in fighting between the forces of the SPLM/A-IO and the National Democratic Movement (NDM), and in Central Equatoria with the forces of National Salvation Front (NAS). The losses could have been avoided if the politicians had acted politically. However, acting politically was a challenge for many of them, having had no experience of coalition building.

While in charge of the group in Nairobi, I faced hostile reactions from my colleagues when we decided to attend a consultation meeting of the opposition forces called by Dr. Lam Akol. Some of them accused me of trying to hand over the movement to Dr. Lam Akol, and indeed boycotted the consultation meeting on the flimsy reason that Machar had not sanctioned our participation. The reason was preposterous because on 20 August 2016, when the meeting ended, Machar was still on the run in the bush of South Sudan and we had not established communication with him. Despite the controversy surrounding our participation, the consultative meeting endorsed all of our ideas in its final communique. This was an important political achievement, especially in respect of the show of solidarity demonstrated by those groups with the SPLM/A-IO and the precarious situation of Machar. It shows how petty some people can be; the consultative meeting was indeed the precursor of the South Sudan opposition alliance.

No political party or movement worth its name refuses to engage in political discussions; it does so at its peril or serious risk to its political survival. This was the problem with the SPLM/A-IO and its self-inflicted paralysis in the wake of Machar's incarceration in South Africa. This paralysis, intended to secure his release, unwittingly led to the movement's voluntary isolation. Machar would not permit the SPLM/A-IO's participation in any forum unless and until he was released from detention. In this connection, the movement turned down an invitation to participate in an opposition meeting that the government of Kenya sponsored in the town of Nyahururu because its leader was under detention.[94] It did not occur to Henry Odwar, who managed that dossier, that the meeting could have been a way to build pressure on the region

---

[94] The government of the Republic of Kenya is rapporteur to the IGAD summit on the conflict in South Sudan. This meeting came as part of Kenya's efforts to bring peace to South Sudan. It was considered important that the opposition harmonized its position, and hence the invitation for the opposition to come together.

to release Machar. The SPLM/A-IO boycotted the Nyahururu meeting on account of Machar's incarceration in South Africa. The decision that the movement could not participate in any political activities because of Machar's detention flew in the face of all logic. It marked the foot-dragging, and outright hostility and isolation of those who advocated for working collectively as an opposition to the totalitarian regime. This culminated in a refusal to sign the opposition charter on lame excuses related to a section in the charter that criticized and described as dead or moribund the Agreement on the Resolution of the Conflict in South Sudan (ARCISS). This excuse in relation to ARCISS was fallacious and misleading because we had resolved that ARCISS was dead at the 2016 meeting of the SPLM/A-IO Political Bureau. Therefore, the real reason for refusing to work within the opposition alliance was Machar's continued detention, and the insistence that he should lead both the armed and political wings of the opposition.

In an internal Political Bureau communication, I criticized Comrade Odwar, the deputy chairman, for the clumsy manner in which he had managed the movement's relations with the opposition groups. I also refuted his assertion that the Obama administration had sanctioned the SPLM/A-IO because of its decision to declare war on the government of President Kiir. This communication did not amuse Dr. Riek Machar; he therefore decided to leak the document to the press, ostensibly to put me in bad light with Nuer public opinion and, indeed, there was a hostile backlash. In my rebuttal, I said the US administration sanctioned the movement because we acted "Nuerly", which I explained was in reference to the public announcement of our intention to go to war.[95] This was enough for Machar to order the isolation and marginalization in the SPLM/A of any comrade in the Political Bureau who communicated with me.

The reality of many African countries is that the tyranny of ethnic numbers determines who in a political organization can wield power. This truism is tragically poking the SPLM/A-IO in the eyes. The low level of political consciousness among many members who purport to support social change in a highly ethnicized society pays back

---

[95] Of all the ethnic communities in South Sudan, only the Nuer people have the audacity to declare publicly their intention to wage a war even before preparing themselves. Others would prepare themselves quietly. This occurred in December 2013 when a few Nuer officers and men organised by Taban Deng Gai started to sing the chorus *"Ban ngieny ke Jieng"*, which literally translates to "We are going to fight the Dinka." This careless talk spurred the JCE into action to develop a strange brand of apocalyptic Dinka ethnic nationalism.

in such absurdities as management of a rebel movement from house arrest thousands of miles away. Although many Nuer members of the movement recognize the absurdity of managing the movement from detention, nevertheless they will not countenance any leadership other than that of Machar. This reaffirms the underlying perception that a Nuer must lead any opposition to a Dinka-led government in South Sudan. It springs from "our turn to govern", the sentiment that national politics and state power is organised along ethnic lines.

This perception of polarised ethnic and provincial lines is bound to boomerang sooner rather than later, particularly in the absence of clear national objectives within the different political groups. It indeed is the driving force behind the proliferation of political and armed opposition, particularly those grounded in tribal militias, the members of which resort to the use of physical violence to achieve their objectives. It shifts the focus to power and hence the question of power sharing instead of addressing the underlying contradictions of poverty and ignorance in society. This leaves intact the oppressive system and renders the national body politics a zero-sum game, putting the country in a state of perpetual crisis. It is a situation that allows ethnic chauvinism and bigotry to trump creation of a national agenda and prevent development of civil society.

South Sudan's society is tribal in character. It is impossible to wish away this sociopolitical configuration. But we must work to prevent dangerous views from taking root, views such as "born to rule" and "ethnic turn", for accidentally advantaged individuals to rise to the pinnacle of power. Although it is a right to try to rise to the principal position in the country, it must not be based on ethnicity. It must be based on established legal and democratic practice, lest such leadership plunges the country into chaos and ungovernability. The current situation of competing social and political forces opposed to President Salva Kiir and his regime presents an opportunity to practise "external" as well as "internal" democracy to arrive at a consensus on how to struggle together against the totalitarian regime. It is completely unreasonable, indeed naïve, for anybody in the SPLM/A-IO leadership or elsewhere to expect all opposition to fall in line under the leadership of Machar as an expression of a Nuer turn to govern South Sudan. Inadvertently, and indeed embarrassingly, the refusal to sign the South Sudan Opposition Alliance (SSOA) Charter juxtaposes the SPLM/A-IO to the government position. It is a serious contradiction arising from the projection of narrow and short-term goals. Being the largest of the opposition groups in terms of numbers, the SPLM/A-IO has forfeited the opportunity to lead the opposition alliance and influence its decisions.

The Decision to Quit the SPLM/A-IO

I have mentioned somewhere that of all the people who joined Riek Machar in his new adventure for leadership of South Sudan, I was the only person who was with him in his first stint in 1991. It is with such an uncomfortable sense of guilt that again I must admit my error in judgement when I enlisted in the ranks of the SPLM/A-IO in July 2014. After four years of struggle to raise awareness and build a scientific understanding of the fundamental contradictions underlying the civil war, as well as building a programme for transforming those contradictions, I have come to realize that it is not easy to conduct political work with Machar.

First, Machar is insincere, corrupt, and a Nuer chauvinist, although he pretends to be a nationalist. He lacks basic principles of organization and therefore runs the SPLM/A-IO single-handedly; even while he was in detention, his appointed deputy had to request permission for most everything. He is incapable of providing ethical leadership, or able to care deeply about those he leads, or to offer them honesty, decency, or commitment. Machar prefers informality to institutionalized political work and ignores established chains of command in the army, communicating military orders to junior officers instead of their commanders. This creates friction and indiscipline in the ranks. Machar at times delegates leaders and cadres to attend conferences and meetings but prefers to receive briefs informally, in the form of gossip from his agents planted in the delegation, rather than from the leader of the delegation. Anyone who operates in a professional and organized manner will find it difficult to work with Machar.

The underlying difficulty in the armed struggle in South Sudan, both with the SPLM/A (1983–2005) and now with the SPLM/A-IO, was and remains the waging of war outside its ideological context. Consequently, the two movements produced the same result — political and military elites interested only in power and wealth. That is where my self-criticism would anchor given that my motivation was not power or wealth but the struggle for social change: I could have done better struggling alongside the many in Juba, who have endured the difficult condition of living under an oppressive dictatorship. I found the SPLM/A-IO a place for political speculation and rent-seeking rather than a revolutionary organization that would inspire sacrifice and commitment to social change. This explains why most of its Political Bureau members would not opine or debate critical political and organizational matters of the movement or the country. It evokes wonder and awe at how they reached the pinnacle of a movement's power without any political knowledge or experience.

Machar's refusal to consider or treat his rebel movement as part of a national democratic revolution dismays me greatly. This stems from his confused political thinking, ranging from right-wing ideologies to a strong belief in traditional Nuer mythology centred on Ngundeng's prophecy. Machar believes he can bring change by just wishing. This explains his hesitation to spell out in clear terms the political objectives of the movement in order to build correct strategies for organizing the SPLM/A-IO and to prosecute the war. It has therefore been impossible to build a common vision of the struggle, making it difficult to create an authentic organization guided by principles, a programme, and shared values.

I joined the SPLM/A in 1986 and also came into the SPLM/A-IO from the perspective that civil war has within it the potential to transform the socioeconomic and cultural backwardness of South Sudan. Indeed, this was the raison d'être for my joining the rebellion. Without it I don't think I would have taken the trouble of leaving Juba in July 2014. The movement and the people needed effective and efficient political and military organization to defeat Kiir's aggression and create conditions for a better future. In this respect, the SPLM/A-IO could have been a tool in the hands of the people to achieve this political objective. The movement, therefore, needed, apart from the military, a programme of political mobilization and enlightenment to unite the masses in the production of a national culture that is capable of combating ethnic chauvinism and bigotry, one that abhors corruption and upholds and protects human rights as well as fundamental freedoms enshrined in the constitution.

Most of the political leaders, cadres, and military generals who have thrown in the towel and left the SPLM/A-IO — either defecting back to Kiir or forming their own movements — complained of the obstinacy and arrogance of Machar. The manner he treats those who disagree with him demonstrates his ever-ready attitude to push people to the precipice. Though I was a senior member of the movement, Machar dropped me from the list of the SPLM/A-IO delegation to the IGAD process to underscore his anger with me over my criticism of his attempts to manage the movement while under house arrest in South Africa.

In 2015, a number of politicians and military figures left the SPLM/A-IO. Among them were the politicians Gabriel Changson, Gabriel Yual Dok, and Timothy Tot Chol; and the army generals Peter Gadet Yak, Gabriel Tang-ginye, and Chuol Gaga. I had then disagreed with them because I thought their decision to leave would not resolve the internal political and organizational contradictions in the movement. I thought it was better to soldier on within the movement such that the resolution of the contradictions would benefit the members and serve the highest interest of the movement. I was wrong.

The SPLM/A-IO leadership is organised like a feudal court full of court jesters who discuss personalities and events rather than ideas and strategies. Machar's leadership is an attraction for rent-seekers and political speculators. Even as a rebel leader, he dishes out government ministerial positions and inflated ranks in the army and police. When people anticipate some sort of personal windfall, in the form of a ministerial portfolio or senior military rank, it is difficult for them to oppose the leader in political or ideological debate with other members. He is likely to win the debate not because he is right but because the people give him blind support in return for rewards and privilege. Changson and others stand vindicated for their decision. Many of those who remained, including myself, have no option but to quit the SPLM/A-IO to pursue a wider national agenda for change.

Politics and struggle for the heart of the country bring people together but not necessarily under the same political party. I now understand why Pagan Amum and the former political detainees — Dr. Lam Akol, Joseph Bakasoro, Gen. Thomas Cirillo — and others who rebelled against Kiir's regime refused to join the SPLM/A-IO. However, I want to make it clear that the point of my departure is not personal but ideological and based on my faith in the people to make change if they are given the correct ideological tools.

Here to Where — *Qua Vadis*?

The struggle for change does not terminate at any particular spot. It is continuous because new situations generate new contradictions, which in turn necessitate struggle to address them. As long as the conditions of socioeconomic and cultural backwardness obtain in South Sudan the people will always rise up to struggle in order to address those contradictions. Therefore, quitting the SPLM/A-IO is not like abandoning the struggle. It is done in order to construct new avenues for struggle that employ the right political and ideological tools.

In Chapter Four I discussed the national democratic revolution as a necessary means for transforming the conditions of underdevelopment. The struggle to realize the objectives of the national democratic revolution requires scientific knowledge of the social and economic processes. This does not come ready-made or like relief handouts. People acquire it through learning and unlearning, through a correct perception of social reality and how to transform it. In this respect, many of us leaving the rebellion are heading towards the struggle by different means, towards the social and political mobilization of the masses to raise their social awareness and political consciousness and to conscientize them to their rights and political freedoms.

The people of South Sudan have gone through two stages of the same transition — from colonial domination to statehood and nationhood — without realizing either peace or development of the national productive forces. For this reason they have remained poor, ignorant, and prone to elite deception and fragmentation along ethnic and provincial lines. We need to make our people understand that ethnicity and ethnic politics — as fronted for by the JCE, the elders of Nuer, Chollo, Bari, and all kinds of elder formations and ethnic associations — are nothing but tools of subjugation and exploitation. These elders, like the political, military, and business elites, are bloodsuckers. We must combat them through education. In this endeavour we must identify and build solidarity with those who have spent the last five years struggling within the law and legality against the state's political repression of basic human rights and fundamental freedoms. We must continue to struggle for the right and freedom to organize independently, as well as for freedom of expression represented in a free press.

References

Achebe, Chinua (1983) *The Trouble With Nigeria*. Heinemann Educational Books, Johannesburg.
Alier, Abel (1990) *Southern Sudan: Too Many Agreements Dishonoured*. Ithaca Press, London.
Beshir, Mohammed Omer (1968) *The Southern Sudan: Background to Conflict*. Hurst, London.
Cabral, Amílcar (1966) *The Weapon of Theory*. Published in Speeches and Writings, Monthly Review Press, New York, London.
Chabal, Patrick (2003) *Amilcar Cabral: Revolutionary Leadership and People's War*. Africa World Press. Trenton and Asmara.
De Waal, Alex (2015) *The Real Politics of the Horn of Africa: Money, War, and the Business of Power*. Polity Press, Cambridge.
Epstein, Helen C. (2017) *Another Fine Mess: America, Uganda, and the War on Terror*. Columbia Global Reports. New York.
Fanon, Frantz (1963) *The Wretched of the Earth*. Grove Press, New York.
Garang, Joseph Ukel (1961) *The Dilemma of Southern Intellectuals: Is it justified?* Monologue published by the Ministry of Southern Affairs, Khartoum, 1970.
Hanssen, Halle Jørn (2017) *Lives at Stake: South Sudan During the Liberation Struggle*. Skyline, Oslo.
Johnson, Douglas H. (2015) *South Sudan: Past Notes and Records*. Africa World Books, Wanneroo, Australia.
Johnson, Hilde F. (2015) *South Sudan: The Untold Story from Independence to the Civil War*. I.B. Tauris, London.
Khalid, Mansour (1990) *The Government They Deserve: The Role of the Elite in Sudan's Political Evolution*. Routledge, London.
Markakis, John (2012) *National and Class Conflict in the Horn of Africa*. Shama Books. Addis Ababa.
Nkrumah, Kwame (1965) *Neo-colonialism: The Last Stage of Imperialism*. Thomas Nelson & Sons, London.

Nyaba, P.A. (2018) *The Curse of Elitism*. In Amir Idris (ed.), *South Sudan: Post-Independence Dilemmas* (pp. 19–37). Routledge, London, New York.

——— (2014) *South Sudan: The Crisis of Infancy*. CASAS, Cape Town.

——— (2010) *South Sudan: The State We Aspire To*. CASAS, Cape Town.

——— (2000) *The Politics of Liberation in South Sudan: An Insider's View*. Fountain Publishers, Kampala.

PaanLuel Wël Media (2013) *The Genius of Dr. John Garang de Mabior: The Essential Writings and Speeches of the Late SPLM/A's Leader, Dr. John Garang de Mabior,* vols. 1 & 2.

Tandon, Yash (2015) *Trade is War: The West's War Against the World*. OR Books, New York and London.

Thomas, Edward (2015) *South Sudan: A Slow Liberation*. Zed Books, London.

Wa Thiong'o, Ngũgĩ (1981) *Detained: A Writer's Prison Dairy*. Heinmann, Nairobi.

Wai, Dunstan (1973) *The Southern Sudan: The Problem of National Integration*. Frank Cass, London.

Young, John (2017) "Isolation and Endurance: Riek Machar and the SPLM/A-IO in 2016–17." Small Arms Survey, Graduate Institute of International and Development Studies, Geneva.

——— (2012) *The Fate of Sudan: The Origins and Consequences of a Flawed Peace Process*. Zed Books, New York and London.